Contemporary Irish Women's Fiction: Gender, Desire and

Writing Wales in English

CREW

CREW series of Critical and Scholarly Studies
General Editor: Professor M. Wynn Thomas (CREW, Swansea University)

This CREW series is dedicated to Emyr Humphreys, a major figure in the literary culture of modern Wales, a founding patron of the Centre for Research into the English Literature and Language of Wales, and, along with Gillian Clarke and Seamus Heaney, one of CREW's Honorary Associates. Grateful thanks are extended to Richard Dynevor for making this series possible.

Contemporary Irish and Welsh Women's Fiction: Gender, Desire and Power

Writing Wales in English

Linden Peach

UNIVERSITY OF WALES PRESS
CARDIFF
2007

British Library Cataloguing-in-Publication Data
A catalogue record for this book is available from the British Library.

ISBN 978–0–7083–1998–7

THE ASSOCIATION FOR
WELSH WRITING IN ENGLISH
CYMDEITHAS LLÊN SAESNEG CYMRU

Published with the financial assistance of the Higher Education Funding
Council for Wales.

Typeset by Columns Design Ltd, Reading
Printed in Great Britain by Antony Rowe Ltd, Wiltshire

For Angela

Contents

General Editor's Preface

The aim of this series is to produce a body of scholarly and critical work that reflects the richness and variety of the English-language literature of modern Wales. Drawing upon the expertise both of established specialists and of younger scholars, it will seek to take advantage of the concepts, models and discourses current in the best contemporary studies to promote a better understanding of the literature's significance, viewed not only as an expression of Welsh culture but also as an instance of modern literatures in English world-wide. In addition, it will seek to make available the scholarly materials (such as bibliographies) necessary for this kind of advanced, informed study.

M. Wynn Thomas,
Director, CREW (Centre for Research into the English
Language and Literature of Wales)
Swansea University

Preface

There is a new confidence in contemporary Irish and Welsh women's fiction. One of the reasons for this is that it is inseparable, as this book will demonstrate, from the social, economic and cultural developments in these countries. Another is the relationship that the authors have to the 'English' in which they write, which may be determined by gender, sexuality, class and/or race. There is for many of them a sense of speaking in a voice that is 'different' about subjects on which their national literatures have been silent or have approached in less candid ways.

Thus, the best contemporary writing has a strong exploratory dimension to it and a sense of 'venturing out'. It is 'new' in that it embraces 'difference', 'rupture', 'interrogation' and 'redefinition'. In many cases confidence in language, a newfound voice and radical subject matter sit alongside ambivalence, complexity and even a sense of 'uncertainty', the result of the author having embarked upon something that is definable as 'new' in the above terms.

In my previous work on contemporary Irish fiction, cited in the course of this book, I have drawn on the postcolonial scholar Homi Bhabha's thesis that when what has been previously marginalized or silenced finds or is given a voice, a 'time lag' occurs between 'relocation' and 'reinscription'. Much contemporary writing from Ireland and Northern Ireland, and now I argue from Wales also, may be perceived as occupying a 'time lag'. Indeed, it becomes in effect an exploration of the nature of the space between 'relocation', the initial movement from marginalization, and 'reinscription', a process of redefinition and revisioning, of which Bhabha speaks.

This transition has been important to the history of black, gay, postcolonial and women's writing. However, it is not so much the transition itself as the nature of the space of redefinition that has interested me in Irish and Welsh writing, where I differ from Bhabha in seeing it as a space of ambivalence and complexity. This is particularly true of contemporary Irish and Welsh writing by women.

For reasons I suggest in Chapter 1, the flourishing of women's writing in late twentieth-century Ireland, Northern Ireland and Wales has been something of a phenomenon. Yet this is the first comparative study of Irish and Welsh women's writing. Its focus is the interrelated themes of gender, desire and power which have proved to be of particular importance to women writers from Ireland, Northern Ireland and Wales and which more than many other subjects have taken them into the kind of liberating but uncertain space of which I have been talking.

Although this book's central concern is with gender and desire, its thematic discussion is much wider, for, as I point out at the outset, these subjects push back the boundaries of identity, nationhood, belonging, community, religion and home. It, therefore, has a relevance that extends beyond the particular authors and texts discussed. But whilst the texts have been chosen with this in mind, they have also been selected so as to represent the variety of women's social, cultural and religious backgrounds in Ireland, Northern Ireland and Wales.

In arguing that the exploration of gender and desire across diverse situations and origins in Irish and Welsh women's fiction is often used to rethink traditional notions of identity, nation and home, I am indebted to a number of cultural and literary critics. These include, again, Homi Bhabha to whom I am indebted for his reconfiguration of national geography in terms of 'difference' and even 'tense cultural locations'; the Welsh critic M. Wynn Thomas for his development of Bhabha's ideas about 'internal difference' into a concept of, in both senses, 'corresponding' cultures; the Irish scholar Conor McCarthy for distinguishing between the different experiences of 'modernity' in different countries and locales;

and the postcolonial critic Gayatri Spivak for her emphasis upon diversity and hybridism which is particularly relevant to Ireland and Wales not only in the general sense but to their developing multiculturalism.

Despite the wider territories into which gender and desire inevitably take the text and the reader, not least because of the way in which they are implicated in social and cultural structures, the subject of desire per se cannot be gainsaid. The recurring interest in desire in contemporary Irish and Welsh women's writing is in the way in which what has been 'silenced' or marginalized' is not only 'different' but 'other'. The focus in the best writing is on exploring desire within the whole complex process of 'othering' and how this is implicated in social definitions of gender, the cultural determination of sexual behaviour and the binary language often used to define, polarize and stigmatize particular types of consensual sexual activity. In addressing this subject, the book necessarily makes use of psychoanalytic and poststructural critical approaches, especially in the analysis of symbolism. But it also draws upon other recent and current ideas. Given the emphasis upon entering a complex and ambivalent space, the French historian Foucault's definitions of limit and taboo are especially pertinent to some of the texts discussed, as is the American cultural scholar Judith Butler's concept of a 'performative' gender identity.

The critical readings in this book are developed through select representations of gendered desire. All of these are symbolically complex, encapsulating the revisionism, anxiety and ambivalence in the 'time lag' with which I began. Taken together, from across the different texts, they present the reader with a variety of perspectives on, and approaches to, desire, gender and power. For example, in a short story by one of a number of emergent black or mixed race Welsh writers, Leonora Brito, a young, mixed race woman begins her touring stage career in Wales, mimicking and mocking the discourses that have defined the black, female body. Unfortunately, her dream ends with her swaying before a coconut tree on a London stage beneath a yellowy moon, redolent of the black artist Josephine Baker who was, of course, much more successful in the theatre and music hall. The moon, a symbol of female aspiration and desire, is

significantly the colour of decay and degeneration. This is a
story that can be productively read in relation not only to
Irish fiction but to the importance of African American dance
as a space in which the black body, especially the black
female body, and black identity generally were 'relocated' and
'reinscribed'. In a novel by the celebrated writer associated
with both Ireland and Northern Ireland Jennifer Johnston, a
woman artist finds her 'true' self in swimming naked in the
sea, aware only of the tide's rhythm and the movement of her
body. The rhythm and boundarylessness of the sea, as potent
a female image as the moon, are appealing to a woman artist
whom all the men in her life – father, son and lover – have
sought to define and mould in their image. In a novel by the
Welsh writer Sarah Waters, which takes us into the risky,
experimental but also paradoxically censorious climate of the
Second World War, two female lovers enjoy consensual,
painful sex. What the episode does is to complicate the kind
of terms that are explicit or implicit in sexual narratives and
stories of passionate desire: 'guilt', 'shame', 'sadism',
'masochism', 'tenderness', 'domination', 'submission' and so
forth. New concepts such as 'performative' and 'fluid' are
brought to bear by the text because the real subject of
exploration is the role of boundaries which these lovers
challenge, collapse and reconstruct at different times and in
different ways throughout their 'play' together. Indeed, the
term 'play' which I employ here is taken from contemporary
sadomasochistic discourse and underlines the 'theatrical'
element in all sexual discourse. However, when 'violence',
'sadism' and 'masochism' enter consensual sexual 'play',
boundaries are important, even though many traditional
boundaries and binarisms are challenged. The 'play' indulged
in by Waters's lovers echoes different types of 'sadism',
'violence' and 'humiliation' which have also concerned a
number of Irish and Welsh women writers. In a novel set in
the Troubles in Northern Ireland by Linda Anderson, the
public punishment of a young woman by her community for
sexual liaisons with British soldiers brings all kinds of
disturbing sadistic desires and fantasies to the fore. Here
Anderson brings out of the shadows, literally and
metaphorically, what has been marginalized in accounts of

the Troubles, unveiling within what is 'other' even more complex layers of silence.

There is a sense in these examples, which are discussed in detail in the course of the book, of a 'time lag' in which limit and taboo are challenged. Indeed, the exploration of desire across the fiction explored in this book ranges from the exploration of mutual heterosexual and same-sex desires in 'permanent' and casual relationships, the discovery of different sexual identities and mutual same-sex sadomasochism, through sadistic fantasies and domestic violence, to child abuse. Many of these are topics on which Irish and Welsh writing in English have been previously silent (or silenced). What brings these different faces of 'desire' together in this book is the movement from the margins that this implies and the influence of the complex and often ambivalent space which is subsequently created upon the language and the aesthetics of the literary text.

Acknowledgements

References to the primary works of fiction are to the following editions, and page numbers are given in parentheses in the text:

Linda Anderson, *To Stay Alive* (London: the Bodley Head, 1984); Vivian Annis Bailey, *Children of Rebecca* (Dinas Powys: Honno, 1995); Maeve Binchey, *Dublin 4* (1982; rpt London: Arrow Books, 1999); *Star Sullivan* (London: Orion Books, 2006); Leonora Brito, *dat's love* (Bridgend: Seren, 1995); Stevie Davies, *Kith and Kin* (London: Weidenfeld & Nicolson, 2004); Emma Donoghue, *Stir-fry* (1994; rpt Harmondsworth: Penguin, 1995); *The Woman Who Gave Birth to Rabbits* (London; Virago Press, 2002); Siân James, *A Small Country* (1979; rpt Bridgend: Seren, 1999); *Storm at Arberth* (Bridgend: Seren, 1994); *Outside Paradise* (Cardiff: Parthian Books, 2001); Jennifer Johnston, *The Railway Station Man* (1984; rpt Harmondsworth: Penguin, 1989); *This Is Not A Novel* (London: Headline Book Publishing, 2002); Catherine Merriman, *Getting A Life* (Dinas Powys: Honno, 2001); Clare Morgan, *An Affair of the Heart* (Bridgend: Seren, 1996); Mary Morrissy, *A Lazy Eye* (1993; rpt London: Vintage, 1996); *Mother of Pearl* (London: Jonathan Cape, 1996); Edna O'Brien, *Down By the River* (1996; rpt London: Phoenix, 1997); Bernice Rubens, *The Elected Member* (1969; rpt London: Abacus, 2003); *I Sent a Letter to my Love* (1975; rpt London: Abacus, 2002); *Milwaukee* (2001; rpt London: Abacus, 2002); *When I Grow Up* (London: Little Brown, 2005); Rachel Tresize, *In and Out of the Goldfish Bowl* (Cardiff: Parthian Books, 2000); Sarah Waters, *The Night Watch* (London: Virago Press, 2006).

Acknowledgements

I am grateful to Professor Wynn Thomas and Sarah Lewis and her colleagues at the University of Wales Press for their painstaking work on this book and, above all, their encouragement and support.

1 Introduction

Contemporary fiction in English by women from Wales, Ireland and Northern Ireland has much to offer the reader interested in gender identity and how desire is mediated by sociocultural discourses. In exploring these themes, this writing often provides insights into the most pressing issues of the day concerning family, community, nation and identity. Focusing on a select range of specific texts, some of which are better known than others outside the academy, this book explores the way in which contemporary women's writing has used the subjects of gender, desire and power to challenge hegemonic historical discourses and to contribute to debates about what is meant by 'Wales', 'Ireland' and 'Northern Ireland'.

The focus of this particular study is upon Welsh writing in English. It must be noted, though, that most writers from Wales who work only in English regard themselves as 'Welsh' and that there are many others who work in both the English and the Welsh languages. In the case of the latter, and more generally through translation and accounts in English of Welsh-language work, there is an increasing amount of exchange between English-language and Welsh-language cultures. Indeed, it would be as much of a distortion to see the one as divorced from the other as to think of Wales as having only two languages and to ignore the importance, especially in the more densely populated parts of Wales, of other community languages. In addition, Wales, Ireland and Northern Ireland have a range of different faith communities, some of which have long histories of settlement in these countries, such as the Jewish communities of Cardiff in South Wales and Cork in Ireland and the Islamic peoples in Cardiff Bay.

Throughout the book, a distinction is made between Northern Ireland and Ireland. The latter term is always used, as it should, to refer to the Republic. It is important to recognize that Northern Ireland and Ireland have distinct histories and many social, cultural and political differences. However, in many respects, the histories, lived experiences and cultures of the two are interwoven one with another. There is (and has been) considerable exchange and social, political and cultural intercommunication between the two, although this does vary from community to community in both Northern Ireland and Ireland.

One of the principal distinctions that this study assumes between Northern Ireland and Ireland has been summarized by Conor McCarthy. He points out that the process of '"modernisation" in the North can be understood in terms of the broader development of social democracy in the post-1945 United Kingdom'. But the Republic enjoyed a 'long post-war boom in the Western capitalist economies' which unravelled not only as a result of the oil crises of the 1970s but with 'the arrival on the Northern scene of more radical reformist movements', such as the Civil Rights campaigns, which demanded more rapid progress in areas such as employment and housing, many directly affecting women.[1] Whereas the nature of the 1960s in the Republic was determined by an extensive programme of reforms, to which Chapter 3 returns in more detail, the 1960s in Northern Ireland highlighted the discrimination against Catholics in many areas of social and civil life, especially employment and housing. The Northern Ireland Women's Rights Movement (1975) is an example of how women's campaigns brought Unionist and Nationalist women together, but campaigns on subjects such as police searches and harassment have generally been Nationalist led.

As a result of modernization, both Ireland and Northern Ireland experienced, at the end of the twentieth and the beginning of the twenty-first century, the rise of a media-oriented, postmodern consumer society which brought them into contact, if not alignment, with wider global processes of change and offered both women and men different ways of perceiving themselves, not all of them positive. Not surprisingly, engagement with postmodern society is a feature of both Northern Irish and Irish fiction, although the most successful works in this respect are written by male authors such as Glenn Patterson in the North and Roddy Doyle in Ireland. Women writers from the North, such as Linda Anderson, whose work is discussed in Chapter 4, have been largely associated with radical alternatives to the more documentary texts on the Irish troubles which have given the impression, as Glenn Patterson has said, that fictional representations of the North have 'stuck about 1972'.[2] Both Northern Ireland and Ireland have produced novels that engage critically with postmodernism rather than texts that in form and structure are themselves postmodern and both societies have experienced crises arising from what McCarthy describes as 'national ambivalence coming into contact with, and frequently articulating with and being expressed through postmodernism'.[3]

As far as the Republic is concerned, despite Ireland's contribution to European modernism at the beginning of the twentieth century, the country itself, as McCarthy says, had little 'experience of Modernist cultural internationalism' and its Romanticism was never fully challenged by 'a socially radical indigenous modernism'.[4] This proved to have a significant impact upon how women were viewed in Ireland and also perceived themselves. While Catholics remained a minority in Northern Ireland throughout the twentieth century, they achieved power in Ireland when the war of independence ended in the creation of a semi-independent Free State in 1922. This came about partly as a result of the fusion of the Nationalist movement and the Catholic Church but also because the Protestants, who had held power for several centuries by passing laws denying Catholics equal rights, did not find their support of Irish independence rewarded in the ways they had expected. The Constitution of the Republic (1937) embraced Eamon De Valera's romanticized vision of a Catholic, rural, isolationist Ireland, dependent upon agriculture and defining a woman's proper place as in the home. Challenged much later than if Ireland had had the experience of industrialization or of 'the socially radical indigenous modernism', of which McCarthy speaks, De Valera's image of Ireland remained in the public psyche and in the consciousnesses of women as well as men for much of the twentieth century. The fact that many women in Ireland lived in isolated communities, in small villages or on scattered farms, meant that the power of the State and the Catholic Church tended to go unchallenged. As we shall see from the way women's experiences are depicted by contemporary women writers from Ireland, this has meant that female aspirations and desires in Ireland have remained inhibited, distorted or denied by hegemonic cultural and economic forces for longer than in Wales and Northern Ireland.

In Wales, Ireland and Northern Ireland, the arrival of television, cinema and other international media provided women with potentially different self-images from the ones with which they had been brought up, some of which were embraced and others rejected. In Wales and, to an even greater extent, in Ireland, the nation has been associated with women. It became increasingly clear to many women in both countries that female sexuality and gender identity had histories bound up with ways in which women had been culturally defined in order to serve Nationalist, and largely male-oriented, aspirations. However, the association of women in Ireland with the Virgin Mother proved particularly complex, giving them status within Catholic communities, while some of the key images, such as the Virgin Mary kneeling at the feet of her son, suggested their inferiority to men. The most obvious demonstration of this kind of ambivalence in Wales is the Welsh national costume worn by women which is still much in evidence today in Welsh Eisteddfodau. Based on the Welsh peasant's dress, and linking nationalism with the rural as in Ireland, it was also a defiant symbol of Welsh-language culture and identity. But it would be misleading to suggest that in these countries there is only one 'Women's History'. Women's experiences are diverse and, as we shall see in the course of this book, influenced by the communities and localities in which they find themselves.

Although this book is not a survey of contemporary women's fiction from Wales, Ireland and Northern Ireland, it acknowledges the different kinds of writing, life experiences and social experiments that constitute what in contemporary Ireland, Northern Ireland and Wales is a diverse body of artistic achievement. Hopefully, it will provide the young scholar or the general reader new to this fiction with an introduction that will inspire further reading.[5] This writing has now reached a maturity and level of excellence where it is the subject of extended critical and scholarly attention.

But the question to begin with is, why focus only on contemporary women's writing and not include literature written by men? In Wales, Ireland and Northern Ireland, there is a strong published history of writing by women, but the issues involved in tracing a history of women's writing have to date been more fully developed in the criticism and scholarship on Irish and Northern Irish literature than on Welsh writing. Christine St Peter points out, in relation to women's writing:

So if a writer or critic draws a circle around women's writing, looks at it apart from the writing of men, this is not a denial of its connection to that larger shared literature [by male and female writers]. Rather such an exercise asserts that the conditions of a woman's work, the subjects of her writing, and the experiences of her life will be, inevitably if variably, connected to . . . the progressive changes of the last generation and the continuing oppressions specific to women's lives.[6]

Without distinguishing at this point between Ireland and Northern Ireland, she highlights 'the importance of women's sexuality, sexual orientation and reproductive lives as sites of conflict and resistance . . . and a ubiquitous sense of the contradictoriness of forces that together are reshaping life on the island'.[7] Whilst not pretending, in the space available, to be inclusive or definitive, this book is concerned with pursuing the importance of the two preoccupations that St Peter emphasizes – the incremental modernization from which women have generally benefited and the continuing discourses which have oppressed them – for contemporary women's fiction in Wales as well as Ireland and Northern Ireland.

Thus, an important area of study as far as literature is concerned that emerges from what St Peter says is not women's sexuality and sexual orientation per se, but the way in which they are situated at the centre of wider conflicting forces in society that seek to configure women and female desire in different ways. The Welsh critic M. Wynn Thomas has coined the term 'corresponding cultures' to mean the different ways in which Welsh- and English-language discourses in Wales have existed together and, as suggested earlier, related, directly or indirectly, to each other.[8] The following chapters explore some of the correspondences and incongruities that may be found within writing from Wales, Ireland and Northern Ireland over the last twenty or thirty years around the specific and important agenda that St Peter identifies.

Gender, power and nation

As has been suggested in the previous section, Ireland and Wales are small countries with different histories, cultures and national aspirations. However, each of them has two principal languages, in addition to further community languages, and a complex relationship to England, Europe and the United States. At the level of the lived experience of their people, and especially women, they are diverse societies, undergoing radical and wide-ranging change, and are full of internal contradictions.

Books in English through the end of the previous century and into the present have conspicuously borne witness to the rise of contemporary writing in Wales and, especially, the Republic. This occurred for a variety of reasons: the world-wide feminist movement; publishing houses such as Honno in Wales and Arlen and, subsequently, Attic in Ireland dedicated to women's writing; the increased presence of women in public life and in senior appointments in higher education, publishing, arts and government; and the fact that more women, like the principal protagonist in the Irish writer Jennifer Johnston's *The Railway Station Man*,[9] have had the means and the time to devote to artistic expression.

For some scholars this might appear to be an over-optimistic interpretation of the publishing of women's writing. The first anthology of short stories by women was not published in Wales until 1994.[10] In her Foreword to this volume, Jane Aaron thinks in terms of a 'present consciousness stepping on towards a future shaped by the shadowy hand of the past'. That 'shadowy hand' reveals itself for Aaron in the way in which some stories in the anthology 'echo the painful and enforced resignation characteristic of many of the earlier texts published by women in Wales . . . disappointment and the wastage of female potential on a massive scale'.[11] The editors of the first anthology of women's writing from Ireland to be published in the United States, five years before the first anthology of Welsh women's short fiction, are much more upbeat than Aaron about their women authors: 'They represent the period during which Irish women "began to look at themselves differently" and to express themselves differently and during which a far wider social range of Irish women have been writing and publishing for the first time.'[12] Thus, Ireland seems to have been ahead of Wales in the 1990s in publishing women writers from diverse social backgrounds. The majority of Welsh women writers who are published by the leading presses have a university background. But the Irish-American editors acknowledge, like Aaron, that achieving publication was a long haul for many women authors because of the male-centred nature of the publishing industry.

Thus, the most obvious rationale for a study devoted to women's fiction is that, despite what we have already said about women's writing flourishing, it is still underrepresented in many critical studies of Welsh and Irish and Northern Irish literature. But another case to be made is that women's writing shares with the work of authors from other groups that have been marginalized or silenced at least the trace of the history from which it emerged. Despite the differences between Wales, Ireland and Northern Ireland and the different backgrounds from which women's literature has come, such writing is grounded in a matrix of empowerment and disempowerment; struggle and confrontation; and categorization and prioritization. As will become clear from this book, sometimes this background is present in the literature in covert ways, as in the Welsh writer Clare Morgan's enigmatic *An Affair of the Heart*[13] which explores the subtleties of heterosexual or same-sex desires. In other works, such as the Irish writer Emma Donoghue's collection of short stories, *The Woman Who Gave Birth to Rabbits*,[14] which recreates the lives of women who have been written out of history, it is much more explicit.

The history from which women's writing has emerged is not simply 'about women', or even 'about feminism'; it is about the way in which women and feminism are implicated in social structures. Thus, such writing is about power, politics, nation, history, religion and education in a broad sense and the importance of each of these to the imaginative formulation, and reformulation, of Wales, Ireland and Northern Ireland. It also shares with that of other marginalized groups a profound concern to create art that interrogates, rather than simply delineating, the different sociocultural contexts in which we all live. It goes without saying that nation and history, and everything affiliated with those concepts, from the Catholic Church in Ireland and Nonconformity in Wales to how each country's history has been taught (or not taught), are central to the dominant discourses around Welsh, Irish and Northern Irish cultures. Central to these concepts is gender, as a manifestation of the defining discourses circulating in a nation and culture at any particular time. This was very much the case when the Irish Constitution was published in 1937, linking women with the hearth and the home. At the same time gender is one of the most potentially subversive elements within those hegemonic discourses.

As the reader moves between writing by women from Wales, Ireland and Northern Ireland, their shared preoccupations become evident, notwithstanding the obvious differences between them. Of these, few stand out more than their recurring concern with themes and metaphors by which the subject of gender becomes a lever to prise open notions of 'nation' and 'history' from a particular group's perspective. In late twentieth-century Irish, Northern Irish and Welsh literary criticism this has led to a configuration of the nation in terms articulated by the postcolonial critic Homi Bhabha, who points out that a nation must not 'be seen simply as "other" in relation to what is outside or beyond it' but 'must always itself be a process of hybridism', incorporating new peoples.[15] The implication of this, which is evident in the texts discussed in this book, is not only that a nation is inevitably more heterogeneous than the rhetoric of national identity allows, but that the composition of a nation changes over time. Thus, when the 'new "people"' articulate their experiences it is frequently in forms of writing that challenge the generic characteristics as well as the content of the nation's literary history. Bhabha argues:

> The nation is no longer the sign of modernity under which cultural differences are homogenized in the 'horizontal' view of society. The nation reveals, in its ambivalent and vacillating representation, the ethnography of its own historicity and opens up the possibility of other narratives of the people and their difference.[16]

A greater awareness of their own 'historicity' and the de-marginalization of new and previously silenced voices are two of the principal forces that have helped extend the boundaries of what was thought of, about twenty years ago, as the characteristics of Welsh, Irish and Northern Irish writing. Thus, this book begins with how a Cardiff-born, black writer, Leonora Brito, challenges the 'ethnography' of the 'historicity' of Wales.

The postcolonial critic, Gayatri Spivak, like Bhabha influenced by the French philosopher Jacques Derrida, takes a different but complementary approach to the subject of national identity: 'One needs to be vigilant against simple notions of identity which overlap neatly with language and location. I'm deeply suspicious of any determinist or positivist definition of identity . . .'[17] She illustrates her argument with reference to her own life, interweaving her education, her intellectual development and the way she has lived in a variety of places, including the United States and Europe, since her upbringing in metropolitan Bengal. The kind of diversity and hybridism that she sees in her own life, geographically and intellectually, is evident in the lives of many of the women writers discussed in this book. Spivak presents an interesting model of how a writer's oeuvre may be seen in relation to Bhabha's model of the diversity and changing nature of the nation: 'I find that I'm still learning and unlearning so much that the earlier things I have written become interpretable in new ways.'[18] This has proved to be the case for many women writers from Wales and, especially, the Irish Republic over the last three decades. Indeed, the process of 'learning and unlearning' which Spivak identifies has been important to the intellectual life of these countries. The subjects of gender, desire, power and affiliated concerns with nation, locality, family and community are at the heart of this process and are also constantly being interpreted in new and different ways.

The subversive potential of 'gender' as a literary device has proved significant in the countries with which this book is concerned. In none of these in the late twentieth- and early twenty-first centuries, despite hegemonic discourses and rhetoric, has there been an essential, singularly focused women's, or indeed man's, perspective or experience. Thus, in all the works discussed in this book there is an overt emphasis upon differences within women's experiences that are bound up not simply with issues of class, race and sexuality but with the different levels of importance these assume at different times and in different localities according to economic circumstances. This is especially true for Emma Donoghue's *The Woman Who Gave Birth to Rabbits* which ranges geographically across the British Isles and what is now Ireland and Northern Ireland and in time from the fourteenth to the nineteenth centuries. Leonora Brito's stories set at different times in Cardiff Bay inevitably focus upon the significance of race but, like the Nobel prize-winning African-American novelist Toni Morrison, she does not allow race to subsume gender or class. Indeed, it is the diversity and complexity of identity and culture, within specific economic frameworks, that provides the springboard for many of the most experimental and radical writings by women in Wales, Ireland and Northern Ireland.

Concerns with gender, power and economics tend to provide fiction with what Clair Willis, in a discussion of poetry from Northern Ireland, describes as 'engagement'. She argues that 'engaged literature' is deemed to be writing that is 'rooted in a particular community . . . but also . . . refuses to be reduced to the level of propaganda for one side or the other'.[19] Clearly, from the perspective of being rooted in particular geographical areas, the texts discussed in this book are examples of 'engaged literature' as Willis defines it. But whilst some of these are anchored in specific physical and/or cultural communities, such as Leonora Brito's stories about Cardiff Bay, others are 'engaged' in the sense of belonging to an intellectual or particular 'sexual' community.

At the end of the twentieth century, some critics argued that Irish, Northern Irish and, subsequently, Welsh writing might be perceived as 'engaged' in a different sense to Willis's as part of a wider postcolonial movement. However, despite interesting debates, not all critics, including those who have built reputations addressing 'engagement' in their country's writing, have been prepared to accept 'postcolonial' as the most appropriate epithet for Irish, Northern Irish and Welsh history let alone their literature. In the Republic, the debate focused for a time around two schools of thought: one of them intent to define Ireland in terms of 'post-colonial' models and another, 'revisionism', focused on reinterpreting nationalism and particular nationalist histories. With the Republic in mind, Joe Cleary has concluded that 'debates about whether Ireland was or was not a colony have rarely got beyond questions of geo-cultural location and constitutional statute'.[20] This summary verdict may not do full justice to the complexity of the debates in Ireland – his title is posed with a question mark – and it may not be entirely fair to apply it to the emergent arguments in various branches of Welsh studies.[21] However, the alternative model that Cleary suggests is certainly appropriate to many of the Irish and Welsh authors discussed in this book. Cleary argues that 'colonialism' should be 'conceived as a historical process in which societies of various kinds and locations are differently integrated into a world capitalist system'.[22] The different ways in which not only Ireland, Northern Ireland and Wales but different communities within them have been at different times 'integrated into a world capitalist system' is evident in their literatures. Two of the emphases in Cleary's model provide a useful context within which to discuss the works explored in this book: that colonialism is a changing historical process and that 'specific national configurations are always the product of dislocating intersections between local and global processes'.[23]

Sexualities

Cleary's emphasis upon the importance of 'dislocating intersections between local and global processes' is all too evident in the history of women's writing in the twentieth and twenty-first centuries. Indeed, this is exemplified at many levels in Leonora Brito's *dat's love*,[24] the subject of Chapter 2, and Emma Donoghue's lesbian novel, *Stir-fry*,[25] discussed in Chapter 3. Contemporary writing is inevitably situated for the author, publisher and reader in regional, national and transnational cultures. The latter is probably what defines for many the 'contemporary moment', but it also triggers an interest in reading cultural and literary histories within this framework. Thus, an important motif in Brito's titular short story 'Dat's Love' is the influence of American music on post-war, black Cardiff identity. Siân James's short story, 'Happy as Saturday Night', from her collection discussed in Chapter 5,[26] set in 'a tough part of Cardiff' (109), is informed by an inevitable contemporary awareness of how social and economic regeneration is bound up with transnational as well as national socio-economic forces.

Thus, women's writing presents us with invaluable perspectives on history, or histories, rooted in discourses about inclusion and exclusion and/or engagements with cultural diversity. However, there are further levels of complexity. Threaded through much diverse, sometimes highly innovative, writing by women are recurring motifs that use gender not only to explore concepts of 'nation', 'history' and 'culture', as I have been suggesting, but to examine the traditional notions of 'gender' and 'sexuality' themselves. Of the numerous motifs and metaphors employed in this capacity, none appears to be more important to contemporary Welsh, Irish and Northern Irish women writers than those of betrayal, confession, secrets and silences. Indeed, there is a plethora of significant texts from Wales, Northern Ireland and, particularly, the Republic that, in addressing these themes also engage with secrecy and silence around desire and sexuality.

One of the reasons why there are so many novels from Wales and, especially, Ireland written around sexuality, secret desires and betrayals may be the importance which religion – Catholicism and Nonconformity – has assumed in these nations at a community, family and, in the Republic, state level. In the sectarian culture of Northern Ireland the abiding concern with dangerous, cross-faith and community relationships has led to an unsurprising preoccupation with betrayal and secrecy. Thus, the subject of betrayal often, and inevitably, triggers an exploration of the extent to which family, community, religion, politics and history have a heightened presence in Welsh, Irish and Northern Irish writing and are interconnected one with another.

Whilst gender has always been recognized as a subversive element within Wales, Ireland and Northern Ireland, as many of the texts discussed in the following pages make clear, its full history and even potential in this capacity has become clearer through more advanced understanding of gender and its link with sexuality which emerged in late twentieth-century critical writing. One of the most revolutionary ideas in this respect, radically questioning the link between gender and sexuality, was the concept of gender as 'performative', a term coined by the feminist critic Judith Butler and explained in more depth in Chapter 2. Late twentieth-century thinking conceived of gender as situated at the meeting place of the determinism of contemporaneous cultural forces and the subversive, regenerative potential of the individual subject. Recent literary, especially feminist, criticism frequently reads literature, particularly women's writing, through this new critical prism whilst the new ideas about gender that were very much in the air in the latter part of the twentieth century re-energized the engagement with gender in new writing. A strong example of the 'performative' aspect of gender identity which resists and subverts cultural pressures is provided by the wartime lesbian Kay, in Sarah Waters's *The Night Watch*,[27] discussed in Chapter 3, who dresses on the boundary that conventionally separates men and women's appearance. In the works discussed in this book, the new energy informing this fresh engagement with issues around gender and sexuality returns in different ways to the significance of culture in the formation of individual, community, regional, national and, increasingly, global identities .

Language and voice

Although there are conceptual and political concerns in many of the works discussed in this book, as literature they are fundamentally concerned with language. When the language in which Irish and Welsh literature is written is English, as Seamus Deane has said of Irish and Northern Irish writing, it is 'dominated by the notion of vitality restored, of the centre energized by the periphery, the urban by the rural, the cosmopolitan by the provincial, the decadent by the natural'.[28]

Irish, Northern Irish and Welsh women's writing share faith in the regenerative possibilities of literature and its capacity to extend and reshape our lives. All writing takes the reader into specific language usage and how we create, enact and maintain identities and meanings through language. Women's writing, like the works of other previously marginalized groups, is often characterized by a heightened consciousness of the importance of day-to-day 'enactment'. By this I mean a strong awareness of how identities, including gender identities, are extended and shaped through day-to-day interactions and differences. Thus, it is not surprising that in contemporary women's writing, embedded in interaction and difference, dialogue is taken very seriously as a manifestation of the interaction and enactment we are talking about. This is an important aspect of contemporary Welsh and Irish writing to which I shall return in the discussion of particular works. At the centre of dialogue in many of the works to be discussed is not only the manifestation of the difference by which gender identity is defined but the 'performative' dimension of gender, referred to above, situated between cultural determinism and the individual potential for subversion.

Notions of family, history and community are frequently employed to further the public discourse of nationhood. However, exploring the concept of 'nation' through these subjects can actually serve to undermine it, exposing not a coherent nation but sites of internecine rivalry. Having its historical roots in engagement with empowerment and disempowerment, referred to earlier, women's writing in Wales, Ireland and Northern Ireland is often multi-layered. Some of the more experimental and innovative works, such as the Dublin writer Mary Morrissy's first novel, *Mother of Pearl*,[29] discussed in Chapter 7, might be seen as struggling to keep its critical scrutiny of the grand narratives in balance throughout the book. Others, such as the Welsh writer Sarah Waters's *The Night Watch*, discussed in Chapter 3, move back in time on more than one occasion in order to unravel the secrets with which they are concerned and deftly untangle the intermingled lives of their protagonists. *The Night Watch*, a story of four Londoners in the aftermath of the Second World War, begins in 1947 and then shifts to 1944 and 1941 in order to reveal very gradually a number of secrets linked to personal tragedies, involving betrayal, that are in turn mixed up with national mourning and loss. Some of these novels are complex because of the interconnection of family, history, nation, politics and religion in Wales, Ireland and Northern Ireland. But they are often made complicated through their search for alternative histories and community perspectives, a topic to which the discussion of Siân James will return in more detail in Chapter 7.

In its unravelling of family, gender, nation and power, contemporary Irish, Northern Irish and Welsh women's writing often bears the trace of modernism more firmly than of postmodernism. There are few examples in Wales, Ireland or Northern Ireland of the kind of ultimate scepticism about myth, meaning and language that we find in the late twentieth-century English novel, in the work of Angela Carter, for example. As in the early and mid-twentieth century modernist text, there is the conviction that an ultimate truth or meaning does exist. Hence, in James's *A Small Country*, discussed in Chapter 4, a young man in the trenches in the First World War does eventually discover a Welsh identity that makes sense to him and which saves him from the nihilism which others found on the front lines.

As much as modernism had faith in what could be recovered from the failures of the traditional Grand Narratives – including the demise of 'traditional' understanding of 'History', 'God', 'Patriotism', 'Duty' and 'Gender' – it functioned as a force of continual 'rupture'. After the First World War, one of the most commonly used motifs to explore the former thinking around 'Patriotism', 'Duty' and 'Sacrifice' was the one highlighted in women's writing in the previous section – 'betrayal'. Given the experience of the trenches and the appallingly high casualty figures, it is easy to see how the First World War gave rise to a deeply rooted feeling among many that they had been betrayed – by the Generals, by the Government and by the old concepts by which they had previously lived.

How the tropes of gender, desire and power have led to a reinterpretation of what we mean by 'History' is the subject of the next chapter, which focuses on two books of short fiction by Leonora Brito and Emma Donoghue that are watersheds in Welsh and Irish writing, uncovering the experiences of generations of women previously unexplored in fiction. However, if 'History' has distorted, or failed to engage with, women's experiences because of the way in which it has been imbricated with gendered social structures, it has also frustrated or silenced, in different ways at different times and in different communities, female desire. Chapter 3 pursues some of the arguments of Chapter 2 in relation to what has been one of the most taboo subjects in the countries with which this book is concerned. It is a study of three ostensibly very different novels by Emma Donoghue, Stevie Davies and Sarah Waters concerned with same-sex relationships. Each of these writers initially achieved recognition for what might be called 'lesbian fiction', but without sidelining their interest in this subject, the texts discussed here examine female relationships and the empowerment of women in a broader sense. One of the assumptions of this book, referred to earlier, is that contemporary women's writing often bears the traces of centuries of struggle for empowerment. Thus, contemporary women's fiction, especially narratives with a historical perspective, highlights the day-to-day courage of ordinary women. Whilst this is all too evident in the same-sex fiction discussed in Chapter 3, it is also true of women's writing more generally, as Chapter 4, examining the extent to which some of the central protagonists in women's writing might be described as 'heroic', makes clear. In doing so, it explores the range of meanings that this term, used previously in Irish literary criticism, might have for contemporary writing. The argument is advanced with reference to a range of authors, including Maeve Binchey who is generally regarded as a writer of blockbusters, in order to do justice to the diversity of women's experience: Edna O'Brien, Jennifer Johnston and Maeve Binchey from Ireland, the Northern Ireland writer Linda Anderson, the Welsh writers Siân James, Rachel Tresize and Bernice Rubens. But the diversity of women's fiction and of female desire is not only the product of different cultures or periods of history. All of us change much over our lifetimes, as a result of experiences, illness and ageing itself, and the difficulties involved in discussing identity because of this is addressed in Chapter 5 with reference to collections of short stories by two Welsh writers, Clare Morgan and Siân James. Because women's writing is so bound up with changing perspectives, personal, cultural and historical, it is not surprising that its most common motifs are connected to the subject of 'vision', a topic explored in Chapter 6, with detailed reference to groundbreaking collections of short stories by the Welsh writer Catherine Merriman and the Irish writer Mary Morrissy. As suggested earlier, gender identity and female desire have been influenced in Wales, Ireland and Northern Ireland by religious discourse. Chapter 7 discusses further works by Mary Morrissy, Siân James and Bernice

Rubens, chosen for the different ways in which they approach 'religion' within a wider framework of 'spirituality'. In doing so, they suggest that 'spirituality' is as fluid and diverse a concept as many others, such as 'history', 'race', 'self' and 'nation', examined in the previous chapters. Like the equally complex and ambivalent concepts of 'gender' and 'desire' with which this book is primarily concerned, 'spirituality' embraces much by which we define ourselves, including ideas about individuality, family and community. Although this book is based, inevitably, on a selection of contemporary works by women from Wales, Ireland and Northern Ireland, it is hoped that the following discussions will stimulate in-depth criticism of other works and authors that it has not been possible to include.

Notes

1   Conor McCarthy, *Modernisation, Crisis and Culture in Ireland 1969–1992* (Dublin: Four Courts Press, 2000), pp. 12–14.
2   Glenn Patterson in Gerry Smyth, *The Novel and the Nation: Studies in the New Irish Fiction* (London: Pluto Press, 1997), p. 114.
3   McCarthy, *Modernisation*, p. 40.
4   Ibid., p. 34.
5   The best, current introduction to Welsh writing in English in Wales is M. Wynn Thomas (ed.), *Welsh Writing in English* (Cardiff: Unversity of Wales Press, 2003). Unfortunately, because it is a survey, there is not the space to include every writer. Although Leonora Brito is briefly mentioned, the women writers with whom this book is concerned – Siân James, Catherine Merriman, Clare Morgan and Bernice Rubens – are not discussed. There are several introductions to contemporary Irish fiction: Gerry Smyth, *The Novel and the Nation*; Liam Harte and Michael Parker (eds), *Contemporary Irish Fiction: Themes, Tropes, Theories* (Basingstoke: Macmillan, 2000); and Linden Peach, *The Contemporary Irish Novel: Critical Readings* (Basingstoke: Palgrave Macmillan, 2004). Harte and Parker, ibid., include discussions of Emma Donoghue and Jennifer Johnston but not of Linda Anderson, Maeve Binchey or Mary Morrissy.
6   Christine St Peter, *Changing Ireland: Strategies in Contemporary Women's Fiction* (Basingstoke: Macmillan, 2000), p. 7.
7   Ibid., p. 4.
8   M. Wynn Thomas, *Corresponding Cultures: The Two Literatures of Wales* (Cardiff: University of Wales Press, 1999), p. 1.
9   Jennifer Johnston, *The Railway Station Man* (1984; rpt Harmondsworth: Penguin, 1989).
10 Elin ap Hywel (ed.), *Luminous and Forlorn: Contemporary Short Stories by Women from Wales* (Dinas Powys: Honno, 1994).
11 Ibid., pp. ix, xiv.

12 Louise DeSalvo, Kathleen Walsh D'Arcy and Katherine Hogan (eds), *Territories of the Voice: Contemporary Stories By Irish Women Writers* (1989; rpt London: Virago, 1991), p. xii.

13 Clare Morgan, *An Affair of the Heart* (Bridgend: Seren, 1996).

14 Emma Donoghue, *The Woman Who Gave Birth to Rabbits* (London: Virago Press, 2002).

15 Homi K. Bhabha, 'Introduction', in Homi K. Bhabha (ed.), *Nation and Narration* (London and New York: Routledge, 1990), p. 4.

16 Homi K. Bhabha, 'DisemiNation: Time, Narrative, and the Margins of the Modern Period', in Bhabha, *Nation and Narration*, p. 300.

17 Sara Harasym (ed.), *Gayatri Chakravorty Spivak: The Post-colonial Critic. Interviews, Strategies, Dialogues* (London and New York: Routledge: 1990), p. 38.

18 Ibid.

19 Clair Willis, 'The Politics of Poetic Form', in Claire Connolly (ed.), *Theorizing Ireland* (Basingstoke: Palgrave Macmillan, 2003), p. 125.

20 Joe Cleary, 'Misplaced Ideas? Colonialism, Location and Dislocation in Irish Studies', in Connolly, *Theorizing Ireland*, p. 103.

21 See, for example, Kirsti Bohata, *Postcolonialism Revisited* (Cardiff: University of Wales Press, 2004).

22 Cleary, 'Misplaced Ideas?', p. 104.

23 Ibid.

24 Leonora Brito, *dat's love* (Bridgend: Seren, 1995).

25 Emma Donoghue, *Stir-fry* (1994; rpt Harmondsworth: Penguin, 1995).

26 Siân James, *A Small Country* (1979; rpt Bridgend: Seren, 1999).

27 Sarah Waters, *The Night Watch* (London: Virago Press, 2006).

28 Seamus Deane, 'Heroic Styles: The Tradition of an Idea', in Connolly, *Theorizing Ireland*, p. 16.

29 Mary Morrissy, *Mother of Pearl* (London: Jonathan Cape, 1996).

2 Unspoken Histories: Groundbreaking Short Fiction

A lot of women's writing is about reclaiming histories that have been marginalized or never previously articulated at all. However, two collections of short stories, one written at the end of the twentieth century and the other at the beginning of the twenty-first, as suggested in the previous chapter, may be regarded as watersheds in Welsh and Irish literature because of the extent to which they explore previously undocumented women's experiences.

Although very different authors, the Cardiff-born, black writer Leonora Brito and the white, Dublin writer Emma Donoghue, who moved to Canada, are each responsible for re-conceiving women's history in their respective countries. In doing so, they also further the understanding of the different ways in which late twentieth- and twenty-first-century women's writing is rooted in a history of struggle, confrontation, empowerment and disempowerment and of how women have assumed control of discourses that have previously marginalized or silenced them.

Leonora Brito's most recent collection of short stories, *Chequered Histories*,[1] extends the global and conceptual reach of her first work, *dat's love* (1995), through exploring issues around mixed race and identity in areas as diverse as the west coast of Africa, Massachusetts and the Cape Verde islands, as well as her own home city, Cardiff. However, in doing so it underlines the groundbreaking nature of her earlier book which has not been fully appreciated but which may have inspired a number of works by Welsh women writers at the end of the previous century and the beginning of the current century concerned with the ethnic diversity of Wales. These include works such as Trezza Azzopardi's *The Hiding Place*,[2] a novel about the Maltese community in Cardiff's

Tiger Bay, and Charlotte Williams's *Sugar and Slate*,[3] an autobiographical account of the growing up of mixed Afro-Caribbean and Welsh race in the slate-mining communities of North Wales. However, the publication in this century and the end of the twentieth century of works highlighting the rich ethnic histories of Wales and Ireland only serves to draw attention to the absence of literary voices giving expression to these experiences.[4] *dat's love* developed from a 'culture of community articulation' created initially by oral history projects in the 1980s and sustained for today's young generations by internet community websites.[5] Barnor Hesse has pointed out: 'Modernity continues to project a nightmarish shadow over the formulations of Black cultural and political identities . . . of timed-spaced tracings of 300 years of African enslavement; the exploitative, violent division of the world into sublime Europe and savage/exotic non-Europe . . .'[6] Brito's work may be regarded as post 'Race' where the concept of 'race' is envisaged as a singular, fixed concept of origins. Brito acknowledges that race can be perceived as a stigma, as it was for many residents in the Cardiff docklands in the mid-twentieth century. But in her work it is a fluid concept, with culturally determined meanings that change and evolve over time and through different geographical contexts. Most important of all is her recognition that this 'postmodern' perception of race can be empowering. It allows us to assume control of our racial origins so that culturally oriented terms such as 'white', 'coloured' and 'black', and even 'Welsh' and 'Irish', need not necessarily define us as they do in the dominant discourses of the day.

Leonora Brito is a fourth generation Black woman, whose immediate family began with two rooms in Christina Street, Cardiff, with family memories of the Spanish enclaves in Butetown where her grandmother danced Spanish valses and Argentine tangos.[7] In this respect, her work is an example of what Clair Willis, as discussed in the previous chapter, called 'engaged' literature. It is important to appreciate that the stories in *dat's love* have emerged from an awareness of the significance of community heritage in Cardiff. This provides us with a valuable point of entry not only into her work but also into the way in which the stories are fragments and pieces of lives lived in the Bay. This is a style that seems to mirror the kind of narratives that evolve from oral and internet histories. The titular story that opens Leonora Brito's *dat's love* is as an exploration of events involving the narrator and a friend when she was younger. The focus upon the relations between the two friends gives the Bay a particular perspective. Brito sees the Bay community, Wales and Cardiff as defined, like the community of the friends, through a relationship to the 'other'. This distinctive way of looking at cultural identities, which we will see in other contemporary Welsh, Irish and Northern Irish women writers, emphasizes the concept of 'boundaries'. Its focus is upon how identities are constructed in and through their relations with each other.

Brito's approach to cultural relations is more subtle than those which are based more exclusively upon notions of domination, subordination or opposition. This can be illustrated in Brito's 'Mother Country' which, ambivalently titled, draws upon the importance of the mother-child relationship in African and Caribbean culture. Ostensibly about a young mother coming to accept her newborn baby, it explores the way in which mother and child are each defined through the relationship between them that is more complex than a 'rejection' and 'acceptance' binarism:

> But she puts out her hand! Amazing, for it is the touch of her hand, her baby hand, with the small white fingers stiff and cold upon the warm, brown flesh of my arm, that starts the thaw – that unfreezes my heart – drip, drip, drip. I put the teat back into her mouth, and watch her tiny fingers uncurling. Entranced, as one by one they uncurl in the warmth of my body-heat, and then wave in the air, palely, like sea-anemones. (46)

Cardiff Bay and Black America

The retrospective, reflective narrative of *dat's love* is not untypical of much short fiction by contemporary Welsh, Irish and Northern Irish women writers that seeks to push back the boundaries around gender, sexual identity, family and community. However, Brito has more in common with the Nobel Prize-winning African-American novelist Toni Morrison than many Welsh short story writers, sharing her concern with how ethnic minority communities and mixed-race peoples can reclaim themselves as the subjects of their own histories and biographies rather than being the objects in other people's narratives.

Butetown, the multicultural docks area of Cardiff, became known throughout the world as 'Tiger Bay', invoked by male novelists and writers such as Howard Spring and John Williams.

Williams was brought up in 'genteel Cardiff' and it was on his return to the Capital from London that he discovered the City 'beyond the tracks'. In many ways this is typical of the representation of the Bay, perceived as an enclave and written about from the point of view of a male outsider looking in. It is this which makes Brito's perspective as an insider and a woman so important. A contemporary history website of Butetown carries a revealing quotation, epitomizing the way in which Butetown's rich, cultural diversity was perceived by the outsider:

> Chinks and Dagos, Lascars and Levantines slippered about the faintly evil by-ways that ran off from Bute Street. The whole place was a warren of seamen's boarding houses, dubious hotels, ships' chandlers smelling of rope and tarpaulin ... children of the strangest colours, fruits of frightful misalliances, staggered half-naked about the streets ... It was a dirty, smelly, rotten and romantic district, an offence and an inspiration and I loved it.[8]

Insiders, as Brito's stories make clear, thought of the 'Docks' as a place where an extraordinary number of different peoples had come together, often sharing a migrant past, and where there was warmth and humour as well as violence and poverty. The Bay is also the kind of community in which the black, American feminist bell hooks found the 'understanding [of] marginality as position and place of resistance' which she argued was so important for 'oppressed, exploited, colonized people'.[9]

Butetown, Wales's first multi-ethnic community, developed over a period of about 150 years during which men (mostly), of over fifty different cultures, followed the trade routes to the bustling coal port, and married Welsh, English or Irish women. In the inter-war period, Tiger Bay was one of the largest ethnic minority communities in Britain. Peoples of African, Middle Eastern and Asian heritages – from India, the Yemen, Egypt, Somalia, Sierra Leone, Liberia, Nigeria, the Cameroons, Gambia, the Caribbean and China – mingled with Maltese, Portugese, Greeks and other European nationalities. What is interesting, as Laura Tabili points out, is that the diverse population of inter-war, ethnic communities such as Cardiff Bay, in the outsider's view, 'shared neither physiognomy nor culture; they were united by a political and historical relationship of colonial subordination'.[10] Following the race riots of 1919, when the city had an ethnic population of over 3,000, Cardiff became linked with Chicago – a tense, industrial city in which ethnic communities were 'othered' and stereotyped in narratives of migration, miscegenation and multiculturalism. The tensions surfaced initially in 1911 when over two nights all but one of the Chinese laundries in Butetown had their windows smashed. But in 1919, when many Dockland's people returned from the war to face economic hardship and no compensation for their efforts, a spate of attacks on black seamen led to a brawl in which a white man was stabbed to death which in turn triggered a week of riots in which homes were ransacked. Brito's Arlene in 'Stripe by Stripe' articulates the cultural memory: 'All that Lloyd George business, and how he did the dirty on all the coloureds in 1919 . . .' (121).

The race riots in Chicago in the same year, also aggravated by economic and employment problems after the armistice, left twenty-three black people dead, 342 injured and hundreds homeless. In both cities whites roamed the streets looking for black people to attack and targeting black homes. After the riots many black people left Cardiff, including 600 who were repatriated to their original homelands. The changing nature of the Bay was famously captured in Selwyn Roderick's documentary film *Tamed and Shabby Tiger* (1967) which recorded the arrival of the bulldozers that razed homes to the ground to make way for a tide of inner-city redevelopment. His daughter, Siân, returned over thirty years later to trace the characters who featured in his documentary in her film, *Where's that Tiger Now?*.

Writing from the perspective of a member of the Cardiff Bay community, Brito sees it, as Morrison sees Harlem in *Jazz*,[11] as a place where it is possible to be more than oneself, and, as Morrison says of Harlem, people can embrace their 'riskier' selves. The Bay, like Morrison's Harlem, is a place of violence, highly charged sexual relationships, and internecine conflict. However, it is also a place where spontaneity, improvisation and sexuality take their cue from the music that fills the bars. In 'Stripe by Stripe', one of the Bay's inhabitants remembers it as 'the New Orleans of a great coaling Metropolis' (117–18) where 'people have fought hard and played hard' (118). The Bay's spirit is epitomized in the 'good time girl' (115), Madame Patti, who is seen as 'rowing and drinking and causing trouble, painting her front door bright yellow while everyone else's was council house blue' (115).

'Sass' and 'performance'

Madame Patti possesses, like many of Morrison's female rebels, what she calls 'sass'. Crucial to 'sass' for both Brito and Morrison is not simply the capacity to get out from under white oppression but the disruption of white stereotypes of black, cultural identity. Each sees mockery and mimicry as important weapons in the armoury of the subjugated. Moreover, music and performance are perceived as central to both the Bay and black America's identity. The dominant contemporary influence on ethnic minority people in the Bay is black American music. This should not surprise us since from the 1920s onwards music and theatre pushed back the boundaries of what it meant to be 'black' in America. The black Broadway musical 'Shuffle Along' which opened in 1921 broke new ground in its content, featuring scenes between black people of a kind not previously shown on stage, and also in the way in which its nationwide tours broke the colour barrier in theatres across the country the following year. Musicals like 'Shuffle Along' played a significant part in reconfiguring black identity, inspiring many subsequent shows such as 'Liza' (1924), 'Keep Shufflin' (1928) and 'Hot Chocolates' (1929), as well as a generation of black playwrights, songwriters and poets. Indeed, the song 'Bye, Bye Blackbird', recorded in 1926 by Ray Henderson and Mort Dixon and referred to in 'Dat's Love', also brings to mind the all-black musical revue the 'Blackbirds' (1928) staged by a white producer for white audiences.

Indeed, performance is the principal motif of 'Dat's Love', which revolves around the funeral of Dooley Wilson, 'much darker than the light-skinned chap in the film' (9) and Sarah Vaughan, 'the coloured young lady with the Welsh name' who is billed as 'the Sepia, Celtic Siren' (14) and wears 'her brownish gold hair swept over to one side, in imitation of some Hollywood film star or other' (16). An immediate real-life model for Sarah is Shirley Bassey, who was born in Tiger Bay in 1937 as one of the children of a mixed marriage between a woman from the North of England and a Nigerian sailor. Although Bassey is generally associated with Tiger Bay, she is more accurately a product of working-class, multi-ethnic Splott. She began her singing career, like Brito's Sarah, on leaving school and was noticed in 1955 by the bandleader Jack Hylton, at about the same time as Sarah was hoping to be spotted, and, like Sarah but more successfully, left Cardiff for the stage lights of

London. Taking the name of a celebrated black American singer, Sarah also brings to mind the legendary black American dancer Josephine Baker, who was the first African-American female performing artist to win recognition in both Europe and the United States. In acts that were both outrageously entertaining and sexy, she performed white stereotypes of black American music and dance in ways that mocked their principally white audiences. In the early 1950s, Brito's Sarah tours the Welsh valleys as a member of 'Jolson's Jelly Babes', making her name through 'blacking up her face and acting comical at the end of the line' (14).

The kind of comical acting which draws the audience's attention to Sarah is exactly how Josephine first got herself noticed. In 1922, she auditioned for the musical 'Shuffle Along' but was not selected. Hired as a wardrobe assistant, she learnt the routines and filled in when a dancer was off sick. Like Sarah, she performed in a clumsy way, winning laughs from the audience, attracting the resentment of her fellow dancers and mocking the routine itself. In 1924, she became a star by performing in 'Chocolate Dandies'.

Josephine Baker, Shirley Bassey and Brito's Sarah demonstrate the capacity of individuals and groups to define their own identities and mobilize these definitions through practices that disrupt accepted traditions and beliefs. The link between practices and performance is a recurring motif in Welsh, Irish and Northern Irish contemporary women's writing, not least because their work applies to wider concepts of identity ideas about performance introduced by feminist critics in the 1980s and 1990s in relation to gender. Consciously or unconsciously, much contemporary writing by women is indebted to radical ideas about gender, sexuality and desire, and the relationships between them, introduced by the American critic Judith Butler, mentioned in the previous chapter, after which gender was seen as a continuous, acculturated process.[12] Butler disrupted the traditional mode of thought through arguing against a predetermined, biological basis for gender identity. In her view, gender is always a 'performance' and is based not only on what one is born into, culturally and biologically, but what one chooses to be.

'Performance' and protest

Brito seems particularly interested in using Sarah in 'Dat's Love' as a focus for different levels of cultural, racial, sexual and gender disruption. It is said that Sarah might have been Al Johnson's illegitimate daughter, a shrewd point since black theatre is the illegitimate offspring of white American theatre. Her career ends on a London stage, 'swaying in front of a coconut tree, under a pale yellow moon' (14); an act reminiscent of the way in which Josephine Baker, naked apart from strips of bananas, performed satirically in jungle stage sets. Sarah's name is a local as well as an international statement about the identity to which she aspires. Whilst her 'real' name is Jones, Sarah takes the name of the man with whom her mother is living. It is an act of defiance as well as a performance: 'her eyes were brown like toffee, and her skin was bright like tin; and if she wanted to call herself after her mother's fancy man, then she would' (16).

A black person changing her name has a particular significance which would not apply to many white people. Kimberly Benston reminds us that in slavery black people were given white names. In this sense, 'unnaming', as he calls it, is an attempt to gain control over one's life and is also 'genealogical revisionism': 'All of Afro-American literature may be seen as one vast genealogical poem that attempts to restore continuity to the ruptures or discontinuities imposed by the history of black presence in America.'[13] Apart from being another link between black culture in Cardiff Bay and the United States in the middle of the twentieth century, Sarah draws attention to how important 'naming' and 'unnaming' can be to people whose cultural origins have been denigrated by a culture other than their own. Whilst this is fundamentally a black American phenomenon, there are many examples of Welsh people, especially after the 1970s when the Welsh language became recognized more widely in Wales, taking Welsh versions of their names or new Welsh-language names altogether.

Sarah's taking her mother's lover's name is also a public retort to the negative view of the Bay held by many from outside, especially in the Valleys which connected miscegenation with amorality and illegitimacy. Although Wales recorded the first mixed marriage in Britain in 1768, miscegenation was a major issue in the denigration of the Bay area, a situation fuelled by the Chief Constable's proposal after the Cardiff riots of 1919 for such marriages to be banned. He was, of course, giving expression to a sentiment of the times. Lucy Bland maintains that as early as 1917 'the press had been full of the horrors of miscegenation, the *Daily Dispatch* for example, having described the black man's "weakness" "for associ-ating with white women" as "The Black Peril"'.[14] Bland also makes the point that the term miscegenation itself has a loaded history with its origins in a spoof pamphlet *Miscegenation: the Theory of the Blending of the Races Applied to the American White Man and Negro* (1864) which implied that Abolitionists sought to free slaves because they desired them sexually.[15] The public attitude to misce-genation in mid-twentieth-century south Wales is illustrated in the real story of a seventeen-year-old girl from the Welsh mining valleys, at about the time Sarah's mother in the valleys took her new lover. This young woman married a Somali seaman in his twenties, Mahood Mattan, who was to be hanged at Cardiff prison for murder in the early 1950s – a conviction that was overturned nearly fifty years later. When the couple moved to Tiger Bay, such was the feeling against mixed marriages that they had to live in separate houses in the same street. At his trial, Mahood's barrister, as was widely reported at the time, peppered his defence with numerous stereotypes of a black man who spoke only halting English, refer-ring to him as a 'semi-civilised savage' and a 'half-child of nature'.

In contrast to the view of sexuality in the Bay held by some respectable classes outside of it, Sarah Vaughan thinks of herself as representing the Bay as a place which combines sexual freedom, an energizing hybridism and a performative sense of self. Like Sula, the central female protagonist in Morrison's novel of that name,[16] and Junior in her novel *Love*,[17] Sarah is a 'trickster figure' who disrupts conventional attitudes and ways of behaving. Just as Sula and her best friend Nel may be perceived as two halves of the Bottom community in Morrison's novel, Sarah and the narrator are the two faces of Butetown. The narrator is an Abyssinian, the largest ethnic group in the Bay. The narrator's attitude toward Sarah is ambiva-lent. Attracted, like her friend, to the group's principal singer, she tries to sing straight in accompaniment to his piano playing and is resentful of her friend's comical routines:

> We were supposed to be funny, but it was Sarah who had been the funny one, going cross-eyed in the background as I sang. She made them laugh, as I was singing. I had to turn round to see what they were laughing at. The piano was slow and lilting. It wasn't him, he played it right. But she made it funny pulling her beret down over her eyes and acting gormless. (17–18)

In many respects, the narrator is comparable to Morrison's Nel as 'always the calm and steady one' (15), but, in describing herself as 'steady and responsible', she betrays envy of Sarah who has 'cheek and daring in her eyes' (15). Like Sula and Junior, Sarah has 'sass', and is 'a wild one, one of those girls who wouldn't take a telling' (15). Her confession that she provokes Sarah into worse behaviour might lead the reader to suspect that she lives her life vicariously through her friend. Sarah sees the Docklands as conservative and the Rainbow Club as being run by 'the friggin' missionaries' (16). In the canteen, she boasts that an older man wants to go out with her. She is crude, she burps in public and also drinks provocatively, for those times, out of a bottle. The argument with the narrator results in her dragging her nails down the latter's face.

The episode highlights the significance of dialogue in contemporary Welsh women's writing, referred to in Chapter 1, as the manifestation of the importance of 'enactment' and 'performance' to female and black people's identities. This is evident in the following lines from Sarah: '"Oh, I'm definitely going! He wants to give me *breathing lessons*; doan he? Says it'll improve my singing voice, ahem!" She coughed.' (17) These lines are partly aimed at the narrator who she knows is attracted like herself to the older man she is talking about. Moreover, she is not only answering a direct question from her work friends – that she intends to see this man – but making a statement about herself and her determination whilst making public her assertive sexuality. In some respects, what she says is less important than the communication of her confidence in herself, her independence and her sexuality. She enjoys indulging in innuendo and double meaning but this is itself an indication of how she thinks of herself as more sexually experienced and adventurous than her friends and work colleagues. In engaging in innuendo, she is in charge of the conversation and the language, choosing to answer her friends in a more complex, albeit amusing, way than they might have anticipated.

Sarah represents the way in which white culture eroticized the black body but also what was perceived by the white community as the dangerous side of black sexuality: 'Love is a bird, that flies where it will.' (20) But the comparison between Nel and Sula also highlights the possibility that the narrator and Sarah, like Nel and Sula, are two sides of the same coin. Sarah's attack on her friend's face is significant given the importance to her act of blacking up and mocking white racist black stereotypes. The attack may well be a transfer of her innermost anger to her friend's face. Conversely, Sarah is the narrator's alter ego. Whilst she is conservative, sober and respectable, she clearly identifies with the need to mock racist stereotypes, otherwise she would not participate in the comedy routine. However, Sarah goes much further and seems to live the protest in ways in which the narrator's Abyssinian background will not allow. To what extent, we might ask, does she want to be attacked, punished for her conservatism, by her more assertive alter ego?

Language and control

Brito's stories illustrate Joe Cleary's arguments, mentioned in Chapter 1, that culturally determined identities are always part of a changing historical process and 'the product of dislocating intersections between local and global processes'. They are set not in a static Bay community but in one that was always changing, and, in 'Stripe by Stripe', is disappearing in the new development of the Docklands. Jack expresses his anger at the apparent Americanization of the district: 'American this, American that . . . Humerican shit don't stink, *hic*. Do it.' (115) Within the collection as a whole, this is ironic because the Americanization which in 'Dat's Love' empowered the community, especially its young people, is now destroying its distinctiveness. However, in this story, too, Brito is interested in how women assume control of situations by taking charge of language. Arlene reacts angrily to her adult son's attempt to order her indoors:

> 'Who's he giving his orders to?' Arlene was hanging over the railings in a flash: 'Who you giving your orders to? I'm your mother I am. That's right!' she called out after him, 'That's right, goan find yourself a woman son, you're not my husband yet!' (120)

Arlene's response, like Sarah's conversation in the factory canteen, is aimed at more than one audience. Initially an appeal to the neighbours, it is then directed at her son. Her swift body movement – quickly leaning over the gate – mirrors the speed with which she becomes verbally confrontational in response to what she sees as his outrageous insolence. Repeating her verbal punches in quick succession is clearly the principal linguistic technique by which she asserts herself. At the heart of her response, where attack is defence, is her reaffirmation of her familial position – 'I am your mother I am' – which again relies upon repetition for its effect but which, in this case, closes off her statement in a way which makes it seem conclusive and beyond argument. She undermines the 'masculinity' her son had shown in attempting to dominate her: 'Goan find yourself a woman son.' She reminds him, and everyone within earshot, of his subordinate position to her whilst implying, what is then fully stated, that he is not yet fully a man because he has not become a husband.

Whilst Arlene seeks to reassert family and community values, it is within the framework of the Bay being redeveloped and the tension between the generations. Throughout Brito's collection, change at different levels becomes the principal motif by which concepts of family, community and history are examined. One of the major achievements is the way Brito uses metaphor to give coherence to stories that, because they concern race, class and gender, are invariably multilayered. The potato's tuberous roots system in 'Roots' is an appropriate metaphor for the complex identity and experiences of a young, black, female Bay resident who recalls her childhood over the period of one summer. The story begins with the planting of the seed potatoes when the earth has been 'crumbled into absolute evenness' (105) and closes with the front garden 'empty, cleared' (112). The change in the garden mirrors the change in the narrator's perception of her father and Mr Talbot from being 'big men, home from the sea' (111). Gradually, all the old reassurances are lost. It is revealed that Mr Blueser, whom she thought of as 'a travelling country blues man' (113), is named after a blouse he mistakenly bought for himself and she notices that the backs of her mother's legs are white. But the key incident, apart from being bullied at school, is the attempt by a man to abduct her on her way home from school which makes her think about being black and what that must signify for her to be approached in this way. At the heart of the story is her growing awareness of difference as she notices that whilst Mr Talbot admires their front garden laid to potatoes, 'His own front garden has a lawn and rockery with a gnome on the top' (111). What she sees are people of a different class for whom there is more order in the world than apparently exists in her own. In the park, when she is playing truant from school, she sees 'old posh people sit on the benches and look at the flowers lined up, row after row in front of them' (109). She finds herself assuming roles that society assigns black children, not only playing truant but becoming a 'black marketeer' selling American tipped cigarettes to her friends. Whilst she perceives difference around her, for her teachers, who mistake her 'for another coloured girl, Carmel, who is two forms ahead [of her]' (109), black girls are all the same. In other words, in white Welsh society in the post 1950s, race subsumes all other differences, including age.

The participant narrator of 'Roots', like Sarah Vaughan in 'Dat's Love', embodies, literally and figuratively, the complexity of being a black-Welsh young woman in the twentieth century. Both think of themselves as located at the boundary between the physical and the cultural body and are vehicles by which Brito explores the nature of this 'space'. But what are central to these stories are the concepts of race and history themselves, which have not been previously subjected to such interrogation from a black perspective in Welsh writing. However, Brito is indebted to the way in which women's writing in Wales, as in Ireland and Northern Ireland, has sought to address the marginalization of women's history and the ways in which different histories have sought to define women in limited and limiting discourses. In this respect, her work, ranging over several Cardiff Bay generations, engages with a dimension of the Welsh past that has been relatively neglected. What is radical about *dat's love*, though, is not only the exploration from a black perspective of a marginalized, multi-cultural community, but the extent to which her stories pursue the implications of the post-History direction that women's writing in Wales, Ireland and Northern Ireland has been moving for some time, emphasizing the diversity of women's experiences across different communities, different generations and different races.

Radical histories

Emma Donoghue has a considerable reputation as a novelist, short story writer and a dramatist. She is the author of two novels set in late twentieth-century Dublin where she was born: *Stir-fry* (1994), about a young student from rural Ireland who is awakened to her sexual interest in women when she moves to the capital, and *Hood*.[18] But she is equally known for her historical novels: *Slammerkin*[19] and *Life Mask*.[20] *Slammerkin* concerns a child prostitute in eighteenth-century London who is eventually forced to flee to Monmouth where temporarily she escapes her true past before it catches up with her and she is eventually hanged for murder. *Life Mask* tells the 'true' story of a scandalous love triangle in 1790s London.

The Woman Who Gave Birth to Rabbits (2002) is a watershed in Irish women's short fiction for the way in which it develops the possibilities arising from the diversity of women's experiences across different communities and different generations. It combines, as Donoghue says in the Foreword, historical research and imagination. Thus, in her words, it is 'a book of fictions, but they are also true'. It uncovers the lives of women, some with famous names and others that have been 'written off as cripples, children, half-breeds, freaks and nobodies'. Her introduction does not simply state the notion that women's writing is born out of struggle but furthers our understanding of how women's writing stands in relation to history in arguing that she uses 'memory and invention together'. If Brito's work is post-'Race', Donoghue's *The Woman Who Gave Birth to Rabbits* is post-'History'. Just as Brito rejects the concept of 'Race' as a singular, fixed term of origins, Donoghue challenges the notion of 'History' as a singular, knowable narrative. 'History' for Donoghue, like race for Brito, is culturally determined and changes over time and through different geographical locations. Her concern is not with 'History', which is always written from particular preconceptions and vested interests, but with histories. Underpinning the engagement with different histories in her work are questions about the writing of history itself. In whose interests and from what standpoint is it conceived? Who is excluded and who is privileged as a result of the particular narrative perspective? How incomplete are particular histories and who is it that benefits and who is it that is disadvantaged by this incompleteness?

The scraps of history upon which the stories are based include the story of Mary Toft (1703–63) who embarrassed the medical establishment in the eighteenth century by pretending to give birth to rabbits; an anecdote about the niece of an apothecary in Ireland around the time of the Act of Union who was forced into a marriage with an English officer suffering from syphilis who had been duped by her uncle; the Welsh activist Mary Lloyd and her friend Francis 'Fà' Cobbe who sought to get an anti-vivisection bill through Parliament in the late nineteenth century; two cousins, Anna Gurney and Sarah Buxton, who lived together in the first half of the nineteenth century and became involved in the rescue of sailors from a shipwreck off the Norfolk coast; the case of a young woman who was one of many upon whom a famous surgeon performed a clitoridectomy without her full knowledge of what was happening; and a maid in fourteenth-century Ireland who, having been found guilty of complicity in her employer's murder of her four husbands and of being a witch, was burned to death. Rejecting traditional, explanatory models of history, Donoghue turns to a conceptualization of space which is similar to that proposed by the cultural theorist Dick Hebdige. Both see cultural and geographical space as, in Hebdige's words, 'a moving cluster of points of intersection for manifold axes of power', which, as Hebdige points out, is 'no less complex and contradictory than historical processes' with which they are interconnected.[21]

Writing and regeneration

Although their work is very different, Donoghue's writing, like Brito's, documents neglected histories and highlights the importance of creativity and critical reflection as a social and cultural force. However, it is a line from the work of another Welsh short story writer, Clare Morgan, discussed in Chapter 5, that encapsulates what it is that Donoghue derives from her resurrections of past lives. In the stories of women such as Mary Toft, Mary Lloyd and Anna Gurney, one feels that Donoghue, to employ Morgan's words, might say, 'I take her hand and step out with her onto the dark surface of the world' (168). This is especially evident in the story 'Salvage' which concerns two female cousins, living together, who have become known as 'The Cottage Ladies'. The title refers most immediately to Anna and Sarah's efforts to assist in salvaging a ship from the rocks off the Norfolk coast but more generally to Anna's efforts to improve the success rate in rescuing as many lives and as much as possible from the recurring shipwrecks. But it also refers to what Anna has 'salvaged' in her own life; a wheelchair user, she had been dropped on the stairs when she was two months old. Like everyone at the shipwreck, she has learnt to recognize what she can do and what she cannot. But she is more determined and more adventurous than many others around her. The progress that she has made in her life has been dependent upon entering a space between 'safety' and 'danger'. At the shipwreck, Anna takes her wheelchair to the sea's edge, pushing back the boundaries of what is 'safe'. In doing so, she shames those who have not used the Patent

Life Saving Apparatus because they believed they could not get near enough to the wreck. When Cousin Fowell enters the water and reaches the wreck, he has to persuade a sailor to let go of a piece of the mast to grab the line from the Life Saving Machine. This provides the central metaphor for the story, and for Anna's life. The sailor has to risk what appears to be safe and enter the space where Anna frequently positions herself, on the edge of danger. What seems safe but is actually not going to save him appears to be more solid than the flimsiness of the rope that will really rescue him from death. The story is empowering because it explores the discourse around concepts such as 'risk', 'safety' and 'possibility'. It is significant that Anna, who has more than one language, is the only one able to converse with the rescued sailors for she is the one most used to thinking beyond limits.

There is a recurring interest in *The Woman Who Gave Birth to Rabbits* in women who think beyond limits. Given the involvement of women in the Irish Republican movement, the opportunity to write about the Victorian, Welsh, anti-vivisection activist Mary Lloyd, the subject of 'The Fox on the Line', undoubtedly appealed to Donoghue. It seems to have provided her with an opportunity to explore not only the tensions and ambiguities around personal commitment to a cause in which one passionately believes but also the way in which involvement in politics often involves unpalatable compromise. The fate of the proposed anti-vivisection bill can be seen as a cryptic reference to the compromise that Michael Collins was forced to make over Irish independence in negotiating with the British Government. Some believe that Collins had been set up by De Valera, who suspected that the best deal that could have been secured at that time was what Collins in fact returned with, but preferred that Collins would be seen as the one who compromised. Whatever the truth, Collins's agreement caused a rift in Sinn Fein in the 1920s, as De Valera might have predicted, and brought into being for a time the Irish Free State rather than a fully independent Ireland. Collins has subsequently been the subject of numerous studies and a film biography that have highlighted the tensions within him between commitment to an Irish republic and the necessity for compromise.

Unlike her friend Francis 'Fà' Cobbe, who is almost mechanistically committed to the cause, Mary Lloyd in Donoghue's story is caught between public life and the quiet retreat she would like to enjoy as a sculptor in North Wales. She is caught between her aspirations as an artist and her ambitions as a public campaigner. Whereas the contribution that writers and artists can make to society and culture is most explicit in their support of public issues, the value of art as the manifestation of a creative, often alternative, way of thinking from which sociocultural development would benefit is often overlooked.

Donoghue also uses anti-vivisection to examine issues pursued in a number of her other stories concerning women and medicine. Mary is torn over whether to spend more time in London with her friend or at her beloved Hengwrt. London offers Fà the kind of radical, open space that twentieth-century feminists such as bell hooks found in the city, while Mary values more highly the spiritual recovery she experiences in North Wales. But Hengwrt is also a place of wider political thought for Mary.[22] There she reflects on her misgivings as a feminist about the campaign against animal cruelty, pondering whether it would be preferable for women to devote themselves to the issues affecting them, such as the gendered nature of medical science, which the anti-vivisection campaigns unwittingly raised. Whereas her friend is singularly focused upon animal cruelty, Mary sees vivisection all around her, linking the male scientists who champion vivisection with doctors who perform experiments on women: 'The surgeons do it simply to kill passion. Simply to make women quieter. Simply because they can.' (34) Whilst a number of Donoghue's stories return to the different ways in which medical discourse regards men and women, the subject of the anti-vivisection campaigns provides Donoghue with a vehicle for suggesting the link between medicine and science. A question left hanging, which is referred to in overt or covert ways in subsequent stories, is the extent to which doctors are physicians or scientists. To what extent are doctors involved in treating their patients and to what extent do they regard them as the objects of wider experiments?

As in many of the stories, Donoghue uses a central metaphor, in this case vivisection, to push back the boundaries of what the story is concerned with. When Mary begins to see vivisection all around her, embarking on a new feminist understanding of science, she acts as a metaphor for what the author is doing in the story itself. Mary becomes interested in how women are subjugated into behaving in ways that please men but harm themselves, epitomized for her in the deformed feet that are the product of the fashionable shoes women wear. Whereas Fà is committed to challenging the accepted norms in behaviour toward animals, Mary finds herself pushing back the boundaries of acceptable and unacceptable behaviours in a much wider sense. The important point that the story makes, which was also made by early twentieth-century modernist women writers such as Virginia Woolf, is that women's lives are determined not only by economic circumstance but also by dominant social discourses that are intricately interwoven. Subjecting these discourses to critical, feminist scrutiny takes one into an elaborate matrix of accepted opinion and, as we shall see in a moment in the discussion of more of the stories, it raises issues about the nature and control of language itself. Nevertheless, Donoghue, like Brito, does not underestimate the influence of financial circumstances upon women's lives.

Women, medicine and science

Unlike Brito's stories, Donohue's have an eccentricity that is sometimes humorous and on other occasions deeply disturbing. An example of the latter is 'The Last Rabbit'. Whilst it is clearly intended as an indictment of the medical profession for the way it treats women, it also leaves the reader with the impression that it is the sheer audacity of Mary Toft's scam that Donoghue found empowering. The episode itself is typical of short fiction by Irish and Welsh women writers in that it explores the subversive potential of gender, to which I referred in Chapter 1. It is multilayered, bringing together the ways in which medicine, law and the wider economic system legitimize privileged gendered and class interests.

The scam in 'The Last Rabbit' is viewed from the perspective of the woman who initiated it. The notion of the confidence trick brings to the fore the 'performative' element in gender identity referred to earlier. At the same time, it highlights concerns with gender politics and economics as determinants of cultural attitudes. It explores how preconceptions about women's bodies, especially those of lower class women, operate in tandem with gender and sexuality to the detriment of women. Mary Toft initiates the trick on the medical profession not for ideological reasons but because she needs the money to support her family; the cloth trade has declined, her husband has been unable to find work and Mary has been forced to obtain a meagre living from weeding hop fields. There is an obvious parallel between what she does, being forced to make use of her body to deceive, and women being forced to sell their bodies as prostitutes out of destitution. Like a prostitute, she sees that she can offer herself as a commodity and as in the case of many women forced into prostitution her husband goes along with it. This parallel is made clear at the end of the story when Mary sees an elderly man having sex with a prostitute in the building in which she has been confined. In many respects, the prostitute, who literally and metaphorically performs 'tricks' for her clients, is the ultimate performer. Indeed, in moaning and groaning as she pretends to give birth to the dead rabbits, Mary mimics the way in which prostitutes 'perform' for their clients. In both scenarios, a woman becomes no more than a body; as Mary observes at one point, women are often not thought of as having souls. But both Mary and the prostitute, paradoxically, also show the power that women have over men. Mary is able to persuade her husband and Mr Howard, the male midwife, to join her in the confidence trick. This power is rooted in the way in which men seem to be dependent upon women in ways in which women are not upon men. Moreover, with the exception of Mr Howard, men in the story are 'other' to the body in that even the Royal Surgeon is ignorant of the female anatomy. That knowledge is generally held by women. The story uses the investigation of Mary's performance to highlight how the male-oriented medical profession, frequently displaying at best an impartial understanding of women's bodies, has subjected women to incredible pain and torture. Mary is actually threatened with prison or an internal medical examination if she does not admit her deception.

The way in which female sexuality was perceived in the Victorian period as potentially subversive and in need of being controlled is also explored in the story of the young woman who suffers a clitoridectomy. 'Cured' is an imaginative reconstruction of a case of a young woman admitted to the 'care' of a famous Victorian surgeon Baker Brown (1812–73), a pioneer of clitoridectomy who performed operations on not only young women but also children as young as ten. He conducts them, the story suggests, on women who come with ailments in other part of their bodies which he attributes to the clitoris. The young woman in this story is suffering from a back injury. But in Baker Brown's mind the operation is justified because otherwise she would have feelings, desires and frustrations that he deems improper, that would distract her from her duties and role as, say, a domestic servant, and would encourage her to touch herself regularly in ways that are perceived as unacceptable.

The story regularly contrasts the verbal and physical investigation of the young patient with the textbook summary of what the doctor can be expected to find. But the textbook is not neutral. It underlines a limited and condescending understanding of women's role in society: 'the patient becomes restless and excited, or melancholy and retiring; listless and indifferent to the social influences of domestic life.' (113) This specific bias in a medical textbook would be of particular interest to an Irish writer because of the way in which De Valera's Irish Constitution defined the role of women, referred to earlier. At the heart of the story is Donoghue's concern with power and meaning as constituted in language. The metaphor which most opens up this aspect of the story is the one that Donoghue uses to describe Baker Brown's internal examination of his patient: 'His hands moved like a pickpocket's, gliding, seeking.' (112) He is as linguistically artful as the pickpocket is physically dexterous. The authority which he has over the woman's body is manifest in the control that he has over language. All his questions to her are leading questions, simultaneously distracting and manipulative:

> 'Are you ever sleepless,' he broke in, 'or do you wake in the middle of the night?'
> 'Only if my back is bad,' she said, aware that she was repeating herself.
> 'Unaccountable fits of depression?'
> 'Well. Not really.' She tried to think. 'Only a sort of lost feeling, once in a while, when I consider my future.'
> 'Attacks of melancholy without any tangible reason?' he said encouragingly.
> After a moment, she shook her head. 'If I'm ever low in spirits, sir, it's for a reason.' (113)

By contrast, her language is naive and deferential. He tries to draw her in a specific direction which she resists because she does not understand either the language or the situation that she is in: 'She thought perhaps if she could tell this doctor all her reasons, all the real and unreal worries that ever lowered her spirits, she would then be able to shake them off.' (113)

The pickpocket metaphor is particularly appropriate because the doctor steals a part of her body and of her very being. The concluding confrontation between them after the operation hinges on the fact that he has betrayed her trust in him. Here she is forceful and in control of her language in a way in which she was not before the operation. But what she is not in charge of is the social discourse around female sexuality, respectability and propriety which Baker Brown relies upon to protect himself. Although she is able to assert herself here, she is still disadvantaged because she does not have an appropriate language in which to articulate her case: 'She imagined the conversation; her brother's face. All the words that came into her head appalled her.' (121) The story makes the point that not only do women have to wrest control over their bodies from the medical profession, they also have to influence the language in which issues concerning them are articulated. When she threatens to tell her husband what the doctor has done, he retorts:

> 'I'm afraid he would not understand which "part" you mean. He is not a man of much education.' A pause. 'How would you describe the "part" to him, Miss F.?' Another moment went by. 'Would you point, perhaps?' (121–2)

In a line that is devastating in its innuendo – 'She tried to gather her spit but her mouth was too dry' (122) – the text makes a powerful comparison between the doctor's examination of her mouth and of her vulva. The reference here is not only to the loss of arousal. In examining her mouth, he is figuratively investigating the organ of her expression, underscoring the way in which women's language and sexuality have both been denied by male discourse. One of the reasons why the doctor has been able to take control of her body and her sexuality is that there is no alternative to female-oriented discourse available to her. Initially, she sees Baker Brown as 'the famous Mr Baker Brown who understood women as no other man in the world did' (111–12) but when she finds her voice, she sees him as 'only a man. A middle-aged man' (122). Her changing view of him reflects her new insights into the medical profession towards which her attitude is no longer as naive as it was, but she still needs to acquire the language to challenge effectively the discourses that legitimize what he has done to her.

Language and complicity

The issue of who it is that controls the prevailing discourses affecting women is central to 'Come, Gentle Night', which concerns an art critic's impotence on his wedding night with his young bride who eventually divorces him. The story is rooted in the various conversations between them, especially the one leading up to the wedding night and the veiled dialogue between them which follows their discovery of his impotence, which neither is able to address candidly. The obvious question is, why the bride stayed as long as she did with a man who could not, and seemed unwilling to, consummate their marriage? The answer lies in the authority which the language and discourse of the husband commands in comparison with that of his wife. In the flirtatious conversation between them on the way to his home, it is obvious from the way in which he determines the content and the direction of the communication between them that he sees himself as the one in charge of them. Having established the precedent that he decides what is appropriate for them, it is inevitable that he is then able to persuade her to accept his spurious argument that the double excitement of travel and sexual relations would be too much for her to bear. But it is not so much the argument as the authority which he is able to invoke that assures her eventual compliance: 'I am asking you to trust me to decide this, as your husband.' (92) Like the Royal Surgeon in 'The Last Rabbit', he has little knowledge of women – being only familiar with statues of headless torsos and armless statues – but his suppression of his young wife's sexual instincts and drives signifies the way in which for centuries male-oriented discourse dictated that women's sexual needs went unrecognized and unarticulated.

How women are entrapped within situations where they appear to be complicit in their oppression is a recurring theme in Donoghue's work. In 'The Last Rabbit' and 'Cured', the explanation lies in women not having control of medical discourse and not being sufficiently in control of language. But in 'Looking for Petronilla', the maid's behaviour is much more enigmatic than that of the women in the previous stories. Unlike these other stories, the narrative is a record of a modern-day woman's research trip to a small Irish town to discover more information about a fourteenth-century maid who, having been left behind to answer for her wealthy mistresses' crimes, was burned to death, apparently without protesting her case.

The story turns on a number of contrasts. The most obvious is that between Alice Kytele's evil, which amounts to only 'a footnote in the annals of war and treachery' (202), and the ordinariness of Petronilla, which is underscored by the commonplace details that interrupt the narrator's search such as the uninterested bookstore assistant discussing her relationships on the phone and the empty hamburger carton in the gutter. The latter also signifies the disposable nature of so much that constitutes a living moment in the wider reaches of time. If Petronilla is too 'ordinary' to be remembered, what is not forgotten is remembered in a very distorted way. Donoghue makes the point that history becomes a kind of 'cartoon' (201). The story contrasts the 'real' history pursued by the narrator, whatever that may be, with the cartoon of history that is everywhere around her: in the painting in Kyteler's Inn where the shoes are from the wrong century and country; Alice's restaurant which has a sign 'It's a kind of Magic' (200); the pub offering 'Live Trad To-Nite' (207); and the poster inviting costumed revellers to a 'Quentin Tarratino Night' (205). This is postmodern Ireland where distinctions between the ordinary and the extraordinary no longer seem to have any validity and history itself is a commodity like everything else. The narrator, seeking the prison which held Petronilla, muses: 'Anything could have been built on the site of Petronilla's last months: a hardware shop, a B&B, a public toilet.' (207)

The story is ostensibly concerned with why Petronilla accepted her fate so uncomplainingly. But it also questions how we have accepted such banalities as Alice's restaurant and 'Quentin Tarratino Night'. A clue is offered in the bartender's version of history when she says, 'I love history, myself [because it] makes you feel more complete' (202). Like the cartoon history manifest in Kyeteler Inn, what appears to make sense is totally meaningless. How can one 'love history' (including what Cromwell did to Ireland?) and when did history ever offer a sense of 'completion'? The mendacity of her language as well as of her thinking seems to entrap the bartender in the postmodern present. Similarly it is the language with which Petronilla grew up that eventually seems to be responsible for sealing her fate. The narrator concludes that she went unquestioningly to her death because she was used to language that positioned her as an object without a mind of her own; 'Her mistress's orders girded her like chain mail' until 'she embraced her death as a final order' (204).

The exploration of women's history, female sexuality, medicine and language in Donoghue's stories means that, like Leonora Brito's, they are multilayered. But, like Brito, she is adept at finding the image or metaphor – such as that of the pickpocket in 'Cured' or of the water's edge in 'Salvage' – that holds the different dimensions of the text together. In one of her more complex stories, 'Acts of Union', it is the Act of Union itself. As mentioned earlier, it is based upon an anecdote about an English officer in Ireland who, whilst drunk, is duped by an apothecary, whom he consults because he has syphilis, into marrying his niece. The multilayered nature of this story is evident in the wedding toast: 'To a most glorious union between two young persons, two families, two nations under God!' (24) Whilst the title refers to the marriage, it also invokes the Act of Union between Ireland and England; between the professional classes evidenced in the guests, including the minister, who join the apothecary for the fateful dinner; between the professional classes and the Protestant church; between the French and Irish rebels and between the officer and the unknown woman who has given him syphilis.

The woman who has infected him, possibly a prostitute, signifies the existence of an underground sexual society to which men have access and mirrors the role that secret societies have had in Irish politics. Indeed, reference is made at the supper table to the secret societies that are operating in the area whose members would think nothing of slitting the throats of their enemies (18). The clandestine nature of Irish politics and society generally at this time is mirrored in the duplicitous nature of the dinner where the soldier is being set up by the others into marrying Mr Knox's niece. What the story highlights is the difficulty of seeing a nation as other than a mass of contradictions. Thus, there will always be some people who will choose to go to the apothecary and others who would prefer to attend the Ferrier for treatment and ongoing debate as to whether Mayo or Donegal poteen is the better, whilst claims for the superiority of Scotch whisky will always signify the Scotch settlement of (Northern) Ireland.

It is possible to read this story at face value and to see it as an indictment of how women are treated. It is a moot point whether the real victim here is the officer or the niece who is forced into this union under the threat that if she does not agree she will be turned out of her uncle's home. The story also highlights Donoghue's recurring interest in the gendered nature of medical history. Whilst the officer attends the apothecary for a cure of his syphilis, he does not even begin to entertain the morality of his behaviour. Meanwhile, the niece's melancholy on losing both her parents is treated in an especially cavalier and misogynistic way. She is simply given pills so that soon 'she'll be lively as a doe' (20).

It is also possible to read 'Acts of Union' as an analogy for Ireland. Divorced from her roots, the niece stands for Ireland itself dependent upon and controlled by elderly men whose affiliations and actions are not in her best interests. Indeed, the English Captain's belief that he thinks he knew her is typical of an outsider's view of Ireland: 'He felt he knew the shadowy thoughts of her melancholic mind, the secret motions of her bosom.' (21) The story focuses upon the Captain's departure leaving unexplored what happens to her after the union with a diseased man which, thankfully for her, she has not consummated. Another question that hangs in the air at the end of the story is the motivation and interests of her uncle who would commit her to a relationship with a man who is suffering from syphilis.

The Woman Who Gave Birth to Rabbits is a collection of stories that are individually ambitious in their fusion of historical research and imaginative creativity and in the scope of their relevance to the twenty-first century. Collectively, they push back the boundaries of our understanding of how women are, and have been, imaginatively, socially and politically positioned by language and discourse.

Notes

1   Leonora Brito, *Chequered Histories* (Bridgend: Seren, 2006).
2   Trezza Azzopardi, *The Hiding Place* (New York: Grove Press, 2000).
3   Charlotte Williams, *Sugar and Slate* (Aberystwyth: Planet, 2002).
4   See, for example, Alan Llwyd, *Cymru Ddu: Hanes Pobl Dduon Cymru* (Black Wales: A History of Black Welsh People) (Wrexham: Hughes & Son (Publishers) Ltd, 2005); Williams, *Sugar and Slate*; and Bill Rolston and Michael Shannon, *Encounters: How Racism Came to Ireland* (Belfast: Beyond the Pale Publications Ltd, 2002).
5   See, for example, *http://www.bbc.co.uk/wales/history/sites/cag/pags/baypeople.shtml*.
6   Barnor Hesse, 'Black to Front and Black Again: Racialization Through Contested Times and Spaces', in Michael Keith and Steve Pile (eds), *Place and the Politics of Identity* (London and New York: Routledge, 1993), p. 166.
7   See her essay in *Cardiff Central: 10 Writers Return to Wales* (Llandysul: Gwasg Gomer, 2003).

8   *http://www.connections-exhibition.org/index.php/xml=parallels/cities/cardiff.xml*.

9   bell hooks, *Yearnings: Race, Gender and Cultural Politics* (Boston: South End Press, 1990), p. 149ff.

10 Laura Tabili, *'We Ask for British Justice': Workers and British Justice in Late Imperial Britain* (Ithaca: Cornell University Press, 1994).

11 Toni Morrison, *Jazz* (New York: Plume/Penguin, 1992).

12 Judith Butler's ideas are expounded in two principal texts: *Gender Trouble: Feminism and the Subversion of Identity* (London and New York: Routledge, 1990) and *Bodies that Matter: On the Discursive Limits of Sex* (London and New York: Routledge, 1990).

13 Kimberly W. Benston, 'I yam what I am: the topos of un(naming) in Afro-American literature', in Henry Louis Gates, Jr (ed.), *Black Literature and Literary Theory* (1984; rpt London and New York: Routledge, 1990), p. 152.

14 Lucy Bland, 'White Women and Men of Colour: Miscegenation Fears in Britain after the Great War', *Gender and History*, 17, 1, April 2005, 29–61 at 34.

15 Ibid., 29.

16 Toni Morrison, *Sula* (1973; London: Picador, 1991).

17 Toni Morrison, *Love* (New York: Alfred A. Knopf, Inc., 2003).

18 Emma Donoghue, *Hood* (London: Hamish Hamilton, 1995).

19 Emma Donoghue, *Slammerkin* (London: Virago (Little Brown), 2000).

20 Emma Donoghue, *Life Mask* (New York: Harcourt, 2004).

21 Dick Hebdige, 'Subjects in Space', *New Formations*, 11 (1990) vi–vii.

22 hooks, *Yearnings*, p. 149ff.

3 Unspoken Desires: Writing Same-sex Relationships

Leonora Brito and Emma Donoghue's collections of short stories discussed in the previous chapter may be compared to photograph albums of people and events that have been forgotten or written out of history. Although very different in many respects, these works reclaim the struggles of women and marginalized groups to acquire a voice and a presence amidst discourses which render them invisible. Each writer 'recovers' the past through the lens of the present which, as is evident in the motifs and preoccupations of their texts, is shaped by twentieth- and twenty-first-century interests, histories and concepts. These include the 'performative' nature of gender, referred to in the previous chapter; the struggle of women to reclaim control of their bodies from male-oriented, scientific and medical discourses; and the reinterpretation of the concept of 'History' itself as something that is often written from the perspective of privileged interests. Both collections reflect women's struggles to wrest language away from what many twentieth-century women writers, from Virginia Woolf to Angela Carter and Toni Morrison, recognized was its traditional, male 'centredness'. As is now commonplace knowledge, reclaiming the 'feminine' from what has been called the 'masculine' orientation or 'phallocentricity' of language has preoccupied not only many twentieth-century women writers but also some of the most significant British and European cultural theorists of the second half of the past century including Judith Butler and Julia Kristeva.

No other subject has pushed as hard at the boundaries of the cultural construction of women and female sexuality as same-sex relationships. But writings about same-sex relationships push back further boundaries, too – of desire, history, family, community and even nation. Of course, this is what happens in the texts with the most sophisticated conceptual reach. In others, the sexuality is the primary interest and the work crosses over into erotic, sensational fiction. The literary critic Rosalind Coward's concern with texts that emphasize 'sex as knowledge' is that there is a danger, as in the erotic, sensation novel, that they 'may well obscure the fact that sex is implicated in society as a whole'.[1] Three of the most significant contemporary figures in Welsh and Irish women's writing, Emma Donoghue, Stevie Davies and Sarah Waters, came to prominence with what might be described as 'lesbian fiction' though it was in fact much more than this. Stevie Davies achieved recognition with *Impassioned Clay*,[2] concerning a seventeenth-century Welsh lesbian and Sarah Waters won critical acclaim for her historical novel, *Tipping the Velvet*,[3] a picaresque novel about lesbian love which traces the life of Nancy Astley from her family's oyster parlour, to her 'career' as a male impersonator, her role as a prostitute and rent-boy, to sex-toy of an aristocrat. The strength of these texts is that they avoid writing about women's sexuality as separate from the wider social structures.

Although more about lesbian sexuality per se than is the case in *Impassioned Clay* and *Tipping the Velvet*, Emma Donoghue's *Stir-fry* (1994) deftly highlights the way in which sexuality is embedded in a range of social structures. It provides a useful starting point for a discussion of how same-sex relationships offer the writer a means of pushing back the boundaries of sexuality and desire without limiting themselves to these areas. Like Erica Jong's groundbreaking *Fear of Flying*,[4] it is based in the mid-twentieth century, but it is different from Jong's novel in being less concerned to equate same-sex relationships with rebellion. Donoghue's book is an exploration of alternatives to the dominant, heterosexual discourse. It also uses issues around gender and desire, as in an account of a university student induction event, to ask more general questions about power relationships and social structures.

The Welsh novel by Stevie Davies, *Kith and Kin* (2004),[5] based on a middle-aged woman's recollections of the 1960s and after, shares much the same period as Donoghue's novel, although the 1960s in Ireland, to which we will return in a moment, had a different cultural context from the 1960s in Wales. Davies's book also shares with Donoghue's novel, along with Leonora Brito's *dat's love* and the novels of the African-American writer Toni Morrison mentioned in the previous chapter, entry into a risky, almost violent, kind of love. At one point, Davies suggests in a phrase that might be

45

applied also to Donoghue and Sarah Waters, 'Love might inhabit a zone of murderous danger and still be love' (41). Although it avoids equating sex with rebellion, *Kith and Kin* is based, like the story 'Dat's Love' and Morrison's novel *Sula* (2003), on a friendship between two young females, one of whom is more rebellious than the other. In fact, the three 'rebellious' women in the texts mentioned, Brito's Sarah, Morrison's Sula and Davies's Frankie, are encapsulated in what Frankie's friend Mara says of her, 'She hadn't proper boundaries' (34).

The desire to push against limit and boundaries as an activity that itself provides an individual life with meaning is a particularly strong motif in both the novels by Welsh writers discussed in this chapter as is the uncovering of the past. In departure from her historical novels set in the nineteenth century, Sarah Waters's *The Night Watch* (2006), the final novel discussed in this chapter, opens in post-war London and then in two sections, as mentioned in Chapter 1, moves back in time from 1947 to 1944 and 1941. What interests Waters is how the Second World War created ambivalent social and sexual spaces and how these influenced relationships between people, especially same-sex relationships between women.

University, sex and Dublin

The epoch with which Donoghue's *Stir-fry* is concerned is not so much the 'hippy' period, as in Davies's *Kith and Kin*, but the product of the liberalizing effect of the modernizing economic reforms of the Lemass era. When Fianna Fáil won the 1959 general election, it ushered in a period of confidence that in some respects is comparable to that in Wales which followed the establishment of the Welsh National Assembly. In the period 1959–66, the reforms of Sean Lemass included the introduction of a state television system, application to join the European Economic Community and relaxation of censorship in relation to film and literature. They created a climate in Ireland in which liberal ideas might be developed and topics around which there had previously been an unhealthy silence, such as sexual behaviour, could be discussed more openly. Conor McCarthy describes how the process of modernization in the Republic can be traced from 1959:

> Up to this time, a chauvinistic economic nationalism had been pursued, that found its ideological basis in post-Independence

isolationism, wartime neutrality and the ambivalences of the political and economic relationship with Britain. This issued in policies based on the development of the agricultural sector, import substitution and protectionism that had been pursued since the Second World War. These policies had now been revealed to be wholly inadequate to the country's needs.[6]

However, in writing of the 1960s, Donoghue, like Davies, provides a critique of the feminist reform of the second half of the twentieth century, focusing on the difference between openness and debate in the metropolis compared with more provincial areas and between the attitudes and preconceptions of different generations. These differences are especially pronounced in Ireland where same-sex experience, even in the 1990s, existed within a fluid, socio-political situation which itself might be described as something of a 'stir-fry'. The 1885 British Acts which criminalized homosexuality were only repealed in the Republic in 1993.

Stir-fry is the third-person narrative of a seventeen-year-old, Maria Murphy, who, as a consequence of the liberalizing reforms of the Lemass era, has an opportunity to leave her small, country town and attend university in Dublin. Maria's process of 'coming out' mirrors the emergence of modern Ireland itself. In my earlier study of contemporary Irish writing, to which I made reference in Chapter 1, I suggested that in the late twentieth-century Ireland moved into a space that was not yet fully defined.[7] As far as the status of women and sexual relations, especially same-sex relations, were concerned, the modernizing improvements of the 1950s and 1960s proved partial and uneven, particularly when Dublin was compared with more remote, rural areas. In Eamon De Valera's ideologically constructed nation state, it was especially difficult in the country towns and villages for women to break from the gendered discourses enshrined in the Constitution. And even within Dublin itself, developments affecting women were not always wholly supported. Liberalism was invariably an urban, middle-class affair where women could participate in suffrage associations and organizations such as the Irish Women Workers' Union. Maria's own movement, physical and psychological, began, as it did for more outward-looking women in rural Ireland, with the arrival of radio and television and with the discovery of feminist texts. In her case, it was a significantly 'tattered copy' of Germaine Greer's *The Female Eunuch*.

Like the Irish novels discussed in the next chapter, *Stir-fry*, as the name suggests, is a conflation of a number of genres. At one level, it is a version of the innocent abroad narrative, as Maria unwittingly ends up sharing a flat with a lesbian couple. It is also a coming-out novel, a sexual *bildungsroman* and, at times, a campus novel. In each case, Donoghue's text disrupts the generic conventions and traditional literary expectations of these familiar forms. A number of feminist texts revise the *bildungsroman* – initially concerned with the rise of a young man in society – in order to explore female subjectivity. But Donoghue goes further and adapts the narrative to a young woman's growing consciousness of her same-sex desire.

Maria's complex dilemmas are anticipated when she first makes her way up the stairs to Ruth and Jael's flat in shadow and darkness. Like *The Night Watch*, *Stir-fry* suggests that freeing desire and sexuality from its fixed referents is a difficult intellectual as well as emotional project. That Maria's journey will involve her finding the courage to do so is anticipated when, with some reluctance, she discards her copy of *Her* magazine on the stairs. Consisting of articles on breast cancer, standing up to the boss, slimming and desirability, it reinforces a largely male-centred, heterosexual socio-gender structure. Sexually, emotionally and physically relocating herself, Maria has more difficulty than Davies's Frankie apparently has in redefining herself. Frankie, as we shall see, seems to adjust to moving across and between different roles and identities. She would not, if she were in Maria's position, consider collecting the magazine again; in other words, contemplate returning to her familiar 'reference points'.

Sexual discourse

Donoghue, Davies and Waters are concerned with the way in which desire is determined, complicated and distorted by the discourses in which it is articulated. Set in the mid-twentieth century but written in the 1990s, *Stir-fry* is a novel as much about the way prejudices and preconceptions are preserved in established and popular discourse as about same-sex relations. It opens with Maria struggling to decipher Ruth and Jael's card advertising for a flatmate. While she is able to work out that they are two feminists, the reference to 'NO BIGOTS' passes her by.

At a literal level, 'stir-fry' refers to the meal that the lesbian couple, Ruth and Jael, serve Maria when she first visits their flat. But it is also the metaphor that Ruth uses in her letter to Maria, near the end of the novel, explaining how the relationships among the three of them proved more complicated than she had expected:

> It's sort of like a stir-fry, that's the only way I can think of to describe it, don't laugh. I thought you could chop up lots of different vegetables and mix them in and raise the heat, and they'd all make each other taste better. It never occurred to me that ginger and fennel might clash. (199)

Ruth is referring to the way Maria has fallen in love with her but is attracted to Jael. This stir-fry is similar to the one in which Mara finds herself in *Kith and Kin* where, attracted to Frankie, she has sex with Frankie's lover and the father of her child.

Stir-fry also shares the concern in *Kith and Kin* and *The Night Watch* with the way in which women have to contend on a daily basis with discourses that disempower them. The extent to which even the educated in the city might be implicated in the oppression of women is evident from an incident Maria witnesses, in which male engineering students throw a fellow, female, student in the University pond. At one level, it is, as one male student says, an act of 'adolescent macho thuggery' (25). But it is legitimated by tradition, like some of the attitudes that Davies's and Waters's characters encounter – each year the engineers try to beat the previous record for the number of young women thrown in the pond – and upon discourses that permit men to abuse women simply out of 'fun'; one student argues that 'if she's going to be in their class for four years she won't want a reputation for not being able to take a joke' (25). The incident has resonance of the ducking stool, one of a number of punishments intended to control female power meted out in early modern Europe to women suspected of witchcraft. As Maria herself points out, 'She's no witch, she's a bimbo' (24).

The images of a close, physical relationship between two women are as important in *Stir-fry* as in *Kith and Kin*, where Frankie and Mara lie together in Oxwich Bay, and *The Night Watch*, where Helen and Julia share a bath. However, in *Stir-fry* they are seen from the outside by a third woman, initially when Maria catches sight of her two flatmates on a table: 'Ruth, cross-legged . . . her back curved like a comma, and Jael, leaning into it, kissing her.' (68) In staring at them, Maria is trying to make sense of what she sees

within the conventional structures within which desire is constructed: 'The kiss, their joint body, the table, all seemed to belong
to a parallel world.' (68) As in *The Night Watch*, Maria begins to
appreciate the subtlety, fine detail and peculiar beauty of the female
body, as when she later witnesses Ruth and Jael having sex: 'She
could see firelight edging over a tangle of limbs. It wavered on Jael's
long brown back arched over Ruth, their arms like the dark
interlacing bars of a hedge.' (98) Here, however, the entanglement is
not simply in the bodies of the lovers but in Maria's complex
reaction, for she is beginning to recognize that she loves Ruth but
desires Jael – hence the stress on how her eyes focus desiringly on
Jael's long, brown, arched torso.

In each of the novels discussed in this chapter, much between
people who have same-sex desires for each other is only half stated.
The language of desire is one that involves silence, pauses, visual
recognition, distractions, innuendo, symbols and missed opportunities:

> Maria slashed through the bead curtain. Ruth's door was shut. She
> stood outside, her fingers against the wood, waiting for the right
> words to come. Not a sound from behind the door. What was she
> expecting – a sob, breaking glass, the snapping strings of a guitar?
> Her thoughts were interrupted by a flush, and suddenly Ruth was
> behind her, toothbrush in hand.
> 'Hi,' said Maria, her back to the door.
> 'Did you want something?' Ruth's voice was barely audible.
> Light caught the wet bristles of the toothbrush. Maria stared at it
> stupidly. 'Just to say goodnight.'
> 'Sweet dreams, Maria.' Ruth shut the door behind her. (210–11)

As I have argued elsewhere, this passage is more subtle and complex
than might at first appear.[8] It is especially pertinent to the concern
here with the interrelationship between desire, language and power.
The passage begins with Maria determinedly breaking through the
bead curtains through which she had previously witnessed Ruth
and Jael making love and becoming more intensely aware of her
own desires. The closed door represents how she, consciously or
unconsciously, perceives herself in relation to Ruth and vice versa.
As is the case with the principal, female characters in Davies's and
Waters's work, the struggle is with the figurative door that Maria
must open for herself. In order for her to do so, she must achieve a
radical shift in her own sense of self. But, more importantly, such
inner change is predicated upon her de-centring language in order

to articulate, as much to herself as to others, how and what she feels. Without the language to articulate her same-sex desires to herself, she is unable to explore them, let alone express how she feels to Ruth. There are suggestions that Maria needs to acquire a more female-oriented language than she has been used to. From behind the door, she does not imagine words but simply sounds.

Ruth's question opens a door for Maria, and for a while both stand together in the time lag it has created. All that Maria can do though is stare at the bristles of Ruth's toothbrush, an object that in the context has obvious connotations of the vulva. Although it is Ruth who eventually physically closes the door, it is Maria who initially closes it in a figurative sense in bidding Ruth 'goodnight'. Ruth's reply, 'Sweet dreams', may be an innocent, automatic response or an acknowledgement that she has seen through Maria, as it were, to her secret, innermost desires.

The conclusion of *Stir-fry* locates Maria in an 'in-between' space. Like many of the women characters in Jennifer Johnston's work which will be discussed in the next chapter, she has emerged from a previously silenced position that has also been, and to some extent still is, marked by secrecy. In doing so, like Helen in *The Railway Station Man* (1984), she is a vehicle by which the text confronts the dominant discourses that have been responsible for her silence and marginalization.

Family affairs

To place women's writing in its full context is to recognize that literature is a product not only of high cultural thought but also of reflections and research into how the lived experiences of ordinary people have changed in particular periods. One of the most valuable advances of the previous century, especially as far as women and minority groups are concerned, is the authority granted the records and experiences of ordinary people alongside the official records and documents of government and public policy. The novels by Welsh writers discussed in this chapter reflect the new-found, late twentieth- and early twenty-first century preoccupation among Welsh writers, including those who live outside of Wales, with family and 'life' stories. Although, as we shall see in later chapters and have already seen in the case of Leonora Brito, these preoccupations are often pursued in short fiction, the novels discussed in this chapter are important for their creative use of the past-present in exploring previously neglected aspects of ordinary women's history.

In the previous chapter, we discussed the work of an author who exemplified the new confidence among Welsh writers in exploring the social, cultural and economic diversity of Wales at the close of the twentieth century and the beginning of the twenty-first century. Although the reasons for this confidence were many, it was undoubtedly bolstered by the successful 'yes' vote in the referendum on devolution and, as referred to earlier, by the creation of the Welsh Assembly. The two 'historical' novels by Welsh writers in this chapter are products of this confidence, even though one was written in London. It is evident in the way in which each text explores what, at the time in which each book is set, was perceived as 'controversial' female desires. This subject in turn is used in each novel to explore equally controversial issues around family, community and relationships more generally.

Davies's novel and Brito's story 'Dat's Love', both highlighting a friendship between two young women, are set in south Wales within a decade of each other. Davies's novel is set in and around Swansea and her characters come to a watershed in their lives in the 1960s. The more recalcitrant figure in each relationship is a blues singer who thus encapsulates the riskier, more dangerous approach to life and love embraced by that genre of song. In Davies's novel, Francesca and Mara are cousins rather than simply friends. But, as in Brito's story, the narrative point of view is provided by the more 'conservative' of the two women, in this case Mara. The longer span of time which the novel provides compared with the short story enables the text to explore the relationship between the two women in more depth and how it changes over time. The different 'selves' which each of them becomes at different times and in different situations is reflected in the different versions of their names that are used in the course of the narrative: Francesca is also known as Frankie and Mara is known as Mars and Marsie. Early in the novel, Mara observes:

> I am no longer the same person. I walk down to the shops for milk, past the house in which Susan is said to be immured in a state of premature senility, and remind myself that I was young then: I am not the same person. Or if I am, I have taken steps to render myself harmless. (24)

Kith and Kin is partly a quest novel, a family narrative, a love story, a novel of home and community, and a narrative of social change. It is based around Mara's discovery of a film clip of her cousin Frankie in her youth which triggers memories of the events leading up to Frankie's suicide which she had suppressed. The relationship between the different parts of the film is imagistic and this visual approach to narrative is embraced by the text itself. Mara's rethinking of her past through and around the film from the BBC archive is paralleled in her daughter Menna's own investigations of her immediate family's past in an attempt to re-establish contact with her uncle. At one point, Mara inverts the normal mother-daughter relationship by becoming more knowing than her parent: 'You were all . . . kind of innocent, really, like big hairy babies.' (76)

Like Brito's Sarah in 'Dat's Love', there is a mocking kind of mimicry to Frankie, centred, as in Sarah's case, on herself as a performer. She sings with 'pouty provocation' and at one point wears a sarong 'with one shoulder bare' prompting the family to see her, and Mara, as 'disgraceful, acting like trollops, ungodly hooligans' (8). Like Sarah, Frankie is a figure who seems constantly to be acting and, like Sarah, she is able to take control of relationships through a command of language that can be equally uncompromising in its protest. Moreover, like Sarah, she inherits controversy around her mother's love life. Frankie's mother, Susan, is more outrageous than Sarah's mother, 'dressed to kill' and bringing 'unsuitable types' home to Francesca. In this case, after her father's death, Frankie's mother takes a man who is seen as 'given to the bottle and blue jokes. Sex. Tattoos all across his shoulders.' (11) Frankie dismisses them as: 'Those concubines, that old lecher and his moll, that pair of dimwits.' (10) Her language here, like Sarah's, is assertive because it is both imaginative and of the 'streets'. Sometimes, Frankie's language reflects an ambiguity that both Sarah and Frankie possess that is to be admired but is also disturbing. At one point, she is said to have sung 'like an angel, [and] like a demon' (80). When Frankie and Aaron are holding Zack, she says: 'Drop him, why don't you?' (126) They assume, in shock at having been spoken to in this way, that she means that they should literally drop her baby. They are appalled by Frankie's callousness. But what Frankie says could be read differently. It could be a sarcastic comment on the way that they are holding him. However, Mara is inclined to believe the former rather than the latter because it confirms an aspect of Frankie that has always bothered her. Mara recalls at one point: 'The bitter beauty of that face shocked me sometimes, and made me draw back, wary and admiring.' (102)

Frankie seems to signify something that is buried within Mara, as Sarah signifies something that is hidden within the narrator of Brito's story. Mara is now employed in a medical institute researching the phenomenon of phantom pain and, finding an analogy to her loss of her cousin, she tries to distinguish between the 'reality' of Frankie and Frankie as a 'phantom' in family memory. At one point, Mara admits: 'There are occasions when, to complicate things, I see someone else submerged in my own eyes, a younger self who looks back from the mirror scandalised.' (16) Sarah ends up on a London stage, singing under a banana tree; Mara surmises at one point that Frankie, too, will end up unfulfilled, 'dying fucked out and friendless' (34). When the adult Mara visits a Susan who is suffering from dementia, she is mistaken for Frankie and actually for a while becomes the young Frankie. On recollection of the occasion when Frankie was spanked for going onto a shipwreck, Mara asks Susan if she had voyeuristically watched the punishment and blames her for sadistically divulging the secret to her stepfather, knowing what he would do to the girl.

This is not the only occasion in the novel, though, when Mara, through some kind of guilt, seems to want to experience a phantom version of Frankie's pain. Another notable instance is when Mara does well in her 'A' levels and Frankie fails her GCEs. She tries to expurgate the guilt by throwing into the sea her blue sandals which she adores. It is a sacrifice not simply of the shoes but of something of herself: they 'smelt of me and told of my comings and goings over the earth and the tarmac' (81). However, this tendency to mythologize Frankie and events related to her comes up against limits, like the earth against tarmac. Indeed, the throw fails because one of the sandals becomes 'lodged in a mass of rubbish, sticking there like any other junk' (81). Mara, thinking of Frankie in the context of her research into phantom pain, remembers that pain was a significant part of Frankie's life outside of the rest of the family. She also remembers Uncle Lew realizing this when Frankie held out her hand for him to beat her, causing her uncle and aunt to worry about what her stepfather might be doing to her.

In some respects, the relationship between Frankie and Mara is reminiscent of the relationship between the young Sula and her friend, Nel, in Toni Morrison's *Sula* rather than of Sarah and the narrator in Brito's 'Dat's Love'. Both novels focus on a relationship between two women which at times is sexual but cannot be simply labelled as such. The relationship between Davies's two young females when they lie together is also comparable to that between two youngsters in a short story by the Welsh writer Siân James, 'Outside Paradise', which is discussed in Chapter 5. In James's short story, the youngsters lie together in some woods; in Davies's novel it is in the lee of a boat on Oxwich Bay. When Frankie kisses Mara, she is drawn like the two girls in James's story into 'the shadow-zone' (78).

But what is really significant here is the language that Mara finds to describe what happens. In the conflation of the earthy and the spiritual and the prosaic and the poetic, she gives voice to a dimension of female experience that is often not articulated by women because they have to wrest language away from the 'masculine' in order to do so: 'She kissed me with such thrilling delicacy that a moth's wing seemed to have brushed me.' (78) She goes on to think of the experience in terms of colours, transcending the usual referents that are invoked to describe love: 'I lay the length of her and, oh it was blue.' (78) Blue is a colour that recurs throughout the text and is particularly associated with Mara; her favourite sandals are that colour. The prose of the novel's narrative is interrupted here by a line that has some of the qualities of lyric love poetry. But Mara also moves out of the traditional literary structures at this point by invoking not only colour but music; Frankie is said to have written a 'piece of music without a tune', something that is pre-structure and, like the Blues, spontaneous, whilst 'trapping me in the mystery of her harp-like guitar' (78).

Thus, one of the most important motifs in this book is not only the way in which Frankie uses language to control, confront and confound, but the way in which Mara assumes such command of language as to be able to configure verbally and appropriately the different faces and situations which Frankie presents to the world. The poetry and the spontaneity which she acquires are appropriate to describe the experiences between them on the beach. In relaying what the young, rebellious, just-out-of-school girl does, she has to find a different, but equally appropriate set of rhythms, reminiscent of the pop American writers of the 1960s:

Busked. Barmaided. Sold icecreams down at Caswell . . . turned up four months later with an all-over tan and a motorbike . . . fucked

around, stopped eating, started again ... Walked barefoot singing
along the cliff path with an acoustic guitar (80)

It is not just the rhythm and the absence of punctuation here that
brings the American Beats to mind but the leading Beat prose writer
Jack Kerouac's favoured technique of turning a noun – as in
'Barmaided' – into a verb, bringing subject and activity together in a
seamless action. Mara's account of Frankie conveys her energy and
the rapid changes in her life. She does so in a prose that tries to
eliminate as much as possible of the barrier language usually puts
between the reader and this kind of vivacity, employing, as in the
phrase 'an all-over tan and a motorbike', the Beat writer's technique
of clipped juxtaposition. Moreover, as in much of the American
Beat writing, energy and spontaneity, the celebration of the present,
is fused with pathos and hints of past tragedies or tragedies to come.
Here, there is anticipation of the tragedy that will eventually befall
Frankie when she is described walking barefoot – suggesting her
freedom but also her naiveté and vulnerability – along a cliff walk.

A recurring aspect of the way in which Mara delineates the
'identities' assumed by Frankie is her tendency to mythologize her
friend in different ways. In the account of herself, Frankie and
Aaron climbing on board the Cleveland wreck, Mara effectively
records Frankie's transition from 'Tomboy' whilst retaining her
interest in her as an 'in-between' character. The image of the wreck
itself is important in this respect because of its own 'in-between'
status: being not quite on land and not quite at sea and being
between two periods of history. When Mara describes how 'the
ship's allure had grown into a spell' and thinks of her 'breasting the
white waves of sand' (52), she might just as well be talking of
Frankie. It is from this point onward that Mara becomes interested
in the way in which Frankie, like the shipwrecked vessel, seems to
be located between the elements:

> The tatty old vest she wore veiled budding breasts; her hair, tangled
> and bleached with sand and salt, was a wild mane. Beside my lumpy
> solidity she seemed like a gypsy girl, I thought, free. (52)

Frankie, in the way in which Mara imagines her, like the way
Morrison's Nel sees Sula and Brito's narrator thinks of Sarah,
appears to be possessed of knowledge that is beyond her years. Her
blues singing is described as 'dark and earthy and dirty' and Mara
notices that 'Her body was sinuous; it knew. Her body knew.' (54)

Later, the young Frankie is associated with the Virgin Mary who, in her role as 'Madonna Dolorosa', weeps for the sorrows of human-kind: 'Her hair was shorn. The calm eyes of a Madonna, resigned to grief.' (67) The Madonna Dolorosa (but one whose weeping is ineffective) is invoked again at the birth of Frankie's child, Zack, when Frankie weeps all day long, 'a tedium of tears which purged nothing and expressed nothing, but fell monotonously as drizzle' (129). The Virgin Mother is explicitly recalled here, too, in the description of the visitors at the bedside: 'Quite a congregation had gathered round Frankie's bedside to worship the boy-child, though conceived in sin and surrounded by tatty pals.' (118) The variety in the language employed at this point once again exemplifies how Mara slips between literary, mythical, prosaic and colloquial lin-guistic registers. Mara moves from subtly invoking Christ's birth, through the references to the 'boy-child' and 'conceived in sin', to language – 'congregation' and 'worship' – which alludes to the biblical event but also broadens the religious frame of reference. Eventually, she provides an end stop that brings the reader once more into the 'reality' of Frankie and her friends. But in recalling the relationship between Frankie and her newborn child, Mara also moves between the New and the Old Testament. Thus, in the account of how Zack is left behind by Frankie and Mara when they visit the United States, she alludes to the story of Moses: 'Zack, like a babe in a folktale Moses basket, drifted away relieved of the ballast of our anxiety.' (156) The Old Testament is also invoked in the name of Frankie's child's father, Aaron, who is actually described at one point in language reminiscent of the Bible: 'Aaron was gentle under their wrath.' (108) In the Bible, Aaron is sympa-thetic to the Israelites, indulging them, offering sacrifices on their behalf and praying that they might be forgiven. Throughout the novel he is a 'feminine' character, with an 'ache of tenderness', who is called by Frankie, 'a girl of a boy' (111).

The allusions to the Bible in the novel are schematic and do not readily suggest a coherent framework for the events of the book. However, they do reinforce an aspect of the 1960s which Frankie and her friends lived through. The invocation at different points of the Madonna, Moses, the Virgin birth and the exodus of the Israelites reminds us that there was a seemingly spiritual and religious rebirth in the 1960s which was itself eclectic.

Moreover, Aaron's 'feminine' presence underlines the fore-grounding of the feminine in that decade together with a 'feminizing' of masculinity in appearance and attitudes at the time which supposedly stressed tenderness and sensitivity. At one level, Mara's account of her friends and those with whom she mixed in her earlier life, for good or ill, echoes this larger apparent social realignment and new idealism. Her frequent changes in register, employing different types of language, is an attempt to try to encapsulate what she felt she was a part of. But it also brings the seeming values of the youth culture of the time up against the reality of lived experience and in particular locales with specific individuals. The overall effect in the text, as it moves backward in time, is to mix the sense of a new beginning, however bogus it later proved to be, with the bitterness of something that was actually waning. There may be something 'feminine' in the way in which the sea and sand is reclaiming the 'masculine' aggression signified by the *Cleveland*, the ship with which Aaron, Mara and Frankie as children are linked for a time. But the really telling, contradictory detail in the account is that 'there were still remnants of the hull, and a funnel poking up out of the sand' (111). In addition to the obvious phallocentricity here, Davies draws attention to how, even in its last moments, the ship does not lose its energy and power as a war ship. This detail makes the identification between the *Cleveland* and Frankie, referred to earlier, more complex than at first appears. Not only do they both occupy an in-between space for the reasons given above, but each is located between what might be described as a poetic 'feminine' and a more aggressive 'masculine' principle. It is this kind of ambiguity in Frankie which interests and disturbs Mara, and is encapsulated at one point in the image of her eating a fruit: she 'watched her skin a plum with a penknife, sink her teeth into the plush meat of the fruit' (127). The imagery here, in the phallic knife and the vampire's bite, suggests the 'phallic woman', an imaginary female type, dating from the Victorian period, and embodying an assertive and sexual independence that challenged the Victorian ideal of the dutiful, obedient and passive wife.

The daffodil

One of the key images in *Kith and Kin* is that of the daffodil from which 'the most powerful scent comes as they perish', redolent of the 'sickly sweetness of other people's sex' (103). The smell – sensual, bitter, repulsive and reminiscent of stale sex – seems to bring together many of the book's motifs. Throughout the novel, there is much that becomes pronounced, compelling and repulsive in its last days. The 'hippy' era itself, associated with flower power, closed in infamous episodes of violence such as the Charles Manson murders. As Frankie's home life breaks up, relationships become more violent and Mara becomes more aware of the violence within others. This includes Frankie herself whom Mara feels at one point had 'an aura of violence' about her even as a child. In their childhood, there is an especially disturbing incident in which Frankie holds the pods of a piece of bladderwrankin close to her real father David's head and 'snap[s] one after another viciously in his face' (27). Susan's complicity in the ill-treatment of her daughter becomes clearer as she gets older, as does Jack's sadomasochistic fantasies toward her: '"This hand, you little madam. See this hand?" . . . We saw the hand. He saw in imagination her bare behind.' (45) Mara witnesses several of the major confrontations in the novel which become more violent and compelling as things seem to come to an end, including the quarrel between Frankie and Jack when she breaks a vase over his head. Even Breuddwyd (Dream), too, is a more powerful symbol when it stands empty, waiting for dereliction to set in. Moreover, at the end of the novel, when Jack turns up, denying any responsibility for Frankie's suicide, he literally smells, repulsively, like 'a down-and-out'. Earlier in the novel, when Jack seemed to be becoming more slothful, lounging around on the sofa all day watching television, Frankie seems to find him most compelling. Towards the end of her life, Frankie herself appears to become more crudely sensual and bitter, on one occasion singing the blues, topless, on a bar table while downing pints. Here, whilst she thinks that she is the subject of her own narrative, she is an object in those of the men who watch her. In many respects, her actions typify the 1960s which at the end of the decade seemed to smell sensual and bitter like the daffodil at the end of its spring. Of course, what Mara realizes is that the 1960s were never the liberal decade that they purported to be and that they privileged the interests of men rather than women. There was a shallowness to the 1960s which becomes evident when Frankie's son Zack returns as a young adult, having changed his name to John. He advises Mara that she should walk barefoot, as he often does, so that she can have a more intimate physical awareness of the earth. Although she reminds him that she often went barefoot when she was young, and got scolded by her parents for it, it becomes clear that for her it was a symbol that 'united' her with other rebellious young people and arose out of media representation of what constituted the 'hippy' movement rather than a deep spiritual conviction on her part.

This is a novel that is an analysis not simply of one family but of several families, mentioned throughout the book in ways that invoke a much older Wales: 'the recurring warring Evanses, Manelauses and Thomases, [are] inveterately fratricidal' (17–18). Indeed, an older, warring Wales is quite deliberately suggested at times, especially in the dispute over who owns Breuddwyd. Frankie's family is said to have become 'split apart into a feud of epic proportions', whilst Jack is described as having 'bonded the tribes in an orgy of reproach' (11). The reference to the families being 'inveterately fratricidal' is significant because, as children, Frankie and Mara seem to take the reader back into an even earlier Wales than that alluded to by the references to 'warring families', 'tribes' and epic feuds: 'We had our own private language before we acquired English or Welsh, which spooked some and charmed others.' (21) The allusion here appears to be to a time when the people of Wales spoke 'Cymraeg'. Mara here cryptically distinguishes between 'Cymraeg' and 'Welsh', suggesting that Welsh, unlike Cymraeg, is defined in relation to English. The cryptic references to a pre-modern Wales, like the allusions to the Bible, reinforce a theme that is important to the novel, to pre-modern Welsh history and to the Bible: the way in which betrayal serves to open the text, including history as a 'text', on to the gendered nature of much 'epic' conflict and of the narratives in which it is explored.

Conflict in London

Although *The Night Watch* is not concerned to the same extent as Davies's novel or Brito's story 'Dat's Love' with a relationship between two women, it has a number of preoccupations in common with Davies's work, including the emphasis upon 'performance' in the construction of women's gender identities. These shared concerns include the dismemberment and fragmentation of families and of individual lives; the sense with which the end of something gives a pronounced bittersweet resonance to everything within that framework; and the relationship between one's sense of self and the cultural and economic realities of a particular time. Whilst twentieth-century writing, outside class-oriented fiction, has tended to stress an existentialist or psychoanalytic approach to the self, *The Night Watch* shares Emma Donoghue's recognition, discussed in the previous chapter, that individual attitudes are shaped by socio-economic as much as sociocultural forces. Given that the novel is set in the Second World War this is not surprising, for wartime conditions meant that economics became more pronounced in day-to-day as well as national life then than it had for a generation.

The subject of alternatives to the sexual norm, pursued by Davies in her account of the relationship between Frankie and Mara, is more pronounced in Sarah Waters's *The Night Watch* in the relationships between her principal characters: Helen, Julia, Kay, Duncan and Mickey. But the socio-economic parameters within which they live out particular sexual orientations or ambivalences are at one level more rigid and at another looser than in the period with which *Kith and Kin* is concerned. The reason for this, of course, is that while both works are by Welsh writers, *Kith and Kin* is set in provincial, peace-time Wales whereas *The Night Watch* is based in a wartime and post-war capital city. Mara and Frankie and the community at Breuddwyd base their identities upon confrontation with the perceived 'establishment' in appearance and political attitudes. But in wartime London, day-to-day living was a perpetual gamble with injury and death which encouraged people to indulge in sexual liaisons in their private lives and illegal practices in their public lives. At the same time, paradoxically, there was a harder-edged, censorious culture which disapproved of sexual promiscuity and black marketeering. Thus, the title *The Night Watch* may be read on many different levels, as referring literally to the night watch, to the novel's exploration of the secret lives and innermost thoughts of its characters or to something more sinister, to which I shall return later. During the war, day-to-day censorship was inseparable from the new-found authority of the state, evident in the novel in the impact of rationing, the new regulations with which one had to live and, at the other extreme, the treatment of conscientious objectors and even fear of what would happen to you should you deface a government order.

Thus, when Helen and Julia take a weekly bath together, they have to make sure that their landlord does not hear them and are only too aware that he contemptuously labels them female eunuchs. His attitude toward women, exemplified in the way he speaks to his wife, is part of a larger culture against which individual women have to struggle on a daily basis. National, post-war discourses informing advertising and popular culture sought to realign women with the domestic and with more conventional female behaviours after the war which had reconfigured women's identities in a variety of new ways. Kay is an interesting character because of the way in which she dresses, more as a man than a woman, preserving the radical space which she found for herself in wartime London. In the post-war capital, increasingly shaped, according to the novel, by the return of older, gender-based ideologies, Kay's day-to-day struggles to assert a different sense of self from most of those around her renders her as 'other'. She has to deal on a daily basis with the kind of conservatism displayed by the baker who greets her entry into his shop by asking her if she knows that the war is over. In *Kith and Kin*, radical female display still pushes at limits but it does so in a space in which the boundaries have been pushed further back than in the immediate post-war years. The other customers in the baker's shop, laughing and gossiping behind Kay's back, indicate the extent to which the boundaries in post-wartime London are closing in on radical femininity.

After the war, a sense that the radical, gendered behaviours which the war had permitted if not encouraged on the home front were coming to an end created in some quarters in the late 1940s a pronounced public display of 'difference'. Before she enters the baker's shop, Kay has to make herself a 'character'. Whilst she is the protagonist in the novel who most obviously does so, there are many other female characters for whom appearance is also a cultural, political statement. In these cases, as in Davies's novel, 'performance', which embraces creative possibilities that push against previously accepted behavioural norms, is important; from the way in which Mickey in a mechanic's overalls and boots assumes a manly pose to the expensive dress sense of Ursula. Mickey, in one of several recurring references to *Oliver Twist*, to which I will return in a moment, is likened to the Artful Dodger. Both are in-between characters: Mickey is not-quite a conventional female and not-quite working-class male as the Dodger is not-quite a child or a man and also, in his mimicry of a respectable gentleman, stands at the boundary between respectability and criminality. Mickey's 'in-between' status is underpinned by the fact that her home is a moored boat, an 'in-between' position, not-quite land and not-quite off land.

The argument about the importance of 'performance' in wartime and post-war Britain is applied to men, too, in this novel, in the way, for example, in which Duncan notices Frazer's clothes. But 'performance' in *The Night Watch* is different from the majority of incidents in *Kith and Kin* where it is often about social and ideological protest and linked to contemporary cultural phenomenon such as the 'hippy' movement. In *The Night Watch*, as becomes clearer in Frankie's case in *Kith and Kin*, 'performance' is a 'survival' strategy at the most profoundly personal and individual level.

Although Waters's book, due to its wartime subject matter, emphasizes socio-economic determinants of human behaviour, it also stresses the psychological dimension of the home-front experience. As the novel twice moves backward into the war, it unravels and makes further 'sense' of the principal characters' lives and preoccupations. In doing so, the first part of the novel, set in 1947, juxtaposes the motif of physical rebuilding with that of psychological repair. The latter, though, is much more difficult as most people after the war are coming to terms with loss on many levels. This is exemplified in the experiences of Vivian and Helen's agency where clients ostensibly come to build their personal futures but spend more time talking about their pervasive sense of loss; by the people, including the physically disabled whom Kay watches visit the doctor's consulting rooms; and also by Kay's own incessant walking of the streets. Indeed, the novel might be seen to take its cue from Vivian's clients for in moving back in time it moves from 'rebuilding' to physical and psychological destruction and from 'recovery' to strategies for survival. One of the 'arguments' of the novel is that there is really no recovery process and the war and post-war are not readily separated.

A key motif, referred to earlier, that links the three parts of the novel and the war and post-war periods is *Oliver Twist*. The novel, adapted in a famous film version in 1947 by David Lean, was part of a cinema 'project' throughout the 1940s of adapting classic English novels for the screen which, because of the way they represented classic concepts of Englishness, had popular appeal. Whether intentional or not on the part of the producers, Dickens's novel was particularly well suited to its post-war context: the labyrinthine rookeries of inner London would clearly remind its audiences of war-torn London and other bombed European capital cities; Fagin and his gang were all too redolent of the black market economy; and the orphan Oliver Twist would have appeared to epitomize the post-war sense of loss and lack of belonging. However, it is not only Dickens's literary influence that can be seen in this novel. The combination of loneliness, sexual and moral confusion, intrigue and anxiety, as well as the deft use of detail, recalls Graham Greene's *The End of the Affair* and *The Ministry of Fear*.

'Other' and taboo

The kind of radical identity that Kay in *The Night Watch* assumes is also important in its role as the 'other', or what was increasingly cast as the 'other', against which the recovering nation could define itself. In this respect, there is a model of cultural identity here which is similar to the one underpinning the cryptic point that Davies makes about the Welsh language being defined in modern Wales in relation to English. However, both Davies and Waters, like Leonora Brito, are interested in a model of culture that is not based on notions of superiority and oppression but perceived as a matrix that would include negotiation and assimilation as well as resistance. Thus, the confrontation in the baker's shop, one of many in Kay's life, has to be placed in a wider context of social relations and encounters. These include even fleeting incidents, such as the one in which Kay approaches a young woman out walking on the street only to see her go off, arm-in-arm with a female friend; one of many references that suggests the importance of the war in bringing women together in more public shows of affection. Waters's book, like Davies's, explores a variety of female and male-female relationships in a diverse range of contexts that deny late twentieth-century categorization based on concepts such as 'lesbian', 'gay' or 'straight'.

Waters's novel does not deny the significance of 'taboo' as a social force. But in *The Night Watch*, as the title at one level suggests, censorious, accusatory and even complicit gazes are obviously a feature of day-to-day reality, from Helen and Julia having to be especially careful about being seen leaving their bathroom together, to Duncan thinking that a former inmate from prison has recognized him, to Vivian's exaggerated reactions in Reggie's car when she thinks that Kay might see her. This emphasis in the novel upon the likelihood of being seen is a product of its wartime setting, referred to earlier, in which communities were inevitably vigilant in their 'watch'. The wartime context is also responsible for the equation in the text between being 'seen' and being 'caught out', stemming inevitably from the black market economy and the looser sexual climate in which ordinary people took opportunities which the ever-present threat of death and destruction encouraged.

The night watch, as mentioned earlier, had a highly ambivalent set of associations in wartime Britain. At one level, it was the eye of the wartime state and at another it looked into what lay beneath the publicity and propaganda. Kay and her women friends see limbs and dismembered bodies sticking out of the wartime rubble and bomb damage that exposes what was once private – often the most private spaces in the house – to public view:

> [Kay] supposed that houses, after all – like the lives that were lived in them – were mostly made of space. It was the spaces, in fact, which counted rather than the bricks.

> The rear of the house, however, was more or less intact. They went through a creaking passageway and emerged, bizarrely, into a kitchen, still with cups and plates on its shelves and pictures on its walls, its electric light burning and its black-out curtains up. (182)

In many respects, this is the most important passage in the novel. It highlights how, in imagining several entangled lives over a period of time, the novel thinks of lives in terms of the spaces that people occupy and how these spaces relate to each other. It also draws attention to the schizophrenic nature of life in the war: the way in which one part of life is collapsing, through the pressures, the destruction and loss, whilst another remains intact.

The novel exposes horrors ranging from the man who accidentally blows himself up with a faulty cooker to what women like Vivian have to endure when they go for back street abortions:

> . . . she felt more exposed, somehow, with only her bottom half bare, than she would have felt if she had stripped completely. It was like something a tart would do. But when she lay on the hard flat couch, she felt foolish in another way – like a fish, with gaping gills and mouth, on a fishmonger's slab. (364)

The images here work together to denigrate Vivian as a woman. But more important they are indicative of the kind of self-images women draw upon when they step outside acceptable norms.

Such images of the Blitz as the novel recreates encapsulate the horrors of the home front which official documentaries of the war suppressed in favour of reports of stoicism and resistance. But at another level, they signify the way in which war renders what is beautiful, sensual and even poetic as a disposable commodity. One of the most disturbing aspects of Waters's accounts of war-torn London is the way in which she juxtaposes the dismemberment of people and the destruction of homes and public buildings. Kay's appreciation of the beauty and sophistry of Helen's body which closes the novel is a poignant reminder of the beauty that survives war. But it is also a response to how the act of recovering body part after body part out of the rubble is desensitizing and despiritualizing. Waters explores through the lives of particular individuals, especially women who are aware of the fine details, intricate delicacies and intriguing flaws of each other's bodies, how one recovers from seeing brutally destroyed bodies without the compensatory symbolism which normally softens and spiritualizes our view of the dead.

The philosophical vein underpinning Waters's novel is summarized in its most pressing question, what is the value of beauty in the face of this kind of violence and atrocity? For Helen, it is important, as she tells Julia, that 'we've still got St Paul's . . . and all it stands for: I mean, elegance, and reason, and – great beauty' (336). Julia, however, thinks differently about 'elegance', 'reason' and 'great beauty' now:

> 'I think it's about our love of savagery, rather than our love of beauty. I think the spirit that went into the building of St Paul's has shown itself to be thin: it's like gold leaf, and now it's rising, peeling away . . . If we have to fight so hard to keep it – if we have to have elderly men patrolling the roofs of churches, to sweep incendiaries from them with little brushes! – how valuable can it be? How much at the centre of the human heart?' (336)

Helen senses in Julia at this point the kind of darkness that Mara senses in Frankie in *Kith and Kin*. However, it is not just that one senses something 'dark' in the other. Eve Sedgwick highlights the importance in writing of same-sex relationships to 'challenge queer-eradicating impulses' by recreating what in childhood was a relationship to 'objects whose meaning seemed mysterious, excessive, or oblique in relation to the codes most readily available to us'.[9]

Whilst Helen and Julia, like Frankie and Mara, occupy different emotional spaces they are drawn one to another. Waters recreates the kind of excessive, mysterious meaning that Sedgwick mentions but within the context of the war which created its own relationships and different codes. In *The Night Watch* what Julia says about 'savagery' determines the kind of sex that she and Helen have together. Julia offers Helen a different sort of sex from that which she was used to with Kay, who was 'more of a gentleman than any real man' (397). She finds the difference and the strangeness exciting, experiencing new desires that are linked to violence and masochism: 'She stretched out her hands behind her head, wishing with some part of herself that Julia had bound her, fastened her down: she wanted to give herself up to Julia, have Julia cover her with bruises and marks.' (394) Their lovemaking pushes back the boundaries of accepted behaviour in the 1940s – Julia has to keep asking Helen to 'shush' in case they are heard by their neighbours. But the sex between them also pushes back the boundaries of the type of sex that women were supposed to enjoy with men let alone other women. Whilst Helen had previously enjoyed what she would describe as 'leisurely love making', now, 'shaken' and 'trembling', she is excited and shamed by the fact that Julia's lipstick on her makes her look 'as though she'd been hit' and 'her thighs and breasts were marked, as if with rashes, from the rubbing of Julia's clothes' (394). The anxiety that they may be overheard and found out is fused with Helen's anxiety about how she is going to hide the marks on her body from Kay. It is not just that the different lovemaking awakens Helen's secret sexual desires. Sex with Julia is the 'other' that enters Helen's subjectivity, creating new-found notions of guilt, betrayal and fear: 'I used to loathe the sort of people who did the kind of thing we're doing. I used to think they must be cruel, or careless, or cowardly.' (395)

The context in which Helen has betrayed Kay by making love to Julia is, of course, the war; Julia muses: 'Everything's dreadfully wrong, just now.' (393) But it is not just that the war has taken Helen into a new, riskier kind of sexuality, referred to earlier, but that she has been enticed by Julia into an almost boundaryless kind of desire. Like the bombed-out house where one side is standing intact, signifying the orderliness and structure of life before the war, but another has collapsed, Helen stands exposed in a way she did not expect, needing the old order to some extent, but fearful of returning. Thinking of Kay, she admits that what frightens her is: 'We might – stop. We might – go back.' (393)

Shame and privacy

The half of the bombed house exposed to public view and the way in which Helen feels forced to dress quickly so that she is no longer naked in front of Julia both suggest a sense of shame in what is 'private'. When Vivian is on the abortionist's table she is worried by the shame as much as by thought of the pain. Shame is a theme that the novel returns to in different contexts from different perspectives. At one level, it raises questions about self-destruction, guilt and betrayal. At another, it introduces the idea that what is a source of guilt in one generation is the nucleus of change for the next. Frazer tells Duncan: 'A man ought to be a source of shame to his father, don't you think? . . . How, otherwise, will there ever be any progress?' (404)

However, private shame, which is often the product of dominant public discourses, is not easily shrugged off. The sexual relationship between Helen and Julia moves from hesitancy to overt sex, in which Julia is still fearful that what they are doing in private will be found out, while Helen postpones such worries until they have finished. The same tensions are explored when Reggie and Vivian make love. She stops him several times; the first time telling him that someone may intrude upon them and the second time insisting that 'someone might see' (65 and 66). Again the emphasis falls paradoxically on the shame in her 'privacy'. Persuaded to move under the shadow of trees, she still looks around anxiously, 'conscious that anyone could be watching' (65). Here her shame is linked, through her obsession that someone could be watching, to what the wartime night watch signified, suggested by the image of the sun as 'bright as a spotlight' (65).

In the war, as the novel demonstrates, 'shame' was frequently juxtaposed with the desire for personal, often sexual and even spiritual, satisfaction. The war redefined 'spiritual' so as to include what for most people now came to be part of spirituality, including love, sexuality, desire, family, home, friendship and community. At one point in the novel, Kay talks about the advantage of entering a cinema when the movie has already started and of then seeing the beginning through the lens of the ending. In many respects, Helen's

'reading' of Julia's body in the bath early in the book becomes
the lens through which we later read of her experiences earlier in the
war. What happens in the novel is that the experience of the horrors
of the home front, the pungent odours of death and destruction,
exaggerate the spirituality to be found in even fleeting physical
awareness, let alone encounters. Kay finds the discovery of sounds
of life in the rubble thrilling, even if it is only the mewing of a cat:

> Kay had heard such sounds before: they were thrilling and unnerving,
> much more so than the sight of blasted limbs and mucked-up bodies.
> They made her shiver. She let out her breath. The site had grown noisy
> and alive again, as if in response to some small electric charge. The
> generator was started up, and the light switched back on. The men
> moved in and began to work with a new kind of purpose. (466)

The sense of something ending producing its own kind of last day's
poignancy, like Davies's daffodil, is also evident in the post-war
section of the *The Night Watch* in the episode where Duncan and
Frazer meet one evening for a drink and go down to the river's
'beach'. Here we may compare the way in which the beach in both
novels is handled poetically. In each text, the beach, situated as it is
between the social boundaries and established patterns of the land
and the boundarylessness of the sea, signifies the 'in-between' which
in Waters's novel, like Davies's, includes the 'in-between' in sexual,
psychological and gender terms but also embraces the ambivalent
positions in which people such as Duncan and Frazer found themselves because of the war. In *The Night Watch* the river, like Davies's
daffodil, gives off a pungent smell. In this case, the odour is stronger
but, as in the case of the dying daffodils in Davies's text, the smell is
also one that pervades a work preoccupied with the aftermath of
various characters' stale sex. At Waters's beach, though, the sun is
lower in the sky: 'The sun was sinking in the sky, and he had a vague
unhappy sense that time had passed – real time, proper time, not
factory time – and he had missed out on it.' (77) The rubble,
unsurprisingly in a war novel, is more overtly linked to the destruction of families, homes and lives – 'stones and bits of broken china,
the oyster shells and bones' (82). In each text, off-shore rubble and
fragmentation is linked to the sense of fragmentation of family and
individual lives left in the wake of death. Thus, in a passage redolent
of Davies's novel, when Vivian rummages through her deceased
mother's wardrobe, she rediscovers not only old clothes, but 'bits of
rubbish . . . photograph albums, old autograph books, old diaries

and things like that' (74–5). Like Mara and her daughter in *Kith and Kin*, she 'reached into the shadows behind the albums' (75). In *The Night Watch*, Vivian's reaching into the shadows also signifies what the night watch does, entering into the secrets and shadows of people's lives and families.

The three novels discussed in the chapter have at their heart relationships between women that recreate the sense of mystery and expectation that Sedgwick argues is essential to challenge anti-queer forces. In Maria's case in *Stir-fry* these forces are embedded in the local and national culture in which she was brought up. In *Kith and Kin* the relationship between Frankie and Mara is situated at the confluence of forces intent on liberalizing female desire and more conservative forces seeking to reassert the old boundaries. In *The Night Watch*, the tensions that Davies describes in her novel are evident in the return to a more conservative epoch after the Second World War and one that was different from the cultures that existed on the home front. Waters uses the metaphor of the night watch to explore the relationship between the 'private' and the 'public', particularly an interest in the shame that comes when the 'private' life is exposed. In all three texts, the notion of the shame that can exist even in privacy is a creative space in which the author speculates about guilt, desire and limit. Although each novel explores the thrill of rebellion, all are concerned with how ideas about 'shame' and privacy are bound up with wider social attitudes and structures. Experiencing the shame that can accompany the 'private', the principal female characters in Waters's novel behave in ways that might be described as 'heroic'. This applies not only to Kay's work as an ambulance driver but to the way in which the women enter radical personal and socially transgressive spaces. The word 'heroic' would refer to their courage in crossing boundaries. All three novels are structured around different kinds of boundaries, ranging from doors and bead curtains, to regular reminders to be quiet and secretive, and to public and community censorship. This theme of women protagonists in contemporary writing occupying what might be described as 'heroic' spaces is pursued further in the next chapter.

Notes

1   Rosalind Coward, *Female Desire: Women's Sexuality Today* (London: Paladin, 1984), p. 184.

2   Stevie Davies, *Impassioned Clay* (London: The Women's Press, 1999).

3   Sarah Waters, *Tipping the Velvet* (London: Virago Press, 1999).

4   Erica Jong, *Fear of Flying* (Austin: Holt, Rinehart & Winston, 1973).

5   Stevie Davies, *Kith and Kin* (London: Weidenfeld & Nicolson, 2004).

6   McCarthy, *Modernisation*, pp. 12–13.

7   Peach, *The Contemporary Irish Novel*, pp. 10–11.

8   Ibid., pp. 112–13.

9   Eve Kosofsky Sedgwick, *Tendencies* (London and New York: Routledge, 1994), p. 3.

4 'Heroic Spaces': Re-imaging 'Ordinary' Lives

Most people would think of 'heroism' as a masculine concept, associated with romantic views of war or life-threatening deeds of bravery. Whilst women have been honoured alongside men for this kind of courage, they have been in the minority, and women's writing from Ireland, Northern Ireland and, more recently, from Wales has extended the concept of 'heroism' to include crossing boundaries between cultures; survival in communities that bombard women with experiences and images that mutilate the private, female self; and 'staying alive' through the traumas of violence and abuse. The first anthology of Irish and Northern Irish women's writing to be published in the United States, referred to in Chapter 1, actually speaks of how 'women writers in Ireland bravely and eloquently explore what it means to define oneself with dignity.'[1] But in cultures that, like Irish Catholicism, invest women with 'heroism' for resisting secular concepts of femininity, finding oneself and achieving control of one's own body can be both 'heroic' and 'anti-heroic' at the same time. Thus, whereas male-oriented adventure fiction tends to interpret heroism in terms of actions and events, women's writing, which is more inclined to look inward as well as engage in public events, is situated at the border between the inner self and external forces.

One obvious type of writing that applies the concept of 'heroism' to the lives of ordinary women is the feminist historical novel. Here, the emphasis is upon revealing the experiences of women that have not been fully articulated. In Emma Donoghue's *Slammerkin* (2000), arguably one of the best historical novels by an Irish writer in recent times, the principal female protagonist occupies a space that is 'heroic' in the way in which she has to survive violence and abuse on a daily basis. The novel charts the street experiences of an eighteenth-century young woman who was hanged at Monmouth, recreating her time as a child prostitute in London, where the community of prostitutes provides her with an empowering network of support, and her period as a maid in a small town in the border country between Wales and England. In fact, *Slammerkin* is very much a 'border' novel. As a prostitute, its young protagonist occupies a space between childhood and adulthood – indeed, in reading of her experiences it is possible to forget that she is only a ten-year-old child. As a maid to a dressmaker in Monmouth, she occupies a position between employee and slave and between the respectable and the lower classes. The former is encapsulated in the episode in which she is whipped by her female employer across the back of a bent over, female servant who is actually an ex-slave. The latter is signified by the 'slammerkin' itself, a dress that opens at the front which is popular with ladies, and also with prostitutes for a different reason, because it opens at the front and makes it easier for them to ply their trade.

A late twentieth-century example of a feminist historical novel from the Welsh feminist publishing house Honno, but not from a Welsh writer, is Vivien Annis Bailey's *Children of Rebecca* (1995).[2] Like *Slammerkin*, it is based on extensive archival research into what might be described as 'people's history' and finds 'heroism' in the lives of ordinary women. The novel is set in the Wales of the 1830s and 1840s and traces the relationship of a young, lower-class, heterosexual couple during their move from rural Carmarthenshire to the notorious 'cellars' of industrial Merthyr. Throughout, it focuses on the 'heroic' spaces which women at the time occupied. Bethan's experiences as a maid reinforce, like those described in Donoghue's *Slammerkin*, the precarious and difficult position that employees occupied in the household:

> Her memory shuddered away from the night when [Mr Roberts] had come to her instead of his wife. His sneering, demanding face, his threatening hands on her throat and mouth and the thrusting pain of his assault on her paralysed body. In his actions he had told her that she was no more than a slave to him, a receptacle for his lust and hatred. (49)

The Rebecca riots referred to in the title of the novel occurred in West Wales during the period 1839–43, a series of protests by tenant farmers who dressed as women against the payment of tolls to use the roads. Their description of themselves as Rebecca's children recalls the words in the Bible spoken to Rebekah when she agrees to go with Abraham's servant, 'let thy seed possess the gate of those which hate them' (Genesis XXIV:60). But women in *Children of Rebecca* also occupy intellectually empowering spaces that capture the rebellious spirit of the period:

> Siôn was both confounded and thrilled by this spectacle. He had never heard of such a thing – women taking it upon themselves to meet in a public house, discussing questions of morality and politics without recourse to menfolk, addressing questions of national importance and reading from newspapers! The most shocking thing of all was to see a woman standing up in public, while men were watching, capturing the attention of dozens of people, without shame, owning and asserting a viewpoint as if that were a right for women as for men. (151)

In identifying and exploring these 'heroic' spaces which women might be said to occupy in their ordinary lives, the counterpoint to a feminist historical novel such as Bailey's is the serious, literary fiction that combines notions of 'heroism' with a psychoanalytic approach to the condition of being a woman. It is a type of writing that draws upon developments in women's literature which can be traced back to the 1960s and 1970s, to the feminist narratives of tangled family relations and divergent desires such as Jeanette Winterson's lesbian, coming-out novel, *Oranges are not the Only Fruit* (1985),[3] and Angela Carter's *The Magic Toyshop* (1967)[4] concerned with the struggle against incest and abuse, and through women's confessional writing of the 1970s and 1980s such as Verena Stefan's *Shedding* (1980),[5] Lisa Alther's *Kinflicks* (1976)[6] and Kate Millett's *Sita* (1977).[7] In such writing, as Maroula Joannou says: 'The central character's understanding or knowledge of herself is often focused on sexual encounter, love, marriage, or divorce.'[8] Although these subjects might appear to be the ordinary, everyday fare of popular fiction, in the serious, literary novel they are usually developed in such a way as to involve a female protagonist in challenging situations. In these texts, this space is 'heroic' because of the way in which gender, desire and power, as explained in Chapter 3, are implicated in wider social structures, and because they thereby involve their protagonists in encounters with difference within the self, the family and the community that are risky and dangerous, as proved the case with the principal protagonists in the fiction discussed in the previous chapter.

The notion of women's lives in modern Ireland as 'heroic' because of the way in which power is imbricated in its gendered social, religious and political structures, originates with the early work of Edna O'Brien. Indeed, her career as a writer may be seen as 'heroic' since her books were banned by the Catholic Church, vilified in the Press and even burned by priests. Her daring trilogy[9] – *The Country Girls* (1960), *The Lonely Girl* (aka *Girl with Green Eyes*, 1962) and *Girls in their Married Bliss* (1963) – follows two young women, Kate Brady and Baba Brennan, from rural Ireland to Dublin and on to London. These novels are different from the English female *bildungsroman* in the extent of the societal repression of female sexuality against which the protagonists have to struggle. Although both women spend much of their time chasing men, an aspect of the trilogy of which some feminist reviewers disapproved, they may be described, like the texts themselves, as 'heroic' because they articulate female, heterosexual desire in a culture in which this subject was taboo. Their naiveté and, at times, stupidity make them convincing as characters and alert the reader to the kind of 'heroism' it is possible to encounter in even ordinary, and otherwise unremarkable, women in an oppressive culture.

The Country Girls anticipates a host of post-1980s novels and short stories concerned with women leaving Ireland, whether for work or because of pregnancy, and the courage that this entails. These include Leland Bardwell's *That Lonely Winter* (1978),[10] Julia O'Faolain's *The Irish Signorina* (1984),[11] Mary Rose Callaghan's *The Awkward Girl* (1990)[12] and *Emigrant Dreams* (1996).[13] O'Brien, as Christine St Peter points out, imagines women's escape from Ireland, because the North and the Republic constitute an island, as a 'further break of waters' and 'another birth', casting it as a specific female heroism.[14] In Northern Ireland, the literature of female exile acquires a particular perspective because it is often linked to an escape from what Gerry Smyth calls 'fatal sectarianism'[15] and St Peter sees slightly differently as a masculine society based on 'blatant militarism'.[16] Such writing includes Linda Anderson's *Cuckoo* (1988),[17] Kitty Manning's *The Between People* (1990),[18] and Deidre Madden's *Remembering Light and Stone* (1992).[19]

O'Brien's more recent fiction, written in a very different vein, is more obviously concerned with 'heroism' in the more conventional meaning of the term. In *House of Splendid Isolation* (1994),[20] set in the Troubles of Northern Ireland, O'Brien explores the 'heroism' shown by an elderly lady, who has a remarkable strength of character from living in rural solitude. She finds herself having to give refuge to an IRA man on the run, but, in the course of a narrative overtly coloured by the author's political sympathies, each acquires a mutual respect and liking for the other. However, *Down By the River* (1996)[21] is perhaps O'Brien's most 'heroic' work, based upon the notorious 1992 case concerning the rape of a teenage girl, 'Miss X', who was prevented by the judiciary in Ireland from travelling to England for an abortion. In the novel, fourteen-year-old Mary MacNamara does not have the language to express what her father does to her and O'Brien reflects this in the description of it: 'It does not hurt if you are not you. Criss-cross waxen sheath, uncrossing, uncrossing. Mush. Wet, different wets. His essence, hers, their two essences one.' (5) Her father's language is evasive, denying the reality in which he is engaged. He speaks determinedly, in short sentences and questions that invoke the innocence of childhood, such as 'And after the spuds, come the strawberries', 'What are little girls made of?', 'Sugar and spice and all things nice' (5). The control that he has over his language and his daughter stands in opposition to her pain and confusion: '"Sugar . . . and spice . . . and . . . and . . ." the voice growing pipey and the mountains and sky bumping into one another.' (4) The shift in perspective here reflects the separation of her knowing and feeling body. In what happens afterwards, Mary, like 'Miss X', is seen as victimized twice, the second time by the way she is failed by the judicial system which is remote from her in geography, age, gender and understanding:

> In the City far away men of bristling goatee beards, men of serious preoccupied countenances, move through the great halls, corporeal figures of knowledge and gravity, the white of their wigs changing colour as they pass under the rotunda of livid light, ribs of yellow hair, smarting, becoming phosphorescent, powerful men, men with a swagger, a character personified by the spill of a gown or the angle of a coiffed wig . . . (6)

This description of the powerful, masculine judicial system stands in contrast to the image presented later in the novel by Judge Mahoney and Judge Hana as, realizing the impact of the case upon the country, they contemplate having to overturn the original court's decision: 'They walk in silence then, the wind pouching in under their gowns and lifting their hems up so that they look like caricatures of men, arms athwart, groping and grasping for respiration.' (286)

Down By the River can be placed in the context of what is almost a subgenre of fiction in Ireland and Northern Ireland, narratives of not only incest and abuse but also wife battering, unwanted pregnancy and criminalized abortion. They are 'heroic' not only in their representation of female 'heroism' but, as St Peter says, in the way the authors 'struggle to give artistic form to radically new content'.[22] Novels such as Jennifer Johnston's *The Christmas Tree* (1981)[23] and Maeve Kelly's *Florrie's Girls* (1989)[24] represent the act of writing itself as 'heroic'.

Power and space

The way in which notions of space and history are mobilized in Donoghue's *The Woman Who Gave Birth to Rabbits* and Stevie Davies's *Kith and Kin* so as to challenge established notions of the self is not untypical of fiction by Welsh, Irish and Northern Irish women authors. But it is especially true of the way in which concepts of place are treated in the work of women writers from Northern Ireland. Indeed, it might be possible to argue that the way in which geography in Northern Ireland is perceived at the beginning of the twenty-first century is indebted to a diverse range of writings by women such as Linda Anderson, Caroline Blackwood, Polly Devlin, Kathleen Ferguson, Joan Lingard, Deirdre Madden, Kitty Manning and Una Woods.

Most of these writers have approached the Troubles in Northern Ireland through their effect on people's lives, bringing to mind Dick Hebdige's thesis, referred to in Chapter 2, that space is 'a moving cluster of points of intersection for manifold axes of power'. This is an important but often overlooked aspect of the work of Jennifer Johnston, who was born in the Republic (when it was the Irish Free State) but has spent much of her life in Northern Ireland, demonstrating the importance of the movement and links between the two. Many of her novels deal with the fading of the Protestant Anglo-Irish Ascendency in the twentieth century, following the way in which the nationalist movement and the Catholic Church became fused, mentioned in Chapter 1. Thus, they provide a contrast to the work of the Dublin-born writer Mary Morrissy, of Catholic origins, and the Northern Ireland, Protestant author Linda Anderson, who are discussed at length later for their equally distinctive explorations of the way gender, desire and power are interconnected.

Although Johnston has achieved considerable popularity and is one of the Irish women writers most widely read in Ireland, the United Kingdom, the United States and Western Europe, winning a number of prestigious literary awards, she has not received the academic or even literary critical interest that she deserves. The adverse criticism of her work has resulted from a tendency to compare her, if not equate her (along with other writers such as Maeve Binchey), with more popular forms of women's writing, and it has included criticism of her sentimentality, her repetitiveness and the improbability of some of her plots. Such comments seem to be misguided, the result of a failure to see that her work – in comparison with that of a number of other writers of recent decades – is best approached through frameworks other than the conventionally historical and realist.[25]

Like Davies's *Kith and Kin*, Johnston's fiction is preoccupied with how the intersection of axes of power appear to be most pronounced, complex and contradictory in a context of things coming to an end. Indeed, like *Kith and Kin*, the best of her fiction may be seen as an interruption of the accepted past-present continuum. Whereas it is possible to see in Johnston's work a preoccupation with decay – of the Big House in her earlier novels – it is important to recognize also that this background often highlights the matrix of gendered power relations with which the text as a whole is concerned.

Johnston's fiction occupies an 'heroic' space because it is concerned, as St Peter points out, with the way in which her principal characters engage, like Davies's radical females, in an 'heroic refusal of tribal orthodoxies'.[26] The non-realistic strain in her work reflects an ongoing concern with the whole experience of empowerment and disempowerment from which women's writing has emerged and which, as Donoghue demonstrates in *The Woman Who Gave Birth to Rabbits*, has been at the centre of women's history for many centuries. Johnston's characters are more accurately and more interestingly seen as sites of ideological conflict or embodiments of ideological positions that are challenged, as is the case with Miranda's optimism in *Fool's Sanctuary* (1987),[27] for example, not just by what happens to that character at the level of the story but also by the larger interplay of ideas within the narrative as a whole.

What makes Johnston's work, and that of other women writers from Ireland and Northern Ireland, more concerned with ideology than that of contemporary Welsh writers is that the discourses with which all women have had to struggle are embedded in Ireland and Northern Ireland in particular political and sectarian contexts. Indeed, this is where the interest of the reader who wishes to take Johnston on her own terms must lie. Critical discussion must concentrate on following the ideological conflicts through the pattern of recurring motifs and through the frequent juxtaposition of thesis with counter thesis.

Johnston's concern with place as the embodiment of competing discourses is complicated because her characters, like those in Davies's *Kith and Kin*, are forever changing. Although her women find themselves in locations that are oppressively gendered, they are able to think beyond the immediate limits of their lives. Locations in Johnston's novels are not only physical places, but sites of various, and usually competing, discourses and of 'real' intellectual struggles. From her early, albeit not especially original, interest in the Big House and the waning of the Anglo-Irish ascendancy, Johnston has been interested in physical premises as sites of ideological, individual, familial and communal conflict. These are exacerbated very often in Johnston's work, as referred to earlier, by the sense of something, usually the old symbolic order, ending. This sense of an order drawing to a close highlights not only the ideological or sociopsychic struggle but the necessity of creative thinking as a way for women to achieve control over their language and over the matrix of gendered, power connections in which they are situated.

Sheds and skinny dipping

One of Johnston's principal texts that is concerned with the importance of creativity in women's struggle with ideologies and cultures that would disempower them is *The Railway Station Man* (1984),[28] focused upon a woman artist. One of the most productive ways of 'entering' the text is through the two locations in which Helen finds that she is closest to her true self: her painting shed and the sea in which she likes to swim naked. The skinny dipping episode is a key signifier in the text and makes the point that whenever men re-enter Helen's life, they seek to impose limits on her.

Helen's response to men coming into her life is different from the reaction to the entry of men into the lives of women in women's popular romance. There, the female protagonist, who in several aspects of her life lives outside the social norms, usually welcomes the return of boundaries and definitions that the man represents. His initial appearance may not be welcomed by the female protagonist, but in the course of the story she undergoes a conversion. This is not the case in Johnston's work, however, where relationships are often more complex than at first appears. The men who enter Helen's life appreciate her as a woman friend and as an artist but the 'boundarylessness' of her art and her deep-rooted desire to place herself, like her art, outside traditionally configured social and intellectual limits confound them.

Given that Johnston's women have to struggle against the way in which social and religious ideologies are imbricated in Ireland and in different Northern Ireland communities, the significance of Father Quinlan is greater than his fleeting appearance may suggest. He signifies a Church which, as noted earlier, has traditionally been closely associated with Irish nationalism and, in the middle of the twentieth century, closely connected with the framing of a constitution that defined women's place in Ireland in the home, and it is so significant that when he buys one of her pictures he immediately wants to frame it. In other words, he wants to contain and define its subject matter redolent of the way that the Church and the Irish Constitution seek to frame femininity. In effect, he wants to impose boundaries around the inner 'boundarylessness' which Helen has found and which finds expression in the content of her work. Ironically enough he otherwise resembles Helen, in that he spends much time on his knees, in his case working on his garden which is his 'canvas'. But it is a place of boundaries and limits.

Throughout *The Railway Station Man*, Helen struggles against forces that would frame and define her that are actually located in her general, spatial environment. These restrictive environments are connected with men, while the liberating spaces are associated with the female and the feminine. In addition to the examples referred to above, she is seen by her grown-up sons only as a mother to be at their beck and call and treated by her father as if she were a child. The narrative drive of the novel is provided by Helen's desire, literally and metaphorically, to discover her own space.

Eventually, Helen moves into a shed where she works. But, as I have stressed in an earlier discussion of *The Railway Station Man*, the male characters do not understand the importance of the possession of space for women.[29] This point seems especially important to the present discussion of gender, desire and power. After spending a night with Roger, Helen has to hurry home to reclaim her own definition of herself that can only happen in a space that is not constructed by others (one of her first actions is to see herself undressed in the mirror). The dialogue between Roger, who follows her home, and Helen is riddled with references that deny her a space of her own. This conversation is significant because it embraces the struggle and confrontation with empowerment and disempowerment that many women have had to undertake on a daily basis.

Helen's enjoyment of skinny dipping arises from her relocation near the sea in a remote area which allows her to swim naked. The freedom of removing all her clothes is not so much a return-to-nature gesture as a return to her self. Shedding her clothes is symbolically a rejection of the limits and taboos which society has imposed on her sexually, ideologically and artistically. Within this context, Helen's undressing on the beach for herself and not for the male gaze, assumes increased significance. In the sea, drifting in her own space, as it were, as in the 'boundarylessness' that she finds in her painting, Helen discovers a new kind of physical freedom. Here she is free of the discourses that would seek to control her body and her thinking.

In rediscovering herself, Helen moves beyond the symbolic, the masculine and the land:

> ... she swam straight out to sea, something that she normally wouldn't dream of doing, fear always keeping her within scrabbling distance of the land. She swam for a good six or seven minutes, thinking of nothing but the movement of her body through the water, the soft cleaving of arm after arm, the rhythm of her stretched legs beating ... (103–4)

Thus, her 'true' sense of self is linked to what is traditionally associated with women – rhythm and water. Surrounded by water, suggestive of amniotic fluids, and thinking only of her body, she discovers an inner, secretive state of being which returns her to what is beyond language.

In Davies's *Kith and Kin* and Waters's *The Night Watch*, this primal depth of female being is something that is achieved in a relationship with another female, but again often only temporarily

– as, for example, when Frankie and Mara lie together as young-sters in Oxwich Bay or when Helen and Julia lie together in a bath. On both occasions, it is a male shadow that looms over them; in Frankie and Mara's case their father's and in Helen and Julia's their landlord's. Significantly, Helen's skinny dipping is interrupted by the tall, looming figure of Damian Sweeney. He behaves very differently in the water from Helen – almost trying to struggle with it and overcome it:

> Suddenly in a great explosion of energy he rolled into the foam and leapt up into the air again. He twirled round, his arms high above his head and then down he went again, rolling again. Up he came and ran through the shallow water kicking great sparkling fountains up ahead of him as he ran. (105)

In this respect, Damian represents the masculine desire for control of language and bodily identity against which women have had to struggle.

Creativity and empowerment

The feminist version of the *bildungsroman* is important to women's writing in Ireland, becoming a form in which its protagonists have to negotiate 'multiple levels of danger and hope'.[30] But it is also important because of the 'trace' it carries of the struggle women have faced historically between empowerment and disempower-ment.

Johnston's novels share with those of other Irish and Northern Irish women writers, and Welsh writers such as Davies and Waters, the attempt to 'radically de-centre and re-centre the value structure of the narrative tradition'.[31] In Helen's case, the 'language' over which she has control and in which she can express herself without the compromise of traditional, male-centred, verbal discourse is paint. Indeed, typical of a painter, her emphasis falls upon changing colours, especially the interplay of light and dark. At one level, the latter represents the movement between happiness and pain in Helen's own life while also encapsulating the experience of living through Irish history as well as the way in which the politics of the Republic and Northern Ireland are interlinked. At another level, it signifies the shifting nature of the struggle for women, as well as for the Irish people generally, between empowerment and disempowerment.

Putting Helen's concern with changing light in a wider perspective suggests Johnston's interest in taking ideas out of their usual contexts and setting them within new frameworks. If we accept that meaning is derived from the customary interplay of signs and symbols within a wider, established symbolic order, then the kind of change that fascinates Helen may be seen to challenge the way different sets of signs and symbols are normally perceived as relating to each other. As she develops as an artist involved in the kind of work that she wants to do, Helen comes to feel, like Davies's Frankie and Waters's Kay, that she occupies a space in which the known is detached from its limiting referents. This preoccupation with disengagement from rigid definition which is pronounced in Johnston's, Davies's and Waters's work, is evidence of the struggle with empowerment and disempowerment in which modern women's writing originated and which is still a part of the lived experience of women.

As she frees herself from the early influences upon her, the art school and her father, Helen's own thinking transcends the limits which they imposed upon her intellectually and spatially. Her paintings which, as I pointed out in my earlier study, are symbolically unframed,[32] do not only take the wild, untamed elements of nature for their subject matter, they are full of the unfettered energy and light that Helen has sought to discover in her own life and which, by implication, she feels that all women artists have striven to find. In the course of the novel, the activity of painting for Helen becomes increasingly physical, exploratory and revelatory. The descriptions of her at work stress her bodily engagement with her art and the physical effort involved – crouching, leaning and stretching. In other words, it is through painting that she discovers a 'language' that does not seek to constrict her intellectual outlook or impose limits upon her relationship to her own body. Painting sets her free intellectually and corporeally.

To read Johnston as a writer who is interested in feminist, 'heroic' spaces might itself appear to adopt a 'heroic' critical position. But it is the direction in which her fiction has been developing since the Big House narratives. Whilst some critics have seen her work as 'sentimental', they have overlooked the way in which it encapsulates and builds itself around the trace of the history which all women's writing inevitably contains. Both Davies and Johnston, despite the differences between them, are interested in women characters who seek to free themselves intellectually and bodily from the usual determining referents. Both stress the importance of creativity in the process by which women assume a voice of their own. In different ways and for different reasons, it is an art form – blues in Frankie's case and painting in Helen's – that enables them to engage with achieving a sense of identity that is disentangled from the determinism of the socially constructed and gendered, linguistic and cultural environment.

Belonging and (un)belonging

As mentioned above, Johnston's *The Railways Station Man* and Davies's *Kith and Kin* each concerns a character who finds her voice through an art form – painting and the blues respectively. In Davies's novel, the search for a voice on Frankie's part is as much for psychological as sociocultural reasons. In other words, she is a product of her family upbringing as much as her epoch. She has been brought up by a father who treats her as a child even when she is an adult, and the same is true to some extent for Helen. The search for a voice and the attempt to belong as a woman to one's own body is also the subject of Johnston's *This Is Not a Novel* (2002).[33]

This Is Not a Novel is written from the perspective of Imogen Bailey, who discovers a set of documents with which she can piece together, like Davies's Mara, the history of her family, in this case to throw light on the disappearance of her brother. It traces four generations of family history, through letters and diaries, from the First World War, through the war of independence to the present day. In this novel, Johnston extends the technique of flashback that she used in *The Invisible Worm* (1992)[34] to examine incest and to explore psychiatric illness, loss, grief and homosexuality.

One of the ways in which the title may be read is as signalling a different type of work from the other post-Big House fiction, even though it is concerned with the nature of the space and boundaries with which women have to struggle and with the search for a woman's voice. This text begins with a situation in the present and like Davies's and Waters's fiction unravels the present by moving back into the past. With a stronger psychoanalytic dimension than

Johnston's earlier work, it concerns a young woman's loss of speech. At the outset, this is perceived as a symptom that stems from the young woman's relation to her self. In other words, she does not hold herself in sufficiently high esteem. This is the view of her parents who send Imogen to a nursing home and of its staff who receive her. It is an opinion that Imogen also seems to accept herself. She admits that she is afraid to disclose anything, even unwittingly: 'The things I don't want ever to speak about.' (157) She finds herself wondering 'again about [her] invisibility' and 'what [she has] done wrong' (122) and, in visiting her brother at university, she 'finds merely another backdrop for the same old world' (138).

The reader is encouraged to think in the same way as the staff of the nursing home for much of the first part of the text. Indeed, what would have been the most obvious external cause of her illness, the death of Imogen's beloved brother, occurs only after her speech loss while she is already in the home and is, in fact, beginning to recover. On Imogen's discharge, her nurse comments that she is going 'Back to Mammy and Daddy'. In fact, she is doing so in more than one sense, for the novel takes the reader back into her relations with her parents which Imogen now reinterprets more insightfully in the light of what has happened to herself.

The unravelling of Imogen's past takes the reader to an incident in which, arriving home unexpectedly, she discovers her mother in bed with the young German man, Bruno, with whom she has fallen in love. In other words, the loss of her speech would seem to stem from her mother's betrayal of her:

> I stood in silence and they never noticed my presence. The smell of him was intensified by the heat of his burrowing body. That was all I could think of, burrowing and the smell of spices. It was as if he were trying to beat his way back inside her body, back into her dark womb. My mother's womb. (184–5)

In this incident, Johnston would appear to be extending the incest theme of *The Invisible Worm* that recurs in Irish fiction. But, notwithstanding Johnston's usual concern with Protestantism, it may also be read allegorically as the way in which mother Ireland, through the 1937 Constitution, betrayed its daughters and in defining them as mothers first, housewives second and women third robbed them of their speech. What women in Ireland have often seen as the oppressive power of the Catholic Church may be seen as having robbed them of control over their own sexuality. Thus,

Imogen discovering her mother in bed with her lover conflates her loss of sexuality with her loss of voice. But as the novel moves further into Imogen's past the situation is revealed as even worse than that for her. Bruno is also her brother's lover.

This incident involving her mother is only understood by Imogen when she comes to appreciate that her mother, like her father, is left with unsatisfied desires and emotional needs and that both are essentially lonely in their marriage. In other words, Imogen would appear to represent the young generation of Ireland, turning from resentment over the way their foremothers have betrayed them, to an understanding of what binds the generations of women in Ireland together.

The novel also reviews the way in which women stand in relation to the emphasis upon the male heroes who won independence for Ireland. This occurs through the way in which Imogen eventually comes to think of her father differently. Again, it is a realization that can be read in terms of the novel's plot or allegorically:

> You see, you must see, that I deserved what I got: I was as unfeeling, unforgiving, unbalanced as the rest, except perhaps Father, who I believe moved in some dreamlike world of his own. I have seen so many like him, men, in appearance, attend to their own work, their families, but in reality live in another world of defeated dreams and longings. Men who have lost, for some reason, the energy of their fathers and hope that in their sons they may regain it once more. (134)

Imogen's return to her parents proves to involve an engagement with the cultures of which they and their relatives are products. Although the two are not entirely elided, Imogen's father's prioritizing of his son over his daughter reflects the Nationalist's privileging of the men of Ireland over its women. In acquiring a voice to reprimand her father for the burden that he placed on her brother, Imogen epitomizes the empowerment of women in late twentieth-century Ireland. She reminds us of the revisionism that challenged Eamon De Valera's version of nationalism that had ushered in the Republic. His vision of a rural, isolationist Ireland, in which a woman's role was to be a mother, distorted the lives not only of its women but also its men. In bringing to her father's attention the fact that the swimming coach he admired so much attempted to abuse her brother, Imogen also cryptically invokes the revelations of child abuse by priests of the Roman Catholic Church, an institution which in the struggle for Independence had become synonymous with nationalism. Typical of the contemporary Irish novel, *This Is Not a Novel* reclaims occluded Irish histories for a more inclusive Irish identity than monological, masculinist, nationalist narratives have traditionally allowed. Imogen's awareness of how she has succumbed to misery is part of the wider empowerment of women in late twentieth- and twenty-first-century Ireland, often involving a critical re-reading of personal and family, as well as national, histories.

As in Johnston's earlier novel, *Fool's Sanctuary*, the naming of a central female character after a Shakespearean protagonist encourages the reader to read the text against the play in which she occurs. The most obvious way of reading that novel is through the connotations of the name of the family home, 'Sanctuary', and the Shakespearean allusion in the name of the central character Miranda. At one level, the reference to *The Tempest* suggests that these texts share scepticism about retreating from life into an island of one's own. In *Cymbeline*, one of the most psychologically dense of Shakespeare's plays, the young heroine, who shares the twenty-first-century Imogen's confusion, enters exile and a long sleep through drinking a magic potion that is comparable to the modern Imogen's period in a nursing home. Whilst Shakespeare's Imogen awakes to find her husband's headless corpse beside her, Johnston's character 'awakes' to the reality of her brother's death. Both their fathers have in different ways 'exiled' their children and, at the end of the text, both are bemused by their lives. Shakespeare's central concern, like Johnston's, is with a country, in his case Britain, derived from the older societies which preceded it. In *Cymbeline*, Britain is seen as having roots in the Celtic worlds at the margins of its Anglo-Saxon centre. In both texts, the nation's journey is symbolized in the heroine who, through her own private grief, struggles against the corruption symbolized by the father and confronts the past.

The 'heroic' daughter

One might not immediately think of Maeve Binchey as a 'heroic' writer because, as St Peter says, she is regarded as the author of rural, Irish village fiction for '"middlebrow" cultural consumers'.[35] However, her fiction is important to this book for its focus, as St Peter says, on women's 'strength, flexibility and resourcefulness'.[36]

Binchey's seemingly popular potboilers contain thought-provoking criticism of the way in which the gender, power and desire matrix functions in Ireland. Often the 'blockbuster' style and marketing of her fiction belie a subtlety which, as in the case of Jennifer Johnston's fiction, has not always been recognized.

Born in Dalkey, Ireland, and subsequently losing her Catholic faith, Binchey is, like Johnston, a prolific writer whose fiction, like that of many Welsh authors, explores the effect of sociocultural change on women's lives, relations between her country and England and the nature of rural society compared with the urban community. Recurring subjects in her work are growing up in small communities, as in *The Copper Beech* (1992);[37] relations between strangers, as in *The Lilac Bus* (1984)[38] and *Evening Class* (1996);[39] family conflict, as in *Silver Wedding* (1988),[40] and relationships between women, as in *Tara Road* (1998).[41]

As in Johnston's case, the 'heroic' daughter is a key motif in several of her works, two of the most important of which are the short stories 'Flat in Ringsend' and 'Decision in Belfield', in *Dublin 4* (1982).[42] The former examines the experiences of a young woman who, like Maria in Emma Donoghue's *Stir-fry*, moves by herself to Dublin. It emphasizes the kind of courage that a single woman, living and working as a stranger in the metropolis, had to possess to survive the loneliness and isolation of city life: 'She had never expected the miles and miles of streets where nobody knew anyone, the endless bus journeys, the having to get up two hours before she was meant to be at work in case she got lost or the bus was cancelled.' (90) The flat which she shares with other young women is divided into bedsitters with only a shared kitchen and bathroom, and is very different from the 'jolly all-girls-together' (103) that she had expected. The division of the house underscores the atomized nature of the Capital, and her misery is intensified through remembering: 'Back home they'd be going to the pictures or to a dance at eight o'clock on a Sunday night. In the hostel some of the girls would watch television in the lounge, others would have gone to the pictures together and go for chips on the way home.' (96)

'Decision in Belfield' explores not only the 'heroism' shown by a young woman who becomes pregnant, but her fortitude in seeking the truth about what happened to her elder sister who had left home as a result of having become pregnant months earlier. Indeed, it is her sister's advice, given when she returns home unexpectedly for Christmas, that results in Pat's dilemma. Like many of the women protagonists in texts discussed earlier, Pat also demonstrates the courage involved in finding a voice amidst silencing family and societal discourses. She finds herself caught between the rhetoric of women's magazines – 'You will be surprised, the Problem Pages said, at how much tolerance and understanding there will be, and how much support there is to be found at home' (128) – and the reality of her parents' attitude and behaviour:

> There would be no support there, no understanding. Pat's mother wasn't going to smile like people did in movies and say maybe it was all for the best and it would be nice to have another baby around the place, that she had missed the patter of tiny bootees. And Pat's father wasn't going to put his arm around her shoulder and take her for a long supportive walk on Dun Laoghaire pier. (128)

The fact that both sisters become pregnant, although the elder claims that it had been a false alarm despite having departed mysteriously for London, highlights the problems for women caused by the state and the Catholic Church's attitude towards contraception. Pat's case is far from unique and a further example of the 'heroism' required of ordinary Irish women, as demonstrated by O'Brien's *The Country Girls* trilogy referred to earlier, in achieving the personal and sexual independence enjoyed by women in other parts of modern Europe. At the heart of the text are different types of discourse which are imbricated in the wider gendered culture of the Republic from the 'Problem Pages' of women's magazines, through the evasive communication of Pat's parents to the convent-influenced discourse of Pat's aunt. It explores the need for women to articulate ideas that will challenge what Pat's sister, speaking for many young women in Ireland, perceives as the dishonesty of even the liberal discourses around sexuality. She complains that their parents 'keep saying they're in favour of getting divorce introduced and they want contraceptives, and they want censorship abolished, but they refuse to face facts' (130). When Pat confronts her parents over what really happened in the case of Cathy's pregnancy, she generally speaks in a series of short, uncompromising statements – 'This family is becoming a bit like nine green bottles' (137) – and asks brief candid questions: 'Are you just waiting for me to go off and that will be the hat trick?' (138) Her style is designed to disarm her parents, as her mother's reaction reveals: 'What is this Pat, what silly game are you playing?' (138) But, it is also based on a new-found confidence in her position and the fact that her own moral perspective is clearer than that of her parents: 'It's not normal. People marry and have children, they don't have them just to export them off a fast as possible.' (138) Her parents are prompted into fairly long responses which are initially defensive but unravel what has up until now disguised the truth. Like many of Leonora Brito, Emma Donoghue, Stevie Davies and Sarah Waters's successfully independent, women protagonists, discussed in previous chapters, Pat speaks as if she is in control of her life: 'And soon I suppose you'll want me to go. Would you prefer if I tried to get into UGC or Galway or maybe England rather than Belfield, then you wouldn't have to have me around the place and you could be all on your own?' (138)

Binchey's most recent work, involving the motif of the 'heroic' daughter, *Star Sullivan* (2006),[43] was written as part of an ambitious publishing project to bring fiction to a public that would not normally read literature. The series includes works by many well-known writers, such as Joanne Trollope, Ruth Rendell, Tom Holt and Minette Walters, who have used the occasion to produce intelligent, innovative works that experiment with narrative and push back conventional, generic boundaries. The perceived target audience has also encouraged the authors to explore the sociocultural discourses and the circumstances that prevent young people, especially, from achieving their full intellectual potential. Binchey's short novel, *Star Sullivan*, demonstrates these points. It is about a girl, Oona Sullivan, born into an apparently dysfunctional family, who is such an ideal daughter and school pupil that everyone forgets her real name and calls her 'Star'. Her 'ideal' attitudes and behaviour eventually cause trouble for her family, friends and acquaintances. She undergoes a rude awakening and at the end of the story receives an award in her own name from her regional manager who turns out to be someone who, as a boy, adored her. In the course of the story, she falls for the boy next door and, as in romantic fiction, he becomes the focus of her life which he invests, without realizing it, with new purpose and meaning. In style and content, *Star Sullivan* is the kind of story one could imagine being published in a woman's magazine. But beneath its bland surface, it undermines the formulaic women's story.

Star Sullivan is the kind of young woman admired in Catholic Irish culture, with its idealization of the female in the light of the reverence in which the Virgin Mary is held. As such, she is part of what Seamus Deane has described as Ireland's 'committed history',[44] shaped by a fusion of nationalism and Catholicism. However, Star is also an example of a susceptible young woman beguiled by the images of female desire and behaviour to be found in the Church and in women's romantic fiction. In other words, any girl following the Catholic Church in Ireland's guidelines would more than likely turn out to have Star's innocence and ways of behaving. The fact that she is no longer known by her real name but by an epithet that signifies her ideal behaviour underscores the dangers of this kind of brainwashing implied in the text. The novel's apparent blandness serves to highlight critically the bland notions of young, female sexuality promoted by the Catholic Church as well as by women's popular romance. The ideal by which Star lives, it is implied, stands in contradistinction to 'real' adolescent and pubescent development:

> At Star's school they were just relieved that Star had a smile instead of the constant sulk and sneer that so many of the girls wore all day. Star did not have a pierced nose or lip, saving endless hours of argument. If someone was needed to help clean up the classroom, or put out the chairs, or change the water in the flower vases, Star would do it without a seven-minute protest, which the teachers would get from the rest of the class. (7)

Star's behaviour exemplifies the Catholic ideals of female duty and obedience. The activities in which she readily engages – cleaning and tidying – are those of the ideal housewife and mother. The absence of 'piercings' suggests 'purity'. The 'pierced' bodies of her friends signify at one level that they are the victims of another set of discourses about the human body at the beginning of the twenty-first century. But, at another level, their bodies are a protest against the Catholic discourse that values the obedient female body, the submissive body kneeling in prayer or penance. Their 'piercings' might also be read as an inverse image of the worshipped 'piercings' of Christ's body.

In keeping with the guidelines of the series in which *Star Sullivan* is published, to write for readers who are not committed to literature, Binchey produces a text which in style and language is redolent of fable. This is especially appropriate to the subject matter because it is a form that has played a major role historically in the Church's efforts to reach the non-literate and, as part of an oral and literature culture, has provided a means of moral and social instruction for children, as is evident in the following sentence: 'Star Sullivan had a head of shiny copper hair, a ready smile and a good nature, and she did everything that she was asked to.' (1) Significantly, her copper hair is not 'fiery', which would suggest the stereotype of the red-headed woman, but 'shiny'. Star, uncharacteristically of a teenager, is defined by unquestioning obedience, and, as becomes clear, by an absence of sexuality and passion. In this respect, she stands in contrast to her sister whose view of her self as a female is determined, equally disastrously it turns out, by the media. Her ambition is to be a model. She is the antithesis of the Catholic Church's ideal destiny for women, which is motherhood. Star, on the other hand, often asks her mother whether there would be another baby 'she could push in a pram up and down Chestnut Street' (2).

The story provides insights into the tensions within the family and the community. But it is narrated from a reference point that is close to, though not identical with, Star's annoyingly bland conformity: 'Some of the people who lived [in Chestnut Street] went to great trouble to keep it looking nice. Others sat there at night and drank lager and left the cans.' (3) The style reflects Star's way of looking at things which can best be understood through what in the mid-twentieth century was called 'object relations' theory. Associated with the post-Freudian, feminist psychoanalyst Melanie Klein, it argues that a child's early experience of the world is based on its experiences at its mother's breast. These include seeing the breast that is offered as 'good' and the breast that is withdrawn as 'bad'.[45] Whilst children see the world in a stark binarism, they grow up to appreciate that it is more complex than this. The world is not simply 'good' or 'bad' and neither are the majority of people in it. Star's way of seeing the world, in Kleinian terms, is literally childlike, reinforced by the description of her as someone who 'pushed other people's babies and played with their cats. On her own'. (2)

This simplicity shapes the way in which Star becomes involved in other people's lives: she falls out with her favourite teacher because she is leaving, not to teach in another school, which Star would approve of, but because the teacher is going to work on a beach in Spain with a married man; she persuades the boy next door to cover for her brother who is handling stolen goods, which results in him coming under suspicion from the police; she protects Laddy by giving him an alibi that turns her parents against him; and she convinces herself that Laddy is sleeping with his father's girlfriend when he is at work. When she falls in love with the boy next door it is sudden, like something in a romance novel. She becomes a modern-day version of Red Riding Hood, buying a skinny red top which signifies her new-found awareness of her body. But she immediately enters a world that is hostile and responds to her in antagonistic ways because she has the innocence of Red Riding Hood. Her ambition is to become a nurse and this betrays her desire to become involved with other people's lives that borders on an obsessive disorder.

There is also a profound theological contradiction raised by Star. At one level, it is because at the heart of the Republic there is paradoxically what has been called an 'anachronistic and modern-ized present'.[46] Star seems to reflect the 'anachronistic' present in that she tends to look back to the pre-Lemass era rather than the post-Lemass era referred to in the previous chapter. Ironically, the way in which she embodies the modelling of women in De Valera's Ireland, which was closely connected with the Catholic Church, actually denies her a meaningful engagement with the Church for she appears to think of herself as having a purity of thought that seems to be greater than that possessed by the Virgin Mary herself. Seamus Deane, discussing the theme of betrayal in Joyce's work, reminds us that Joyce argued, in writing of Oscar Wilde, that in the Catholic Church one cannot reach the 'divine heart' without sin.[47] The 'divine heart' has many meanings: the maternal figure, the mother, Mother Ireland, the Church itself and the Virgin Mother. It is only when Star begins to 'sin', in persuading Laddy to cover up for her brother and lying that she has spent the night with him, that she embarks upon the road that will, eventually, bring her closer to her family and her mother. In being a pure ideal without the 'sin' of those around her, Star exemplifies the Catholic ideal. But possessed only by the Virgin Mother, it is what women are meant to aspire to with the Church's guidance.

Star Sullivan can be read in a number of ways. Even the reader not familiar with critical discourse and analysis will appreciate that Star is too 'pure' for her own good. More experienced readers will recognize how female desire is suppressed and how women are encouraged to take instruction rather than initiative.

Troubled bodies

The argument initiated in Chapter 1, that all women's writing carries a trace of the history from which it emerged, is complicated by the specific histories of Northern Ireland. This is especially evident in Linda Anderson's fiction in which, as in many works about the Troubles by women writers, there are traumatic moments that are part of the wider lore of living in, and of being a citizen of, contemporary Belfast. *To Stay Alive* (1984),[48] set in 1979, the beginning of the second decade of the Troubles, is comparable to Waters's *The Night Watch* in several respects. It is concerned with how war breaks down the accepted symbolic order and permits behaviours that seem to redefine what being 'human' means (or reveals what being 'human' has meant all along). I have argued elsewhere that this novel is structured around a series of disturbing events that push at the boundaries of ethical behaviour.[49] Anderson's novel is typical of many novels written about war by women, certainly those written about the Northern Ireland Troubles in the 1980s and 1990s, in that it is concerned with the impact of the violence upon ordinary people's lives. In this respect, *To Stay Alive* shares with *The Night Watch* a late twentieth-century concern with 'histories' rather than 'History' and with community stories. Both texts pursue lived experiences of communities in contradistinction to the official histories. In both texts, the focus of this suffering is usually the female body.

To Stay Alive, like *The Night Watch*, leaves the reader with graphic images: in Waters's work of the limbs protruding from the rubble of bombsites and the conduct of an illegal abortion. In the previous chapter, I argued that the images in Waters's novel were especially disturbing because the mutilated corpses of war are presented without the compensatory religious images that normally accompany the representation of the dead. Anderson's novel takes its structural cue from the slide show which is given to British troops at the beginning of the text. At one level, the episodes in this novel demonstrate, as St Peter says, 'the multiple ways that private relationships even among lovers are poisoned by the mutilating world'.[50] However, in the context of this book's theme of gender, desire and power, they might be said to exemplify how women are engaged in 'an heroic struggle against the false forms of heroism' that was current at the time. Indeed, *To Stay Alive* is written from a particularly 'heroic' perspective; it is a study by a Protestant writer of 'the ghastly experience of humiliation inflicted on the Catholic population'.[51] For Anderson, this involves the articulation of previously unacknowledged sadistic desire in the 'gendered' nature of the 'humiliation'.

The images and events interwoven in *To Stay Alive*, referred to earlier, are all the more disturbing because they not only offer the reader little by way of compensatory symbolism, they invert the consoling religious images which are so evident in intellectual and public life in Ireland and Northern Ireland. They push at the limits of the 'acceptable', evoking sadomasochism and a brutality which in the assault on the novel's female protagonist conflate various kinds of sexual domination.

One of the most initially disturbing images that confronts us in Anderson's novel is that of a dead dog. Dan, a Catholic medical student and one of the key protagonists, retrieves his wife's pet that has been used for target practice by a British paratrooper. This is the first example of the violence that surrounds Dan and his young wife, in Catholic West Belfast, who find themselves caught between the occupying British army and the IRA. Their friend Aidan, also, is the victim of a revenge killing and one of their neighbours is killed in crossfire.

As Dan's wife's pet, the dog is part of her family, her emotional life and indeed her femininity. As a British army target, it is placed outside these domestic/familial/loving/feminine referents and seen as something to be hunted, as a rat or rodent, or even tortured. This change of signification says much about the different way in which the 'human' stands in relation to 'life'. As in Waters's novel, 'being human' is a concept that has to embrace love and also savagery. What has happened to the dog is not simply a matter of 'insensitivity' but of enjoying cruelty and inflicting torture.

Like Waters's novel, *To Stay Alive* takes us into the 'heart' of war in two respects. It takes the reader into the physical centre of the Troubles, as Waters takes us into the physical centre of the Blitz. But, like Waters's novel, it also takes us into the psychology of war. In both texts, this psychology is not simply a product of war per se. Both texts are concerned with what stands revealed in war. Anderson's title is ambivalent, suggesting the desire in war not to be killed but also the determination to 'stay alive' in the sense of not being brutalized.

The use of the pet dog for target practice would seem to signify a model of colonial identity based on oppression and suppression which some of the Welsh writers discussed previously would appear to resist. But the incident of the dog in West Belfast, as we have suggested above, is more complex than might at first appear. Moreover, the arguments about 'being human' that it raises are even more complicated by the gendered suggestion. The episode cryptically introduces ideas about male-female relationships. It is significant that the dog is female, is a woman's dog and that the soldier who kills it is male. The soldier not only represents what from a Republican perspective signifies violent conquest and oppression but also demonstrates a type of 'masculinity' which is itself based upon violence, the boundaries of which embrace the working-class people of Belfast as well.

Punishment and boundaries

The wider, gendered matrix of behaviour, at the centre of which the soldier stands, is encapsulated in another of the novel's most disturbing images: the public punishment of Marta O'Hanlon, a slide of which is included among those shown to the British army in an orientation briefing. Whilst the slide confirms the kind of insights into the community which the army wants its soldiers to have, it is also an allusion to the struggles and confrontations which constitute women's history in Belfast. It is redolent of Heaney's well-known poem, 'Punishment', about a young female victim of communal discipline. But it is also different from Heaney's poem in several important respects. The voyeurism that is implicit in Heaney's text is explicit and even more brutal in Anderson's account where the emphasis is upon violation, meanness and misogynism:

> Another slide. A young woman tethered to a lamp post, her head covered with some oily liquid, her full breasts partly bared by a rip in her shirt.
> 'This is Marta O'Hanlon.'
> 'Ohhh, I'd love to martyr her,' Shiner whispered.
> Her hair was cut off by a group of women. They poured red lead over her head until it dripped into her eyes. Men ran their hands over her body and urinated against her while women cheered them on . . . (24)

As I have argued in a previous discussion of this particular episode, the slide brings to the fore what is generally buried within the wider communal knowledge of Belfast.[52] First, there is the behaviour of women who associate with British soldiers and the summary punishment of offenders by the paramilitary groups. Second, there is the cynical chauvinism of the British army that is not broadcast in mainland national news. But what is especially significant is that the soldiers' reactions are elided with the abuse heaped on the female victim by her 'own people', as it were. Like the Welsh women authors we have discussed, Anderson is interested in exploring a model of cultural identity based upon assimilation, confrontation and resistance which offers a more in-depth understanding of cultural relations than the oppressor and oppressed binarism. Anderson's account complicates Marta's punishment by highlighting how it is women who cut off her hair and how, presumably, it is the same women who watch the men, maybe members of their own family but certainly of their own community, humiliate her by urinating on her and then, in what has connotations of a perverse, sexual sadomasochism, run their hands over not simply her body but her naked body. There is a similar incredulity here to that expressed by Mara to Frankie's mother in Davies's *Kith and Kin*, referred to in Chapter 2, that she must have watched her lover beat her daughter.

This elision of the boundary between gendered behaviours is one of the complicating aspects of Anderson's novel. At one point, Dan's wife Rosaleen reminds her neighbours what was done to another young woman in the neighbourhood who was accused of being 'a whore to the entire British army': '"They fixed it so they would be the last guests," said Rosaleen, picturing the wet slick of blood curling from the punctured womb.' (47) Moreover, in Marta's punishment not only do we see a case of cold-blooded, public violence but an act that seems to subvert the religious iconography which frames the role of women in Irish Catholic communities: the paint is redolent of the blood from the crown of thorns; the rip in her shirt suggests the spear wound in Christ's side; and the behaviour of the men and the women echoes the mockery that Christ endured from the Roman soldiers. Moreover, in the echo of the crucifixion in the slide viewed by the soldiers, as in Leo's broken body later in the novel, there is a reminder, often hidden within the religious idealization of the cross, that it was a shameful and, at the time of the Passion and death of Christ, a common form of judicial punishment.

The perverse desire which seems to be present at Marta's punishment is inscribed in the gender politics throughout the text. At this point, it is useful to turn to the attack upon Rosaleen at the end of the novel which furnishes the text with its most disturbing image.[53] Rosaleen prevents herself being sexually assaulted by four soldiers by vomiting upon one of them. The assault is both ideological and sexual, shrouding perverse desires connected with the exercise of power over the powerless. As in Marta's punishment, it is difficult to separate the verbal abuse and the physical assault. Indeed, when we compare what happens to Rosaleen with Marta's punishment, it seems that Rosaleen's mistreatment has confirmed the sexual sadistic tendencies expressed by the soldiers as they watched the slide of Marta's humiliation. The soldier who imagines that he would like to 'martyr' Marta is not only displaying the way he regards her but revealing the way in which he thinks about women more generally. The boundaries that should protect the women from the kind of intimate assaults they are forced to endure have broken down. Like the dog caught in crossfire, they have been removed from one set of referents which respects their identities and dignity as human beings to another which reduces them to available 'objects'. Whilst Marta is physically bound, an object upon which sadomasochistic fantasies can be projected, both women are bound by discourse. In Rosaleen's case, it is a discourse that includes betrayal, sexual immorality and gender and, in the way the soldiers think of her, femininity, Catholicism and sexuality. Because she is a Catholic, Rosaleen, who is not at church on a Sunday, is labelled a 'heretic' and a 'bad girl'. This reminds us that the torture and execution of women by religious courts were a means of curtailing female power as well as religious subversion. Once again, her experiences become a prism through which the reader might look again at Marta. For, like the punishment of witches, the disciplining of her is about curtailing female sexuality and independence.

As the prospect of rape gets nearer, Rosaleen is reduced to an 'it' and to 'Irish' (183). But once again, Anderson complicates the oppressor and oppressed paradigm. The attitude of the soldier who comes forward is shaped by an adolescent masculinity that is linked to the exercise of power over women, which is not confined to the army: 'Acne ran wild on his face. He was leering at her like a deadly adolescent who practised his menace in a mirror.' (183) His friends tease him when Rosaleen vomits over him, 'You make them come at the wrong end . . .' (184) The conflation of public and private, perverse desire hinted at in the account of Marta's punishment is made more explicit here. The most violent words he uses are those he whispers, secretly, into her ear.

Rosaleen's reflections on the crucifixion, after she has been attacked, give us an alternative reading of the event. Just as Binchey criticizes the model of the ideal daughter, Anderson here overturns – but much more explicitly – the theological ideologies of the day:

> She re-read the New Testament in amazement, hating the Jesus she found there. A righteous prig blasting fig-trees, turfing money-lenders out of the temple. And his cruel impossible demands! . . . Not that he forgave his opponents. No, they were destined for 'everlasting torment', which he described with gloating malice. And, oh, how he wanted to die! He invited it, insisted. Elected his own betrayer. (85)

This is not, of course, the way in which Catholic women were brought up to see the crucifixion of Christ. But then the Catholic upbringing of women idealized the Passion, the role of the Virgin mother and the family and did not confront the way in which men brutalized and violated women. What Rosaleen does here, given the emotional pressures which Catholicism usually exerts on individual minds, is intellectually and emotionally 'heroic', in being 'blasphemous'. Approaching blasphemy from the point of view of an angry, abused woman, the novel suggests that from a feminist perspective, it can actually be seen as courageous because it pushes at the boundaries of socially sanctioned limits and taboos.

One of the key signifying events for Catholic framing of female behaviour and sexuality is Mary washing the feet of Christ, which is a demonstration of how women would have cared for the body of the crucified Jesus. Traditionally, it is the Passion of Christ that would be thought of as 'heroic'. But from a feminist perspective, it would be possible to argue that it was instead the devotion of the women to the crucified body of a dangerous, subversive, religious thinker that was 'heroic'. The image of the caring, dutiful and devoted woman is invoked in the episode in which Rosaleen cares for Leo. But here the emphasis is upon the violence and the brutality which he has suffered and the scene complicates the simple binarism of the caring female looking after the tortured male body. It begins with Rosaleen acting out a role that seems to be passed from mother to daughter. But nursing a broken body is seen here not as an act of subservience but as one of 'heroism' since Rosaleen and her mother, like Kay in the Blitz in *The Night Watch*, have to confront injuries that are horrific. They are made all the more so because Leo is family.

> When Rosaleen came back with cold compresses, Leo was stretched on the settee. His face, usually so proud and brazen, was swollen with bruises and tears, his trousers hung in tatters over burnt legs. Rosaleen kneeled, breathing in his close panicked odour and placed a cool cloth on the charred skin, making him wince.
> 'I'm sorry, sorry,' she murmured, turning to stop her tears splashing on his sores. 'Moral degenerate,' she read uncomprehending. There was a notice pinned to his shirt with 'Moral degenerate' scrawled over it! Rosaleen snatched it away.
> Their mother was patting and soothing him: 'My love, my love, who did it to you? Why? Was it Protestants? Where did you go?'
> His speech was snarled and ugly, as if his tongue was thickened: 'Tattoo. They said . . . next time.' (88)

The passage moves from Leo's body violated by 'the new priesthood', to how he has secretly abused the bodies of, presumably, prostitutes, and eventually to how he has abused his own body through drugs. His action is placed in a wider context – the way in which men are responsible for inscribing the female body with a particular text that legitimates the abuse of women.

To Stay Alive conflates different examples of how those with power use the powerless. It underscores how this is legitimated and made possible by the way those with power and authority 'other' the bodies of those they exploit. Most of these incidents draw attention to what is often denied but is always 'encrypted' within scenarios of exploitation: gender and sexual politics.

Trauma

The concept of the heroine occupying 'heroic' space is one that embraces crossing over, as in many of Jennifer Johnston's novels, from one religious and political culture to another; embodying and eventually struggling against the realization of an ideal within oneself as in Binchey's *Star Sullivan*; and trying to 'stay alive' in many senses of the word in the complexities of Northern Ireland. The 'heroic' space is a trope that has taken Irish authors, as in Linda Anderson's *To Stay Alive*, into harrowing subject matter. The family is not the private sanctuary that the Church preaches it should be and innocence and childhood are not synonymous. These are recurring tropes in Irish fiction by both female and male authors, where they are frequently linked to Catholic rural or small town contexts and to issues around premarital pregnancy, as in Kathleen Ferguson's *The Maid's Tale*,[54] or incest and abuse, as in Joseph O'Connor's *Cowboys and Indians*[55] and Edna O'Brien's *Down By the River*.

Although not always as harrowing or as frequent as in Irish fiction, a traumatic childhood event is a subject in contemporary writing by Welsh women, too. In Siân James's *A Small Country* (1979), as in Johnston's *This Is Not a Novel*, the trauma arises from an act that is witnessed rather than suffered, but in the Welsh Jewish writer Bernice Rubens's highly unusual and original work *I Sent a Letter to my Love* (1975)[56] it is endured by the protagonist. Each of these novels is focused upon a female character who is of low self-esteem or frustrated by the circumstances of her life and who also feels unloved, and unwanted, by one or both her parents. In Rubens's novel, Amy Evans, born and brought up in Porthcawl in south Wales, lives all her life with the belief that she is ugly. It is ironic that her first name, of French origin, means 'beloved woman'. She is ignored by her parents, because her brother, disabled in childhood by rickets, receives all their attention, leaving her isolated, jealous and miserable. Unlike Rubens's Amy, James's Catrin is stunningly beautiful but, like Amy, she is treated with indifference by her parents who privilege her brother over her. Johnston's Imogen, too, is shown little love by her father, who again takes most interest in her brother, and by her professional mother, whom she comes to hate with the same intensity with which Catrin, at the outset of *A Small Country*, loathes her father. Given the way in which she seems to be regarded by her parents as some kind of mistake, it is ironic that, as already noted, her first name derives from *Cymbeline*, where it is generally presumed to be a misprint for Innogen.

'Miserable' is one of the most often used epithets in Siân James's *A Small Country*, a novel about an early twentieth-century Carmarthenshire farming family: the daughter, Catrin Evans, is 'less miserable' as a probationer nurse than at home; her father's lover is 'miserable' when he temporarily leaves her to return to his dying wife (144); newly married women are said to become 'miserable when they wake up in reality' (178); seeing Catrin's brother off to war, his friend Edward feels 'miserably lonely' (156); and the young maid looks 'miserably embarrassed' when Catrin's father proposes to her following his wife and lover's deaths (177). Although both male and female characters experience misery, the epithet 'miserable' is applied more often to women in James's novel than to men.

The association of misery with women has a long trajectory in psychoanalytic writing which can be traced back to Sigmund Freud. Primarily interested in the inner psychic worlds and conflicts of women, he distinguished between 'mental suffering, misery and disablement' and 'neuroses' which are 'miseries of a particular kind' with 'particular causes'.[57] This distinction is particularly apt as far as James's novel is concerned. Although at one level *A Small Country* is a sociohistorical family narrative, it also has a strong psychoanalytic dimension.

James initially approaches the origins of Catrin's misery more overtly from a 'social' rather than a 'psychic' perspective. Certainly, it is possible to see the relatively isolated, farming culture of south Wales in *A Small Country* as having been drawn, to employ the feminist, psychoanalytic critic Jacqueline Rose's words, as 'a socially delimiting and self-binding institution'.[58] This is how Catrin purports to see it:

> Catrin spent a miserable Saturday . . . The idea of marriage had always been so abhorrent to her . . . And if the broadest of the jokes were anything to go by, the wedding breakfast was only a preliminary to a farm-yard kind of coupling, leading as inevitably to the first pregnancy; the bride of a few months by this time pale and big-bellied, the finery of the wedding and the presents forgotten. (75)

However, the 'heroic' space that the novel is particularly interested in exploring is the boundary between the social, external and the inner, psychic world. The word 'heroic' seems appropriate here because Catrin's childhood and adolescence have been about achieving an inner, emotional stability that one would more likely associate with an adult than a young woman of her age:

> For three years at least, Catrin had known about her father [and the woman he leaves home for], seen all the signs her mother had been too trusting to notice; how happy he was all day Saturday with Saturday night before him; the glazed, faraway look in his eyes on a Sunday; a man who had lost his road. She had known for years. (12)

As Catrin eventually confesses to Edward, after her father leaves home to live with the teacher with whom he has been having an affair: 'I have to get away, Edward, I must. I don't do mother any good. It's only Tom and Nano she wants. It'll be worse than ever now that Father's left home; we'll live in a sort of half-mourning all our lives.' (48) It is significant that Catrin wants to leave home and become a student at an art college. As with Johnston's Helen, creativity is central to the way in which she reinvents herself and to the concept of self-development that has in turn been essential to the 'heroic' space that she has been forced to occupy.

Like Johnston's Imogen, Catrin's inner pain is the result of what Freud might call 'trauma', but it is not one that has occurred, as in Freud's case histories, in very early childhood. It is revealed that when she was nine or ten years of age, Catrin saw her father and a maid having sex in the hay loft. Confiding this to her brother's friend, she relates the episode in an unusually clipped, matter-of-fact way: 'I saw my father up here with Maggie; she was a maid we had then. They were lying on some bags of grain in that corner over there. They didn't see me.' (34). In order to tell Edward this, she has to take him to the hay loft. Thus, her father's secret place becomes her secret space and in confiding in Edward she admits him into it as well.

In interweaving accounts of Catrin, her father's new partner and Edward's fiancée, *A Small Country* explores ways in which desire disrupts the norms and expectations of family and social relationships. The motif of desire, as in Waters's *The Night Watch*, is a vehicle for exploring loss, loneliness and unfulfilled needs. For women in late twentieth- and twenty-first-century Wales, there are two aspects to this which James's novel examines. The first, referred to earlier, is connected to the socially limiting nature of the rural environment in which Catrin was brought up. An important irony in the novel is the similarity between Catrin and her father's new woman friend which Catrin herself does not see: they each seek to resist the inevitable destiny of women in Welsh rural communities:

> She tried to imagine choosing furniture and curtains, but couldn't. She tried to imagine herself cleaning and shopping and preparing meals for Gareth, but couldn't. The unfinished house she was looking at made her feel nervous and inadequate.

> As Miriam Lewis, schoolmistress, she had duties and obligations . . . Having to conform, doing what the neighbours did, going to chapel on Sunday; being not only a wife, a daughter-in-law, probably a mother, but a member of a respectable, red-bricked society. (57)

Catrin observes: 'Girls stay at home. That's how it's always been.' (31) The second aspect of the novel's exploration of desire is its psychoanalytic dimension. In maturity, Catrin comes to recognize that in desiring Edward, who is someone else's fiancé, she has adopted the same role as her father's lover. In other words, she finds herself cast in the role of the 'other woman':

> He couldn't help himself, she thought, any more than I could help falling in love with Edward Turncliffe. Nothing – she knew it – could keep her from Edward, neither family nor career nor the knowledge of hurting Rose whom she had liked and admired. She was no different. No better. Perhaps no one was. She had been too young and green to understand. She patted her father's arm, forgiving him. (129)

Whilst this experience brings her fresh insights into the emotional and social condition of being a woman, it also suggests the impossibility of really knowing even those to whom we are closest. Although it is possible to read this novel psychoanalytically, it retains the view that behaviour is often in the end contradictory and unfathomable. Thus, when Edward, following his marriage to Rose, visits Catrin to explain why he married her, he is said to be 'lightheaded with pain and joy' (167); Miriam is drawn to a school gate where the sounds so familiar to her in her previous life as a teacher bring her both pain and pleasure (146–7) and, unable at one point to see herself as 'a wife, a daughter-in-law, probably a mother' (57), she ends up like one of the maids with whom Josie had casual affairs. After the death of his wife, Josie derives 'a certain satisfaction from the idea of being an outcast; he needed to feel that he was being punished, ostracized from society' (175). Catrin, like Johnston's Imogen, discovers that our psychic space often allows us to assume contradictions and different conditions within it, including dominance, submission, guilt and innocence. This is evident in the way in which Catrin is able to shift, with seemingly equal conviction, from wanting to be an art student in London to being a trainee nurse in Cardiff.

The 'reality' of fantasy

A Small Country calls into question the 'reality'-seeking principle as the key driver in individual behaviour. Edward's letter expressing his new-found patriotism suggests that 'reality', or the 'reality'-seeking principle, is invested with a definition and importance which it does not always deserve. He and Rose resist the intrusion of the other 'reality' that comes with stories from the front line: '"We're both lucky," Edward said, infected by her courage. "We're the fortunate generation."' (154) His first physical involvement with Catrin is unexpectedly aggressive, almost violent:

> Edward had been so looking forward to the drive, and was so thrown by this turn of events, that he, too, lost control of himself. He grabbed her by the shoulders and pulled her towards him and kissed her hard on the mouth. Only a moment she resisted, then her lips opened for his kiss and she was kissing him back. Their eyes were open and amazed as they went on kissing each other without a word. Soon his hands were opening the buttons which had so enchanted him and pulling aside skirt and petticoat.
> 'Let's go into the field', he said, his voice parched and rough.
> 'No.' She was crying now and rearranging her clothes. 'No.' (49)

Edward's behaviour here is only fully explicable when we bear in mind the way in which he has been fantasizing about her. He does not simply grasp Catrin the person; he tries to take hold of the object of his sexual fantasy that she has become:

> He desired Catrin, ached for her, couldn't stop thinking of making love to her. He couldn't look at her face without imagining her strange green eyes opening wide in surprise against the passion of his kiss. The buttons on her blouse, the frill of her skirt, her small feet, even in the clogs she wore on the farmyard, excited him so much that he had to look away. (43)

The focus on detail – 'the buttons on her blouse, the frill of her skirt, her small feet, even in the clogs she wore' – eloquently expresses how intense and obsessive his desire has become; the 'frill' is almost linguistically the 'thrill' of her skirt. In considering situations such as these, Jacqueline Rose suggests that there is a 'choice': 'you either pay attention to the reality, the social reality of the event . . . or you talk about fantasy and the circulation and interminability of meaning'.[59]

In *A Small Country*, change at a national level is reflected in Catrin, who moves from the remote rural areas to the city, and who, through her private misery, struggles against corruption symbolized by her father and confronts the family's past. In the Shakespeare play to which Johnston's novel alludes, a corrupt court sits along-side a secret court-in-exile in Wales. In James's novel, the corrupt present-day Wales, where fathers 'exile' their daughters, betray their families and have casual sexual relations with the hired help, is contrasted with the fantasy of an older, family-oriented, Welsh-speaking Wales. In thinking about his Welsh identity during the War, Catrin's brother writes of himself as 'belonging' to a culture and history from which, through his education, his social mobility and his place as an Oxford University student, he has always been separate:

> I think of myself as the product of a different society, not better, not worse, but completely different, with a completely different history. Our grandparents, all four of them, spoke only Welsh, had never been out of Wales. How well worth preserving these differences seem to be. When I think of the civilization we're fighting for, I can only think about the patch I know best. I like to think of its radical tradition, its passion for learning; all the craftsmen and labourers who tried to make an academy out of the village chapel . . . And yet I am here with Welsh chaps whose families in one or two generations in industrial South Wales have completely lost their language and presumably with their language their consciousness of being different, their own special way of life. (172)

In other words, like Amy in Rubens's novel to which I shall return in a moment, he locates himself in 'a brand new exciting lineage, an inheritance of beauty and family feeling'. Not necessarily in a derogatory way, his nationalism is as much a product of 'fantasy' as 'reality'. But, like 'distance' and 'intimacy', the two do not necessarily cancel each other out. Although at one level *A Small Country* belongs to the family history genre, it eschews a socio-economic narrative, pursuing the part that fantasy and psychic drives play in determining the destinies of the principal players. Catrin's brother reclaims his Welsh identity when he comes to face the fact that Welsh farming is in his blood and reviews the apparent break-up of his family. These all engage with an imaginary Wales which invokes a familiar trope in Welsh writing in English: the importance of the rural to 'authentic' Welsh identity.

Thus, fantasy is neither simply the product of 'reality' nor a projection of internal anxiety or depression upon it. It is a complex component of 'reality'. How complex is suggested in *A Small Country* by the comparison of Miriam's suicide with the war in which it occurs. At one level, Miriam's suicide is the product of the death drive which Freud assumed was the principal cause of war. But whereas Miriam's death is, at least partly, the product of her misery and guilt, Catrin's brother and Edward, like thousands of others, go to war because not to do so would make them feel guilty. In other words, while at one point in the novel the death drive is the product of guilt – generally speaking psychoanalysis sees violence as the outcome of guilt – at another level it is an attempt to avoid guilt. Moreover, Tom and Edward also fantasize that they are going to war in order to play their part in defending freedom. The assumption is that freedom from guilt and individual freedom are synonymous. Yet this is not always the case. Catrin finds that she is happier in the controlling and dominating environment of the hospital as a probationer nurse than she ever was in the 'freedom' of her home farm.

Inventing oneself

Bernice Rubens's novel *I Sent a Letter to my Love* shares with many other contemporary Jewish texts an emphasis upon suffering that has to be worked through almost on a daily basis. This is exemplified not only by the central female protagonist but also by the elderly woman who comes regularly to the post office for a letter from her missing husband. The trauma of the central protagonist, Amy, begins when she sees herself as 'other' and unattractive:

> She retained all her life the squat nose of her childhood, stubbed on to her face like a plasticine afterthought, a chin too long for any practical purpose, and eyes so close together that it seemed the sole function of the bridge of her nose to keep them apart. (4)

Amy's anxieties about her appearance are triggered when she catches sight of one of the senior school girls. In other words, in looking at herself, she also sees what wider culture defines as 'desirable', against which she judges herself. The impact that this has upon her is evident in her behaviour: 'a wilful child, given to sudden rages and tantrums, who spat with hatred at her elder brother, who ran screaming down to the beach in anger or in unison with the gulls.' (4) Rubens challenges the opposition of the 'social' and the 'psychic' by highlighting the cultural boundaries of the body. Whilst setting up Amy as the victim of her own views of herself, Rubens attributes her low self-esteem to the gender ideologies that determine her identity as a female. Thus, the older girl whom she envies is noticed partly because of Amy's unhappiness with herself but also because she exemplifies the wider cultural prejudices from which Amy's private, psychic processes can never be free.

The importance of Amy's re-presentation of herself to her sense of self-worth cannot be underestimated. She assumes the persona of Blodwen Pugh, juxtaposing a first name that as a child she always associated with angels with the name of the shop on the Pier where it was possible to purchase designer clothes from Paris. In this assumed name, she places an advertisement in a lonely hearts column in a newspaper. When her brother, unwittingly, is the only person to reply, she is sucked into a drama that she tells herself she sustains because her letters have become a lifeline for him. But his correspondence is also the first intimate letters that she has ever received and she becomes dependent upon his re-imaging of her in them: 'She has beautiful hair, the colour of sand, which she ties back in a bun. I often wished she would let it loose, so that she wouldn't look like my nurse all the time.' (82) Within the fantasy that she then creates, Amy becomes a more confident and sexual woman: 'Together they would explore the perilous and dark corridors of joy which, all their lives, their each and separate disorders had forbidden.' (118)

In bringing together the loss of a Welsh and a Jewish past, Rubens focuses upon the capacity of the imagination to recreate, and not simply inherit, a fixed history. The photograph album that Amy purchases in Porth, containing the pictures of someone else's family, is intended to provide a 'history' for Blodwen. But, in addition to an immediate family, she thinks of herself buying 'a brand new exciting lineage, an inheritance of beauty and family feeling' (94). At one point in the novel, her brother, who is similarly alienated from traditional Welsh roots, even invokes the issue of colonialism and its separation of slaves from their family roots by comparing his leg irons to those of a slave.

In her imagined existence as Blodwen Pugh, Amy pretends that she lives not in Porthcawl – where 'cawl' is both a reminder of the gulls and of her pain – but Porth, signifying separation from her misery. In her new identity, not as Amy or Blodwen but Amy/Blodwen, she lives, imaginatively speaking, in both Porth and Porthcawl. The idea that the psychic space of identity is large enough to accommodate both 'belonging' and 'separation' informs the principal narrative. Whilst her brother is physically separate

from Amy/Blodwen, through their exchange of letters they are apart
but intimate at the same time. The complex plot which Rubens
develops demonstrates that 'distance' and 'intimacy' are not necessarily locked in an opposition and cancelling each other out.

It is not long before Blodwen begins to consume Amy:

> She wrote to him of her body, of Blodwen's warm and welcoming
> flesh, and with loud and tidal words she stoked his fires. As she wrote
> she understood that there was equal pleasure in giving as in receiving,
> and that both she and Stan would grow fulsome and blessed in their
> verbal exchange. She told him of her summer days in Porthcawl, of her
> Dad who taught her to swim, of her uncle who was always playing
> tricks. She wrote about Tommy and the ventriloquist and she asked if
> he ever thought the doll was real. She enclosed a photograph of
> herself, and added what had now become an obligatory P. S. 'I hope
> the snap is to your satisfaction. Also the lock of hair.' (118–19)

Her supposed question to Tommy asking whether the doll was
'real', is tellingly appropriate for she has become her brother's 'doll'
in several senses of the word. The identity which Amy assumes as
Blodwen Pugh, her brother's 'girlfriend', becomes more real to her
than her identity as his sister. Forced to meet her brother as
Blodwen, her role as a performer within an invented drama is
underscored by the fact that she has to hire an actress to stand in for
her. Amy receives a letter from the proprietor of the acting agency
describing their actress Marion Morgan's experience of him:

> It seems your brother entertained Miss Morgan with a viewing of
> obscene photographs. Moreover, there were marks on all parts of her
> body that signalled some kind of assault, and had he not been confined
> to a wheel-chair your brother surely would have raped her. (169)

Here Marion/Blodwen is a phantasm on which Amy's brother has
projected, through his letters, his frustrated sexual desires. But, of
course, they are fantasies that have been encouraged by Amy/
Blodwen's letters to him: 'She wrote to him of her body, of Blodwen's
warm and welcoming flesh, and with loud and tidal words she
stoked his fires.' (118) However, despite this, when she receives
the somewhat threatening report of what happened from the agency,
she is stimulated more than disturbed by it:

> She had to write to Stan immediately ... She then continued to
> describe in general terms how her body had burned in his presence,

steering away from all specifics to which she had no clue. It was no mean assignment. She begged him to write to her quickly, 'hot letters,' she wrote. (170)

Through its concern with the role of fantasy in engagement with 'reality', Rubens's novel grapples with what Jacqueline Rose believes is 'a pressing question for feminists': the extent to which women are implicated in fantasies that are ultimately oppressive as well as thrilling.[60] In relation to this, Rose provides a useful framework within which to read psychoanalytically based contemporary fiction. Rose takes issue with the way in which women have historically been seen in psychoanalytic writing as implicated in oppressive yet thrilling fantasies because, as she points out, in this formulation, 'danger is still something that comes from outside – patriarchy makes female desire dangerous to itself'. However, she welcomes how, even in this paradigm of enquiry, 'the terms of femininity, passion, and danger have at least started to move'.[61] On the whole, Rubens, James and Johnston shift the terms of the debate along the same lines as Rose, focusing upon the problematic nature of desire itself. In Rubens and James's novels, men are involved in what are virtually assaults upon the women they desire. In doing so, the texts raise the subject of violence and where to locate it.[62] And it is a question with which the novels of Rubens, Johnston and James all engage. In Rubens and James's texts, violence is bound up with fantasy.

The 'heroic' spaces that women enter in these Welsh novels involve, as in the Irish texts discussed, crossing boundaries: Catrin crosses the boundary between outraged daughter and the 'other' woman, a figure who is originally partly responsible for that outrage, and Amy crosses the boundary between 'sister' and 'lover'. At one level, it is possible to see the original spaces that they occupied as 'heroic': Catrin as an independent young woman alienated from her father, and Amy endlessly suffering because of her appearance and family circumstances. But time brings about changes in the protagonists' lives that move them to a new space, to desires that are risky and dangerous. It also makes it difficult to define the Catrin and the Amy that we are talking of. The difficulty of speaking about the 'self' when the self undergoes such change is discussed further in the next chapter.

The kind of 'heroism' discussed in this chapter has always been a significant feature of narrative that is situated on the border between fiction and autobiography. But it has really come to the fore in two innovative twenty-first-century works from Wales. The first of these, Rachel Tresize's *In and Out of the Goldfish Bowl* (2000),[63] is an account of the childhood and adolescence of a young woman, Rebecca Trigianni, growing up in the post-industrial Rhondda Valley. It is a retrospective narrative of short chapters, subdivided into vignettes from Rebecca's life which, the reader can presume, mirrors the journal which Rebecca tells us she keeps and which her brother reads at one point, discovering his sister's promiscuity. The structure of the book is determined not only by the content of the remembered events but also by the gaps between them and the developing voice within them.

Whilst, at one level, *In and Out of the Goldfish Bowl* is a 'literary' first-person novel, the writing is shaped by the kind of honesty and the sudden shift from one subject to another that one might expect to find in a private diary. As a child, Rebecca read avidly and had an imaginative capacity beyond her years. Thus, the reader experiences a retrospective voice whose rawness and sophistication are both believable. But the novel is also simultaneously convincing and disturbing in the extent to which it is both vivid and restrained.

Only when we get to the end of the narrative do we discover that Rebecca's inner strength comes from her grandmother's 'heroism' displayed in the kind of wartime occupations for which medals were not often awarded and in working all hours in order to bring up her family. Despite her drug taking, depression and suicide attempts, Rebecca has her grandmother's strength of character which enables her to 'survive' abuse by her stepfather and physical, verbal and emotional violence from her mother. As a result of drink and promiscuity, her mother ceases to display the 'heroism' of holding down three jobs and keeping the family together after Rebecca's father leaves them. It is something that Rebecca is too young to appreciate at the time but at the end of the novel she comes to realize that whilst she has seen herself as somehow 'strange' compared with most other people in the post-industrial south Wales valleys, many more of them than she realized have had to contend with and 'survive' similar abuse and violence. She discovers that what she thought was 'extraordinary' was in fact 'ordinary'.

The retrospective narrative is based on a sense that Rebecca's present is always 'pre-sent', first suggested in the novel by her initial suppositions about what had been formed for her in the womb before her birth. At one level, the morbidity in her accounts of her obsession with death is a product of the adult Rachel's viewpoint. But, within the unfolding narrative, they are also omens of what is to come. Rebecca appears to have been deprived of the innocence and the love that children should experience by the depravity of the particular family and community into which she is born. In employing the term 'dysfunction' to describe her family, Rebecca invokes the sociology of social, community and economic breakdown in contradistinction to her own insider or participant's analysis of survival. The novel suggests that what is involved in living in economic, community and family poverty is not adequately captured by academic-laden, sociological discourse about them. The gap here between discourse and experience mirrors the discrepancy in the novel between the lived experience of rape and the way 'rape' is talked about carelessly in everyday conversation. Rebecca's own explanations of her drug taking, shoplifting and self-harm might not always have the psychoanalytic depth that the reader, aware of everything that has happened, might want her to provide. But they have the authenticity of someone who is trying to overcome the horror of having been raped by her stepfather. Rebecca's choice of the phrase 'father-father' for her biological parent is ironic because, in terms of the ideal family she momentarily thinks about, Rebecca never finds a true father. Similarly, only in fantasies about love with another woman does she find the tender love that she has not found with men, with the possible exception of her relationship with Daf.

In and Out of the Goldfish Bowl extends the way in which the day-to-day 'heroism' displayed by women in contemporary Wales and Ireland is explored in fiction through its vivid delineation of depression, the medical condition that destroys the capacity for positive thinking, and self-harm, that is generally perceived as an attempt to achieve control and to release negative feelings of guilt, shame and emotional numbness. Rebecca's self-harm takes the form of cutting and overdoses of pills. Whilst it is unclear whether Rebecca actually wants to kill herself, self-harm is generally perceived as a more positive act than suicide. It makes the participant feel more alive; gives them control over an aspect of their lives which Rebecca is also trying to achieve through her journal; acts as a safety valve which again is a function of the ongoing journal; and through the bloodletting takes away feelings of guilt and shame. In Rebecca's case her use of the term 'self-punishment' emphasizes the guilt her stepfather makes her assume for the flow of blood from her self-punishment mirrors that which followed the first act of rape upon Rachel as a child.

In and Out of the Goldfish Bowl shares with other contemporary Welsh works, such as Charlotte Williams's *Sugar and Slate*, the 'heroism' of pursuing a search for identity in a divided family, community and nation. In Charlotte Williams's book the 'heroism' lies in her courage in pursuing her African-Caribbean bloodline from her father, the Guyanese painter and writer Denis Williams. But there is also a day-to-day 'heroism' on her part in the way that she copes with the sense of difference and isolation in being 'black' in the white, North Wales holiday resort of Llandudno in the 1960s. *Sugar and Slate* highlights the 'heroism' necessary for a mixed-race woman who, when her husband gets a job in her place of ancestry, travels to a country which despite the familial link is culturally remote and removed from her. Whilst in North Wales she is seen as an outsider because she is 'black', in Guyana she is regarded as an outsider because she is perceived as 'white'. Her day-to-day struggles in Llandudno and later in Guyana are mirrored and emphasized by the experiences of the young African men who come to North Wales to train as missionaries. But, as in Tresize's novel, there is more than one 'heroic' woman. Like Rachel's mother, Charlotte's has held the family together during difficult times. Despite her upbringing in an orphanage, she provides her family with a centre of cultural gravity, rooted in North Wales, Welshness and ultimately 'slate'.

In pushing back the boundaries of different types of abjection associated with the trauma and psychological consequences of child abuse in Tresize's novel and with the isolation and loneliness in being of mixed race in Williams's book, there is a kind of 'heroism' in the act of producing the narratives themselves. These somewhat edgy works, like the other texts discussed in this chapter, challenge our assumptions about home, community, race, nation and identity. And above all, Welshness.

Notes

1   De Salvo, D'Arcy and Hogan, *Territories of the Voice*, p. xxi.
2   Vivien Annis Bailey, *Children of Rebecca* (Aberystwyth: Honno, 1995).
3   Jeanette Winterson, *Oranges are not the Only Fruit* (London: Pandora Press, 1985).
4   Angela Carter, *The Magic Toyshop* (London: Virago, 1967).
5   Verena Stefan, *Shedding* (New York: Daughters Publishing Co., 1978).

6   Lisa Alther, *Kinflicks* (New York: Alfred A. Knopf, Inc., 1976).

7   Kate Millett, *Sita* (London: Virago Press, 1977).

8   Maroula Joannou, *Contemporary Women's Writing: From the Golden Notebook to The Colour Purple* (Manchester: Manchester University Press, 2000), p. 104.

9   Edna O'Brien, *The Country Girls* (London: Jonathan Cape, 1960); *Girl with Green Eyes* (London: Jonathan Cape, 1962 (first published as *The Lonely Girl*)); and *Girls in their Married Bliss* (London: Jonathan Cape, 1963).

10 Leland Bardwell, *That Lonely Winter* (Dublin: Co-Op Books, 1981).

11 Julia O'Faolain, *The Irish Signorina* (London: Viking, 1984).

12 Mary Rose Callaghan, *The Awkward Girl* (Dublin: Attic Press, 1990).

13 Mary Rose Callaghan, *Emigrant Dreams* (Dublin: Poolbeg Press, 1996).

14 St Peter, *Changing Ireland*, p. 42.

15 Smyth, *The Novel and the Nation*, p. 142.

16 St Peter, *Changing Ireland*, p. 104.

17 Linda Anderson, *Cuckoo* (London: the Bodley Head, 1988).

18 Kitty Manning, *The Between People* (Dublin: Attic Press, 1990).

19 Deirdre Madden, *Remembering Light and Stone* (London: Faber and Faber, 1992).

20 Edna O'Brien, *House of Splendid Isolation* (Boston, Mass.: G. K. Hall, 1994).

21 Edna O'Brien, *Down By the River* (1996, rpt London: Phoenix, 1997).

22 St Peter, *Changing Ireland*, p. 47.

23 Jennifer Johnston, *The Christmas Tree* (London: Hamish Hamilton, 1981).

24 Maeve Kelly, *Florrie's Girls* (Belfast: Blackstaff Press, 1989).

25 Peach, *The Contemporary Irish Novel*, pp. 101–3.

26 St Peter, *Changing Ireland*, p. 74.

27 Jennifer Johnston, *Fool's Sanctuary* (London: Hamish Hamilton, 1987).

28 Jennifer Johnston, *The Railway Station Man* (1984; rpt London: Penguin, 1989).

29 Peach, *The Contemporary Irish Novel*, p. 104.

30 St Peter, *Changing Ireland*, p. 50.

31 Ibid., p. 15.

32 Peach, *The Contemporary Irish Novel,* p. 103.

33 Jennifer Johnston, *This Is Not a Novel* (London: Headline Book Publishing, 2002).

34 Jennifer Johnston, *The Invisible Worm* (London, Sinclair-Stevenson, 1992).

35 St Peter, *Changing Ireland*, p. 136.

36 Ibid., p. 144.

37 Maeve Binchey, *The Copper Beech* (London: Orion Books, 1992).

38 Maeve Binchey, *The Lilac Bus* (London: Arrow Books, 1984).

39 Maeve Binchey, *Evening Class* (London: Orion Books, 1996).

40 Maeve Binchey, *Silver Wedding* (London: Arrow Books, 1988).

41 Maeve Binchey, *Tara Road* (London: Orion Books, 1998).

42 Maeve Binchey, *Dublin 4* (1982, rpt London: Arrow Books, 1999).

43 Maeve Binchey, *Star Sullivan* (London: Orion Books, 2006).

44 Deane, 'Heroic Styles', p. 21.

45 See, Melanie Klein, *The Selected Writings of Melanie Klein*, ed. J. Mitchell (Harmondsworth: Penguin, 1991).

46 Deane, 'Heroic Styles', p. 14.

47 Ibid., p. 21.
48 Linda Anderson, *To Stay Alive* (London: the Bodley Head, 1984).
49 Peach, *The Contemporary Irish Novel*, pp. 61–7. This book has provided the opportunity to reread some of the principal events of the novel through the tropes of sexuality, gender and control.
50 St Peter, *Changing Ireland*, p. 114.
51 Ibid., p. 114.
52 Peach, *The Contemporary Irish Novel*, p. 62.
53 Ibid., pp. 65–6.
54 Kathleen Ferguson, *The Maid's Tale* (Baldoyle, Co. Dublin: Torc, 1994).
55 Joseph O'Connor, *Cowboys and Indians* (London: Sinclair-Stevenson, 1991).
56 Bernice Rubens, *I Sent a Letter to my Love* (1975; rpt London: Abacus, 2002).
57 Sigmund Freud, *An Outline of Psychoanalysis*, ed. J. Stratchey (1949; rpt London: Hogarth Press, 1969), p. 41.
58 Jacqueline Rose, *Why War? – Psychoanalysis, Politics and the Return of Melanie Klein* (Oxford: Blackwell, 1993), p. 90.
59 Ibid., p. 233.
60 Ibid., p. 106.
61 Ibid., p. 106.
62 Ibid., p. 93.
63 Rachel Tresize, *In and Out of the Goldfish Bowl* (Cardiff: Parthian Books, 2000).

5 The Changing Self

In Chapter 2, Leonora Brito's *dat's love* was seen as post-'Race' and
Emma Donoghue's *The Woman Who Gave Birth to Rabbits* as
post-'History' in their rejection of a singular, monolithic understanding of each. The Welsh writer Clare Morgan's *An Affair of the
Heart* might be seen as post-'Self' in that it is underpinned by a
rejection of the 'self' as a singular, fixed concept of individual being.
The concepts of race and history, and the way in which particular
races and histories have been conceived, have changed over time
and with different geographical and cultural contexts. The concept
of 'self' is similarly one that at different times and in different
cultural contexts has been seen differently. Thus, for example, it has
been associated with an autonomous, coherent sense of individuality; with the fulfilment derived from belonging to a wider community; with a regenerative relationship with the natural world; with
an unknowable and sometimes dark psyche; and with a shifting,
fluid, inner consciousness.

In other words, the postmodern perception of 'self' is of a
concept as fluid and complex as race and history. The impact that
this has had upon Morgan's work is evident in her concern with the
difficulty of one person understanding another, even those with
whom they are most intimate. As the title *An Affair of the Heart*
suggests, her collection of short stories is about desire. However, the
concept of desire that informs it is postmodern in that desire is not
seen as simply natural but as the product of particular times,
contexts and life circumstances. Desire in her work is often enigmatic and as such leads the reader back to a complex and unknowable 'self'.

The passage of time

One of the most enigmatic stories in *An Affair of the Heart*, 'Second Bell', is a reflection by an older woman upon an ostensibly minor event in her schooldays. It is not an incident that seems to lead anywhere especially significant, so one of the puzzles for the reader is, what is there in this episode that makes it so important to the narrator that she wishes to return to it so many years later? Another problem is that the story tantalizingly fails to get to the bottom of the incident itself, which is almost as enigmatic at the end as at the beginning.

The story concerns ten minutes in one school day before the second bell is rung, when the narrator invites a fellow pupil, Saluki, who is very different from her, to a special place to play at something. Throughout the story, the narrator's self-consciousness and nervousness stands in contradistinction to Saluki's composure and sense of superiority. She is more smartly dressed than the narrator, is cleverer and more ambitious. It appears that she comes from a wealthier and more privileged background. It is not made explicit why it is that Saluki has been invited to the shrubbery. The excitement for the narrator seems to lie in the spontaneity of the invitation and in the opportunity to be close to Saluki, to have won her interest for a short time and to have become the focus of her attention.

The reader is given the impression that the narrator is not normally someone that Saluki would have chosen to spend much time with or even notice. In this respect, the narrator enters a kind of limbo with Saluki which is outside of the normal school space as well as being outside of time. This is underlined by the explanation as to why the shrubbery is a special place for her; it is where she claims to have buried a dead bird. The truth is that having got Saluki to the shrubbery, the narrator is not sure what to do next. Subtle references to her noticing the way Saluki carries herself and her movements, to the oncoming spring and to the sap beginning to rise suggest that the narrator has a sexual interest in Saluki but whatever desires she feels she probably does not understand and certainly does not know how to act upon them. The state of limbo is brought to an end when Saluki tells her candidly that she does not believe the story about the bird. In response, the narrator thinks of telling Saluki that she will dig up what remains of it. What she would dig up, of course, would be 'time', of which the jagged, ancient sound of the bell is also a reminder. The narrator's desire for Saluki is for something which itself seems in a state of limbo, outside yet part of the particular moment in which it is located:

> But she had already turned and ducked out of the shrubbery under the silver limb, was already five feet away, ten, fifteen, I could see the neat set of her shoulders poised over her hips, the thick, black plait swaying gracefully as she walked, the shape that her body was already taking on, like my mother, like all mothers, the same compactness, and the swing of her bottom and her thighs as she walked away from me, never hurrying but covering the ground in a way that was unstoppable, as the tide does when it washes out the shapes that you have made along the shore. (131)

This narrator's specific memory is a combination of what is outside of time with reminders of time. It is a reflection upon what occurred, and the meanings which she finds in it are a product of those reflections, not necessarily what she felt at the time. What the narrator remembers, or now realizes with hindsight, is that Saluki at that moment in her life seemed to be reluctant to engage with time. Before the bell rings, she consults her watch, yawns and walks purposefully from the place of death and decay.

Unknowable 'others'

Despite the differences between their works, the stories of both Donoghue and Morgan are often reflections upon seemingly small incidents or events. This is exemplified in an admission from Morgan's short story 'Vertigo': 'The incident is like a tiny hiero-glyph scratched on the fabric of my mind with the tip of a pin.' (152) But whereas Donoghue's deliberations take her into unwrit-ten histories, Morgan explores the enigmas of postmodern desire and of the postmodern 'self'. Both writers are fascinated with the lives of others, especially other women, but Morgan's starting point is that they are ultimately unknowable.

This idea is encapsulated in 'A Place in Wales' in the image of 'the dent in the pillows' (64) which the husband leaves in the bed after he has got up. This disturbing story is dominated by the enigma of the husband who appears to be recovering from a nervous break-down and is seeking to write a novel as a kind of catharsis. In fact, his hopes of finding in the countryside the peace and quiet he craves in order to be creative are not realized. The story compares his blocked creativity with the release which his wife finds in her spinning wheel. But the structural opposition at the heart of the story is that between his wife's intimacy with him, deliberately choosing at one point when they go to bed to lie naked against his back, and her estrangement from him. The latter is evident in the way in which he gets up early, possibly to kill himself. The possibility of his suicide signifies how far removed he is in his mind from her. The point is underlined by the image of the empty hook, which 'looked startlingly solid, casting a short blunt shadow' (65), from where she believes he has taken the belt, which is one that she has made, to hang himself.

Like 'A Place in Wales', with its central image of the crocheted belt, 'a tight mosaic pattern reminiscent of the headband she thought might have adorned the forehead of some ancient Inca deity' (63), all of Morgan's stories are woven around images. The narrator in 'Living Memory' tellingly suggests: 'What gave your life significance was the pattern of images of things.' (160) In the tight mosaic of 'A Place in Wales', the image of the wife undressing and lying naked against her husband's back works because the entire story seems crocheted out of images: the painstaking way in which her husband laid the fire; the blackness after rain in the hills; the abjection associated with the fleshy, sprouting, unplanted bulbs; the death-like emptiness of the room in which he was supposed to be writing; the endless permutations of colour and patterning in her work; the empty hook; and the pages with no more than the title of his proposed novel and his name.

'L'Hotel des Grands Hommes'

Of all the images in *An Affair of the Heart* none is more significant than the central image in 'L'Hotel des Grands Hommes': 'When the sun hit the roofs you could see it shimmering off again and everything was very white, there was white behind the colours of things which was stronger than the colours themselves.' (101) Throughout the collection, Morgan seems to be interested in what lies behind desire which seems stronger than the desire itself.

'L'Hotel des Grands Hommes' is set in a Paris hotel room. A little reminiscent of Hemingway's short story 'Cat in the Rain', it concerns a couple who have come to the French capital to sort out their personal problems. The final weeks of summer correspond with the potential end of their relationship. Although there are references to the French language, each language seems to occupy its own space within the text and there is little interrelationship between the two, highlighted when Tony asks the waitress for extra coffee in poor French. This mirrors the way in which the couple themselves occupy different imaginative worlds within the confines of their narrow hotel room.

The impression that the sunlight over the roofs creates a 'white' behind the other colours which is stronger than them is manifest in the recurring use of the halo effect throughout the story: in the splendour with which Marsha and Tony see Paris on their arrival; in the way Marsha, encouraged by the hotel's name and location, places the great French authors, and subsequently the American writer Raymond Carver, on a pedestal; and in Marsha's ambition to write the Great English novel. The halo effect with which Marsha invests everything around her is at odds, like the French and English languages in the text, with reality. Marsha appears to be motivated by how she thinks things should be and what she thinks she should do – such as renting a villa in which to write – rather than how things are and what she really wants to do. The incongruity of Hugo and Zola occupying the same tomb mirrors the mismatch in her marriage. But it also highlights the contrast between her aspirations to be a great English novelist and how little progress she actually makes on her book. This shortfall between aspiration and achievement in turn seems to epitomize her entire life. The oncoming autumn signifies a realism that at the end of the story is overtaking the idealism of the summer. The puncturing of the summer's halo, as it were, mirrors Marsha and Toby's new views of Voltaire and Marsha's realization that Carver and his wife do not necessarily get on well together, rather like herself and Toby, and that he may be different from what she had imagined.

Fencing

The image created by the sunlight on the roofs in 'L'Hotel des Grands Hommes', of a white behind the colours more intense than the other colours themselves, is inverted in another story. In 'Fencing', the stranger who repairs Eleanor's fence has irises in his eyes that are made dense by the whites around them. But Morgan's interest in the halo effect and the magnification of perception remains the same; for

Eleanor the visitor's words 'built themselves into a monument that dominated the room' (90). Whilst Marsha and Toby seek to resolve their differences, it is the unexpected difference, created by the arrival of Carver and what they discover about Voltaire, that produces the rupture in their lives. Similarly, it is the difference which enters Eleanor's life with the stranger that she finds exciting and which promises change for her.

Untidy and tramplike, the stranger could not be more different from Eleanor. His dark shoes are tied with white laces; her shoes are 'pinkish and made of soft leather done up neatly' (89). The stranger is characteristic of a number of the male characters in *An Affair of the Heart*; he has a strong, physical and, in this story, erotic presence. But what he most significantly shares with many of Morgan's other men is his enigmatic quality, again highlighted by the whites of his eyes that are 'slightly creamy and impenetrable' (90).The stranger confides in her sufficiently to give Eleanor quite a lot of personal information about him, although she does not necessarily believe all of it, yet he still remains mysterious and unknowable.

If 'L'Hotel des Grands Hommes' carries a trace of Hemingway, the influence of D. H. Lawrence underpins this story in the subject of a tightly organized, middle-class woman living alone, with literally and symbolically a fence around her, awakened sexually by a physical, working-class man. In Lawrentian fashion, he undermines the way in which she has defined herself. Everything now seems to look different to her: 'Her plain white curtains looked ridiculous. Her dark flowers in their terracotta pot seemed absurd.' (93) When she eventually pays him for his work, she, not untypically, gives him the money in an envelope which he, not uncharacteristically perhaps, rips open leaving a jagged edge.

At one level, this cryptic, sexual image encapsulates also the difference between them – her neat containment and his rough-and-ready expressiveness – which offers the potential for growth but also conflict. In 'A Place in Wales', the image of the wife lying naked against her disturbed husband's back signifies the intermingling of intimacy and estrangement that now characterizes their relationship. In 'Fencing', the image of Eleanor deliberately choosing to lie naked in her bed while she listens to the stranger showering in the bathroom encapsulates her more intimate knowledge of her drives and desires and, paradoxically, the estrangement from herself that has prevented the fulfilment of them. This mirrors the fact that she has some, quite personal, knowledge of him, but he is still unknown to her. What worries her is the compromise that fulfilling her needs with him at this point in time may involve. As the stranger says in talking with her about living alone: 'And there's the question of yourself. All the accommodating. You get to wondering in the end if there's anything left of you.' (92)

Whilst the stranger repairs the fence that is a psychic as well as a physical fence, the text reminds us that it is both a symbol of her imprisonment and also her freedom. The story is about a dilemma. The question is whether she will take the man to her bed, thereby breaking down one fence. But, as the reference to her pondering the knots of his backbone suggests, knots being a feature of both wood and his spine, he might become only another 'fence'. In this respect, 'Fencing' approaches the theme of 'accommodating', which is raised in the relationships in 'L'Hotel des Grands Hommes' and 'A Place in Wales', from a different perspective.

Limbo

In addition to their concern with the accommodation which relationships involve, with the blending of intimacy and estrangement, and with the enigma of desire, 'Fencing', 'L'Hotel des Grands Hommes' and 'A Place in Wales' are characteristic of many of the stories in *An Affair of the Heart* in their preoccupation with 'limbo'. The women in all three stories are faced with different options and it is the consequent different states of limbo which the texts use to examine incongruent and enigmatic desires.

Micah in 'The Chocolate Factory' frequently inhabits 'her favourite limbo state' (78). In fact, there are several such in this story. At one level, she is referring to the dream state that she frequently enters, 'where anything was possible' (78). One of the images used to describe its heightened nature is an extension of the roof image referred to above in 'L'Hotel des Grands Hommes': 'It was almost as if something else was behind [the skyline], there was what you saw, and then something under what you saw.' (79) This 'something', like the colour white that Marsha sees behind the Paris rooftops and the erotic presence which the stranger brings into Eleanor's house, makes the female protagonist in the story feel something beyond the immediate present which she 'couldn't identify, which made her feel restless and strange' (79).

At another level, Micah's reference to a 'limbo state' might be taken to refer to her home life with her mother and, unlike her girlfriends, with no man in her life. Her white father left home when she was born and now, whilst it is her mother who goes out to work, she remains in the house, getting her mother's meal ready for her when she returns. It is almost as if the mother has the traditional role of the father and her daughter the traditional role of the mother. Further, the concept of 'limbo' might be applied to the fact that Micah, having failed her exams, occupies a space between school and work prior to her starting a job in the factory.

All three aspects of Micah's life to which the term 'limbo' might be applied are outside of time, which seems to have been temporarily suspended. Clearly, she cannot remain at home forever without finding employment or returning to education and she cannot spend the rest of her life as a surrogate spouse to her mother. Neither can she inhabit the dream state as she is inclined to do. The point is made forcefully to her when she is told in the factory to stop dreaming. This terminates all three limbo states: it puts an end to her tendency to dream, brings her out of the limbo between school and work and, since it is in the factory that she meets her first man friend, it ruptures her close relationship with her mother in an all-female household. But in taking her out of three states of limbo it also draws the reader's attention to a further such state that she occupies. In the factory she earns the nickname 'peppermint' because she smells of peppermint chocolate. However, the term is one of abuse for someone of mixed race – being darker on the outside than the inside – which suggests to the reader a more uncomfortable knowledge into which Micah will inevitably grow.

Masculine enigmas

The man who buys Micah chocolate and asks her out is once again characteristic of the male in Morgan's stories even though here he is not fully drawn. He has an enigmatic, very physical presence that is as much forceful as it is persuasive. But not all the men in *An Affair of the Heart* are physical, erotic and mysterious; some are oppressive and linked with violence or the potential for violence.

The husband who deserts his wife Marged in 'Charity' demonstrates a potential for violence. At one point, he speaks to her 'with that look she didn't like in men, the mouth too relaxed, and the pupils of his eyes taking on a dark look' (73). In 'A Small Storm Over Paddington', the husband who has married in haste has an overbearing presence that his wife had not expected: 'He was like a bull, yes, a bull that shakes its head and steps out ponderously with a slow roll of his shoulders.' (132) In 'L'Hotel des Grands Hommes', Marsha's husband enters their hotel bedroom from the bathroom with an erection which she finds almost frightening.

The most overt and developed concern with male violence, however, is in 'Losing'. Although written in the third person, it is narrated from the perspective of a young girl. The first part of the story charts her growing up through her changing identification with the seasons. This gives her inner life an intensity which underscores what is only hinted at in this part of the narrative, that she has grown up with a fear of men. It is suggested at the outset that her mother has had a number of men friends. The man who seems to be with the child for most of her life appears, like Jack in Davies's *Kith and Kin* (2004), to be an aggressive presence in the home. This is evident in the threatening way he asks her what she is staring at when he is trying on a pair of socks that her mother has made for him, as well as in the negative, almost snarling, comments he makes about her learning the piano. However, the violence becomes most explicit in the second part of the story and it concerns her piano teacher, Mr Bristow. As she reaches the age of puberty, she finds his physical presence more worrying and unwelcome. This is enhanced by her own sense of uncleanliness when she begins to menstruate, 'a kind of subdued horror in her own fleshliness' (120), and by her mother's warning: 'Be sure you don't have anything to do with boys or men.' (120) Eventually, she witnesses Bristow's assault upon his wife and daughter. The detail of the violence is unusual for this collection of stories. But it is necessary to convey the enigma which surprises the adolescent narrator almost as much as the physical assault itself: 'He seemed the same. Quiet and tidy. You would never have thought there was any harm in him.' (122) When she hands him the bantam eggs, he speaks his only word of Welsh in the story, 'Diolch', as if to summon up gratitude from a deep reservoir of sensitivity that is somewhere within him and she watches his fingers trembling as he tries to carry the eggs gently into the house. Her witnessing this domestic violence is linked to her fresh awareness of detail around her that is in turn associated with her puberty: 'As she approaches the kitchen door she sees with unrepeatable clarity its every detail, including how "the paint was peeling a bit down the one side, like green flakes quivering in the wind."' (124)

The title of the story refers to her not only losing blood but also innocence. On the positive side, she discovers her newfound sense of herself as 'part of a single system' (124). On the negative side comes an enhanced sense of violence in the image of the buzzard and the sound of her mother's partner chopping wood, the repetitive 'phut' echoing the earlier sound of Bristow's boot against his wife's pelvis. Indeed, throughout *An Affair of the Heart*, desire is linked to nature which is itself violent. But it is also interspersed with the domestic in imagery that is often disarming, as in this story in the reference to the buzzard 'like a mobile over a child's cot' (123) and in 'A Small Storm Over Paddington' in lines such as 'The light when you go in the room seems at first to have that savage element that you can get on a winter hillside with the bracken dying' (138).

Desire and androgyny

Despite the actual or potential male violence in some of the stories in *An Affair of the Heart*, in many of them the women discover their own physical presence. This is certainly the case for Eleanor in 'Fencing' and in 'Charity' where Marged, cut off as a deserted wife from everything she dreamt of, discovers a new physical sense of being as a female wrestler: 'And yet, how solid the sweat had felt running down her back, and down her ribs at the sides under her arms . . . She never knew for certain whether she had been more herself at those times, or less.' (75) Moreover, a number of the stories are concerned with a sense of being that seems to transcend conventional notions of gender. Frequently, the imagery in the stories, such as the bull imagery to describe the husband in 'A Small Storm Over Paddington', lends them an abstract, non-human quality; in others, as in Marged's memory of having been a wrestler, the physical body at that moment of time might not have any specific gender; and in 'Fencing' the gender identity of the protagonists seems subsumed by the different physical presences and relationships to their own bodies that each has.

In this respect, 'Vertigo' is an especially interesting story because for the most part the narrator could be a man or a woman in a relationship with Maddy. Although the narrator turns out to be a man, the ways in which he initially notices Maddy suggest that he is more likely to be a woman. This is evident in the way in which, before as readers we know for certain that he is a man, he admits to being attracted by 'the way a hand configures with a wrist, the timing of speech or silence' (144). Certainly the physical details he notices most about her are not those men are assumed to prioritize: 'I remember watching Maddy's hands (which I never got to like) and noticing how the tips of her fingers were square, and her palms squarish too.' (145) There is also the way in which he carries his books in the crook of his arm and the way he talks about Maddy after she has left after spending the night with him for the first time:

> I didn't think, as you sometimes think when a woman has just left you, of what I'd done to her . . . I thought instead, or perhaps it is true to say I visualized, because Maddy was there on the back of my eye clad in nothing but light, the way she turned her head and looked at me. (146)

Even when he eventually refers to his genitals, the language is more feminine than we might expect – 'My genitals lay along the fold where my belly and leg meet' (146) – and, as a woman more so than a man might, he studies the inside of his leg for a bruise. His description of the bed she has left is again one that we might be tempted to describe as 'feminine' rather than 'masculine': 'The bed was sculpted and the sheets were folded back onto themselves in waves of stone.' (147) Even when we realize that the narrator is a man, there is the sense not simply that this is a male perspective written by a woman but that the author is still pushing back the boundaries of an androgynous concept of sexual being. This becomes explicit when the narrator confesses to a sense of self that transcends gender as such:

> At the centre of myself is a well, a bottomless well. Am I the cylinder of darkness, or the shaft of something inexplicable that contains it? These are the questions I come to again and again in my recollections of Maddy. And yet, Maddy was a woman. And yet. In my relation to Maddy, I was a man. (149)

This important admission hangs in limbo around 'And yet'. There is here a sense of incredulity that displaces the conventional gender binarisms in which affairs are usually conceived and written about. The terms 'woman' and 'man' seem incongruous to the profound awareness of being encapsulated in the imagery of wells, cylinders and shafts. What the narrator is seeking to capture throughout much of the account of his relationship with Maddy is a state of limbo, which is not only outside of gender but also outside of time. The admission, eventually, that he has responded to Maddy as a man and she to him as a woman takes them both not only into gender but into time for the concepts of 'man' and 'woman' are inseparable from time. The story is underpinned by awareness that a relationship which does not last forever mirrors life itself. It takes further the interest in limbo informing this collection by focusing upon the condition of isolation which sex and death are perceived as sharing.

Physical definitions

The relationship between the sense of self, time and bodily change is explored further in the titular story 'An Affair of the Heart' and in 'A Day in the Life of Princess Crystal'. 'An Affair of the Heart' concerns a young man in Paris who, over the course of part of a day, worries that his girlfriend has left him, although when he returns home this proves not to be the case.

The story moves back and forth in time. Jean-Claude remembers some of the occasions when he went to bed with Maddy as well as things that his mother and aunt have said to him. But the story also moves forward in time to when he begins to go bald, to when he leaves Maddy for a short-lived affair with a younger woman, to his first major illness in his fifties, to when he is perceived as a morose old man and even to his own death. Through this shifting, horizontal view of his 'self' the story takes a vertical slice focusing upon how Jean-Claude's sense of himself is bound up with his relation to Maddy's physical presence in his life.

Jean-Claude's desire for Maddy is intricately involved with his creative, selective configuration of her, in terms not only of her personality and her behaviour but also her body:

> Maddy had such fine ankles, all bone and fragile tendon, and the flesh dipped into a hollow between bone and tendon in which Jean-Claude liked, when they were in bed sometimes, to rest the bulb of his thumb. (22)

So detailed is the intricate interweaving of his private thoughts and his highly personalized perceptions of Maddy that his sense of self is difficult to separate from her changing body, signifying time:

> ([he] saw that she was an ordinary woman with breasts that were already somewhat elongated, a woman who smiled too much in bed and breathed his name at inappropriate moments) – nothing, he realized with a final sense of chagrin, stayed the same. (25)

The changing nature of another's body as a mirror to an individual's changing perception of themselves is a recurring motif in *An Affair of the Heart*. In 'Charity', referred to above, Alessandro thinks about a woman who answered her door to him when he was walking the streets with his collecting box:

> He thought of her body and knew what it would be like, because he had measured the decay of his own. He had measured the decay and hated it. His own age, other people's ages; he hated the fact that youth was naturally fuckable and age was not. (69)

In addition to time, the 'self' in another story, 'A Day in the Life of Princess Crystal', is dependent upon the circumstances of birth. The story concerns two friends who are very different partly because of their backgrounds: Jennifer is Irish and Marielle is Anglo-German. The story traces their relationship from when they first took a home together to what happens to that relationship when Marielle marries and has a child. Her marriage is a milestone in her changing sense of self because her sense of being is bound up with her husband and is very different from the way in which she and Jennifer thought of themselves in relation to men when they were young women. The story in effect asks, when and where did the 'true' Jennifer and Marielle exist when their lives are viewed over a period of several decades?

The title of the story refers to a tale that Marielle reads her child. One detail in it is very significant: that Princess Crystal, because she was a princess, was able to admire 'her silver reflection in the green gloom' (36) of the forest and remain young and beautiful. Not so, however, Jennifer and Marielle. Jennifer particularly understands this because mortality and the tenuousness of life rests heavy upon her shoulders.

Outside Eden

Siân James's short fiction shares with Clare Morgan's a principal interest in what was referred to above as the postmodern 'self'. That is to say, the concept of the self as complex, fluid and enigmatic that emerged in the late twentieth century in opposition to the immediate, post-Renaissance rhetoric of the 'self' as autonomous, fixed, knowable and bound up with ideas about transcendence of earthly contexts. How far the self can be seen as independent of and able to transcend biographical, social and cultural contexts has been a moot point in Western philosophical, religious and literary discourses. As in Morgan's work, James explores the determining influences upon who we are, the way we think and the language we use. But, like Morgan, she also privileges the way in which the 'self' is bound up with enigmatic desires and behaviours. This is evident, for example, in 'Not Singing Exactly'. Here, the young, married and hard-up narrator, shoved on the High Street by a well-dressed woman, inexplicably even to herself, decides to steal from the shop she has come out of in an illogical act of revenge. In fact, it is not the only seemingly inexplicable thing she does in the story. She is almost surprised to discover that at the age of sixteen she has allowed herself to become pregnant by a young man who is generally regarded as a bit 'rough'.

The exploration of desire in James's *Outside Paradise*[1] is flagged by the title of the first story, 'Love, Lust, Life', and by the title of the collection itself. The allusion to the Garden of Eden is appropriate because it draws attention to sexual knowledge, to love and lust, which in the Genesis story was the legacy of the expulsion from Paradise. Like Morgan, James is interested in the extent to which our sense of self as individuals, and especially as sexual beings, is dependent upon the changes which occur within our bodies over time. In 'Strawberry Cream', the sense of self of two young girls, one eleven and the other fourteen, is a product of pre-pubescence bodily change. The narrator's passion for strawberry cream signifies her half-understood yearnings. But how they feel, and the development of their desires, is a product also of the hot summer, the boredom of living in a small community and of listening to the stories told by other girls. The fact that the older girl comes from a wealthier family and attends public school is also part of her attraction for the narrator. She is desired as the 'other' because she represents difference.

In the course of the story, the two girls cross over the river and into the woods, a traditional, fairy-tale location for events that threaten young women, and there the narrator and her friend explore each other's semi-naked bodies. Circling her friend's breasts with her fingers, the narrator eventually sucks them, an activity that looks backward to when she was a child at her mother's breasts and forward to when she will be a lover. This backward- and forward-looking allusion to time stands in contradistinction to the periods they spend together each afternoon which seem, like the unchanging summer, to be outside of time. The fact that they confine themselves to activities above the waist because they do not yet understand the lower parts of their bodies is indicative of their location in a limbo between childhood and adulthood and between childlike innocence and adolescent knowledge. They and their bodies, of course, are not outside of time and the summer eventually gives way to autumn.

The different 'selves' that we are at different points in our lives is a subject which recurs overtly and covertly throughout *Outside Paradise*. In 'Hester and Louise', the narrator's grandmother as a district nurse in a family photograph is contrasted with 'the untidy old woman she's become' (59). However, the narrator's assessment of her as an elderly person cannot be taken at face value. It is inseparable from the narrator's own age, her adolescent development and the cultural and peer influences upon her as a young girl living in London. This is reflected in the way she contrasts her grandmother with her grandmother's younger friends, the Arwel sisters: 'I could never understand how Gran had the nerve to treat them so casually, even rudely, when she was ugly and poor and they were so beautiful and so rich.' (63) The past tense here, 'I could never understand', together with the mature reflection throughout the story, suggests that now she is older herself she may have a different view.

While the short story often employs a traditional, chronological view of the self, historically it has been more inclined than the realist novel to eschew linearity in favour of analysing the different forces that converge at a specific place at a particular moment of time. The Arwel sisters are apparently 'right' for the narrator at this moment in her life when she is interested in things bodily and things material. The flirtatious behaviour of the sisters between themselves goes almost unnoticed while the physical attention they show her is welcomed. The way they treat her – brushing her hair with an ivory-backed brush and moisturising her face, neck and shoulders – and the luxurious nature of their house with thick carpets everywhere are indicative of what the narrator aspires to and values at this point in her life. But, as in 'Strawberry Cream', it is the difference associated with class and taste which exudes superiority that is part of the enticement, encapsulated in the contrast between the sisters' moisturizing creams and the grandmother's carbolic soap.

The title of the collection also refers to other meanings associated with being 'outside paradise'. In Western Hebraic religion, paradise represents what has been lost to us but is always a ghostly presence at the margins of our consciousnesses. It accounts for the pervading sense of estrangement that supposedly haunts us throughout our lives and is not assuaged until we come 'home' to Christ. At the core of James's collection of stories are estrangement and the different ways in which this has been and can be defined for women.

Many of the female protagonists in *Outside Paradise* are alone: the narrator of 'Not Singing Exactly' through circumstances brought about by an abusive parent and later by the imprisonment of her husband; the narrator of 'A House of One's Own' by family circumstance and inheriting a house in a village which is new to her; Hetty in 'Billy Mason from Gloucester' because of the amount of time she has given to being a carer; the teenager in 'Hester and Louise' because she has been sent away from her home in London to her grandmother in Wales by her busy parents; and the narrator of 'Strawberry Cream' because she is an only child in a small Welsh community. However, in a number of the stories in this book women are empowered by different female relationships, even if only temporarily: the narrators in 'Not Singing Exactly' and 'A House of One's Own' by their relationships with their mothers; Hetty in 'Billy Mason from Gloucester' by her friendship with the farmer's wife, Mrs Evans; the teenager in 'Hester and Louise' by the Arwel sisters; and the narrator when she was a pre-pubescent girl in 'Strawberry Cream' by the presence of an older, exotic girl who becomes her summer friend.

The idea of returning 'home' as a metaphor for the discovery of Christ, referred to above, and the Father is not coincidental. Again in Western thought 'home' is linked to 'paradise'. This interest in exploring the interconnection between family, home and sense of self recurs throughout *Outside Paradise*. As a recent study has pointed out, 'the word "home" has multiple meanings . . . shelter, hearth (i.e. emotional and physical well-being), heart (loving and caring social relations), privacy, roots (source of identity and meaningfulness), abode and paradise ("ideal home" as distinct from everyday life)'.[2] Of course, returning home for a woman can mean returning to restricting roles and obligations. Throughout 'Billy Mason from Gloucester', there is a sense of Hetty being haunted by loss, and at one level that is the absent presence of a home life in which she can be at the centre. It is summarized most cruelly by the community ribaldry that greets her trial for helping a deserter: '"That's one way of catching a man"'; '"Aye. She burnt all his clothes and wouldn't let him out of bed for three months"'; and '"An old maid's revenge. I reckon he'd have been better off in France"' (32). At one level, the deserter is the stranger that she craves to enter her life and end her solitude. But he also reduces her life to a sequence of roles and activities. It is the only story in *Outside Paradise* that has overt biblical connotations in that the deserter's broken body and his bleeding feet are reminiscent of the broken body of Christ and, in bathing his feet, Hetty is redolent of Mary washing Christ's feet. These allusions conflate the notions of 'returning home' and 'returning to Christ', highlighting how both discourses – that of the traditional hearth and of Christ – entrap women in limited versions of womanhood.

The complex position occupied by the unmarried Welsh woman at the beginning of the twentieth century is encapsulated in a conversation between Mrs Evans and Hetty:

> 'Are you in trouble?' Mrs Evans asked her. But then realised she couldn't be; she was surely too old, had never even had a sweetheart as far as she knew, she was as tall as a man, her chest was flat, her hair scraped back in a bun. 'Are you unwell? Are you having heavy bleeding, something like that? It's quite usual, you know, at your time of life.' (28)

What comes immediately to Mrs Evans's mind is the unmarried pregnancy that disrupted many homes for young women, driving them very often to the parish and/or prostitution. The initial language in this passage – 'Are you in trouble?' – is ironic because of Hetty's age and because it is the kind of evasive language that was used to describe unwanted pregnancies in 'respectable' homes, not quite facing up to what had happened. But whereas women are exiled within the language of sexuality, as Donoghue demonstrates in a number of the stories in *The Woman Who Gave Birth to*

Rabbits discussed in Chapter 2, the elderly or post-sexual woman is pushed to the margins of the community as well as of language. Mrs Evans because she is a wife and part of a productive farm has a voice and position in the community which Hetty as an ageing spinster – 'her chest was flat, her hair scraped back in a bun' – does not have. There is a contrast between the 'respectable' language in which sexuality is discussed, involving words that even when they refer to the opposite still reflect the ideal values of the home – 'trouble' and 'sweetheart' – and the candid discourse about the female body in which women indulge. Thus the tone changes sharply: 'Are you having heavy bleeding, something like that?' Now Mrs Evans's language pinpoints the reality which was not talked about openly in the 'home' but constituted almost a secret discourse among women.

Language and desire

The different ways in which different generations of women talk about desire is a recurring trope in *Outside Paradise*. In 'Love, Lust, Life' a fifty-year-old woman in hospital with a friend of the same age notices the difference between themselves and the younger nurses: 'Of course, as we're both in our fifties, talking about sex didn't come naturally to us. We'd often notice the pretty young nurses drawing together, looking naughty, having a giggle, but they were a different generation.' (7–8) James highlights a further difference and that is related to class. The narrator is a middle-class woman who recalls the memories of Molly, a farmer's wife, from that time in hospital. In this respect, the story anticipates subsequent narratives in the collection in that it is the contemporary working-class women who seem more able to take control of the language of desire in talking with other women. However, in remembering her secret liaisons with a builder she talks more vividly and at greater length about her sexual experience than even the working-class narrators of 'Not Singing Exactly' and 'A House of One's Own':

> And every day afterwards, all the time he worked for us and later, I made love with him, had sex, committed adultery, sinned, sinned, with the same joyful and shattering abandon, relishing every new and extraordinary and undreamed-of thing we did together, he leading and pleading and petting and praising and me following, obeying, wanting everything. And then wanting it again. (16–17)

The language here is different from the somewhat 'flat' way in which Molly describes sex with her husband. She finds an eloquence in which to do justice to the orgasms that she experienced. For the first time, she weaves phrases and clauses together in contradistinction to the staccato succession of sentences in which she normally talks. Most of what she says here is one sentence. The language of the church or chapel – 'adultery', 'sinned' – stands in contrast to the bodily language which reflects the sensations that she experienced: 'joyful and shattering abandon', 'relishing', 'pleading and petting and praising'. As the prose develops and becomes more vivid it also becomes more 'poetic', employing alliteration and assonance, blurring the boundaries between words and phrases so that the experience of 'joyful and shattering abandon' begins to get under the skin of the dialogue itself and determine the nature of the language.

In contrast to the account of sex with the builder, Molly's description of sex with her husband is coldly structured, reflecting the controlled, unexciting nature of the experience itself: 'Just a strangely primitive rite that happened once a week or so, accompanied by a lot of grunting and sweating on Glyn's part and not much more than silent acceptance on mine.' (12) If the word 'abandon' determined the language in the account of sex with Mike, the description of sex with Glyn seems determined by the word 'acceptance'. It is as if Molly is describing something that happened to others. In the previous account the language encapsulated the sense of physical and emotional participation, but here the language reflects only estrangement. In the former description, there is almost a return to childlike pleasure, highlighted by the repetition of 'and', a word which a child tends to overuse in constructing narrative.

Molly's experience of adultery risked her expulsion from the home, from 'paradise'. This was almost the fate which befell the Arwel sisters in 'Hester and Louise' when they were discovered naked together in bed with an Italian prisoner of war, which resulted in them both becoming pregnant and their lover being shot to death. As Molly says: 'You'd think I'd want to forget it. All the intrigue and lies, the interrupted phone calls and the hurried, famished meetings.' (17) But Molly retains a 'paradise' in her mind: 'Even if I was a Christian and hoped for eternal life, I couldn't renounce the memory of it or deny that it was the greatest, most wonderful experience of my life, because that was the time I came alive as a woman.' (16)

Ideal homes

The narrator's sense of self in 'Not Singing Exactly' is inseparable from her home life, which has certainly not been a 'paradise', either with her overtly strict and violent stepfather or married at sixteen to a man who turns out to be a minor criminal. He is eventually imprisoned for several years and she resorts to stealing in order to supply her children with clothes. She ends up trapped between two homes that are forms of homelessness: 'I, just eighteen and trapped forever in this long damp room, my only glimmer of hope that Dave would drop down dead with a heart attack so that I could move back home.' (37–8) The complex nature of the home as signifier is particularly apparent in this story because in addition to physical abuse and verbal intimidation the narrator has to take on the burden of her mother's as well as her siblings' pain. She remembers that her mother:

> . . . cried for about an hour and I didn't know what to do except make her more and more cups of tea. I hadn't realized before that she was frightened of him too, Dave I mean. He could be a devil. I don't think he ever beat her up, not as far as I know, but he used to lay into my brother for any little thing, coming in late, spilling his food, losing his anorak, anything, and it used to turn her stomach . . . (34)

Home for her brother is a nightmare because of the constant physical punishment he suffers but also because he is clearly under constant surveillance. The punishment ceases to have any relationship to his misdemeanours but is one vehicle of oppression in a generally intimidating environment.

The contrast between 'home' as the ideal, safe abode and a place of violence and abuse is brought into sharp focus in 'A House of One's Own' where a young woman of Welsh extraction from Liverpool inherits a small house in a North Wales village. Here, too, the desire is for a home where one can realize and express one's own sense of being. The community's clergyman is shocked to learn that her father had abused her when she lived at home. Instead of mourning his death, she and her mother had celebrated. Her adult view of a home is different from that of someone of his generation and religious background; she thinks only of the men friends and parties that she can have there. However, she does find that being a house owner and member of the village has what she sees initially as a 'conforming' effect upon her. In fact, a house of her own becomes a 'home' where for the first time she can think about having roots. Her desire to have men and drink in the house seems to be a way of assuming control over a domestic environment which in the past has been a place of intimidation and harassment.

It is not only parental violence and abuse that destroys the concept of the home as haven in *Outside Paradise*. James is interested in the way in which the concept of 'home' can take on different meanings as, over time, we change ourselves. There are moments in our lives when we require not simply the privacy of the home as opposed to the outside world but privacy in the home itself from other family members. Such a time is adolescence when sense of self is defined by the need for privacy and control over one's own immediate environment. In 'Hester and Louise', a teenager is reluctant to stay with her grandmother because she now needs more privacy than when she was younger. She tells her father in no uncertain terms: 'I don't have any privacy. And I'm not a child any more. I have my periods now and I have to wear a bra. And I'm not going to bath in a back kitchen and you shouldn't expect me to.' (61) For the narrator's sister in 'Not Singing Exactly' where, as is often the case, children are at the heart of the family conflict, violence and intimidation, the physical assaults she suffers are accompanied by a violation of her most intimate privacy as a young adolescent: 'he'd once taken the strap to Rose when she was fourteen, pulled her knickers down and laid her over the bed.' (37) The home in this context becomes a site of oppression, pain and humiliation. It is also a site of subversion where the narrator is able to forge a relationship with an older boy in opposition to her stepfather's wishes. But because that subversion is in response to parental oppression, it is a gesture rather than a real striking out for freedom which in the end amounts to exchanging one prison for another. When she got married she believed somewhat naively that having a place of her own would give her a supportive space over which she would be able to exercise control.

What the young teenager in 'Hester and Louise' finds in the home of her Gran's two women friends who offer her the use of their bathroom is the ability to relax and be herself. This is because their 'family' life is very different from the dominant ideology of the family which can be seen as emphasizing a 'form of togetherness, intimacy and interest in each others' business that can actually deny this privacy'.[3] But what she also comes to realize is that in their home Hester and Louise have the core of their being and this is not the case for her in her parents' or in her Gran's home. Although the narrator of 'Strawberry Cream' is only eleven years of age, the same-sex relationship that she has with an older friend flags up how, if she were to grow up into a lesbian woman, she might not fit easily into the heterosexual values of her parents' home, since the traditional values of the normative 'home' are heterosexual.

Empowerment and disempowerment

Many of Siân James's stories are first-person narratives by women who are often young, invariably unconventional and, although they are the victims of circumstance, able to empower themselves, as is evident in 'Not Singing Exactly', 'A House of One's Own' and 'Happy as Saturday Night'. Certainly, they are protagonists who have a presence in their communities.

In 'Billy Mason from Gloucester', set around the time of the First World War, Hetty's concern for injured animals and birds is well known in the community and makes an impression on her head teacher when a blackbird follows her to school. Mrs Evans also clearly respects Hetty's concern for wildlife and her regular inspection of her husband's rabbit traps, to which she responds by protecting Hetty from the violence of the farm while she works there. However, there is a disempowering aspect to all of this. Her life revolves around caring: initially for her mother, for wildlife and, eventually, her father who having deserted his wife for another woman returns home once Hetty's mother is dead. The story addresses a major question in Hetty's life, are animals and sickening relatives dependent upon her or is she dependent upon them and upon other people's dependency upon her?

Julia Kristeva, to turn to a European psychoanalytic critic for a moment, argues: 'A woman is trapped within the frontiers of her body and even of her species, and consequently feels *exiled* both by the general clichés that make up a common consensus and by the very powers of generalization intrinsic to language.'[4] The relevance of this to the female situations explored by James is that her women protagonists often occupy a paradoxical position. At one level, they are exiled within the dominant language and, at another level, pushed to an intellectual, emotional and physical space on the margins of the dominant discourses. Hetty offers a type of resistance which is based upon quiet, physical and often covert activity. This is not the case, though, for many of James's protagonists.

Kristeva believes that women find compensation in the maternal in language; they are more easily able to identify with the presymbolic and with sounds, music and rhythm in lullabies and ultimately the poetic. This, for Kristeva, reinforces the significance of the mother and daughter bond. In a number of stories in *Outside Paradise*, mother and daughter relations are based on a sense of exile but this is as much physical as linguistic. The majority of James's female protagonists not only reclaim the social initiative but take charge of the 'symbolic'. This can be seen in 'Not Singing Exactly', where the title itself indicates a distancing of women from their traditional linguistic associations in lullabies and song, 'A House of One's Own' and 'Happy as Saturday Night'. Despite the narrator's admission in 'A House of One's Own' that 'no one believes in me anymore' (81), she is disarmingly assertive in her dealings with others. She confronts the vicar with 'I'm a big, bad sinner, I'm afraid. An alcoholic, for one thing' (76); and she responds to her elderly female neighbour's complaint about noise which had never come from her uncle: 'Pity he didn't disturb you a bit. I bet you were a good looking lass fifty years ago.' (82) Her outspokenness is part of her sense of her identity and how she feels she has been empowered, especially after her father's death, by her mother's assertiveness. Returning us to the theme of how our sense of self changes as we change over time, she recalls, 'We had quite a good sort of life for the next ten years. Lots of rows and shouting, specially when I got to be thirteen, fourteen and wanting my own way about everything.' (79) Like that of Brito's independent, working-class women, her assertiveness is conveyed in the way her speech is invariably structured around unequivocal, short and combative statements: 'I own this house, this garden and that little stunted tree by the back wall' (72); 'I am not one of the saved' (76); and 'My mum was a big woman like me . . . she drank a lot and had lots of men friends' (79). But the bluntness of the language also reflects the stark way in which she sees things. Her attitude is summarized by the respect that she acquires for the vicar: 'I don't think he'll fob me off with fairy tales.' (82)

Indeed, the no-nonsense, female narrative voice seems to interest James, as much as Maeve Binchey in *Dublin 4* (1982), discussed in the previous chapter. The narrator of 'Happy as Saturday Night', brought up in 'a tough part of Cardiff' (109), is another example of the blurred boundaries between self and environment. Like the narrator of 'A House of One's Own', she has little time for sentiment and romance; she is candid about the need of young women such as herself to be aware of men, is disarming about sex, admitting that 'I'm always turned on by words like fuck and shag' (112), and frankly recalls a boy in school showing the girls his 'thing' (113). What is seized in this story apart from the initiative is a language which is normally seen as 'male' rather than 'female'. James appears to find in her working-class, Welsh protagonists a reclamation and ownership of the symbolic whereas Kristeva stresses women's estrangement from it. But, despite Kristeva's focus on the female and the pre-symbolic, she provides us with an insight into what James, and Leonora Brito too, are striving for in the language of their assertive female protagonists. As Anna Smith summarizes Kristeva: 'Innovation in language then, must maintain an investment in shocks, disturbances, and the opening of boundaries to an outside.'[5] James and Brito's most independent female characters appear in their language and behaviour to find innovation in shock and disturbance.

There are women, like Molly in 'Love, Lust, Life', who experience moments when they come alive as women with a male lover. There are others who experience joy and pleasure in sensual pursuits with other females. The concluding pages of 'Happy As Saturday Night' contrasts the violence and aggressive sex which Janice experiences at the hands of her husband with the comfort she finds by getting into bed with the narrator: 'And I moves right up against the wall and puts my arm around her, and after a while she stops crying and we gets nice and warm.' (117) Desire in *Outside Paradise* is bound up with violent parents, abusive relatives, misogynistic local communities and predatory strangers. In these stories, an abused child remembers: 'Oh, I remember the way he'd kneel over me, pushing his fingers into me front and back, pretending it was fun and that I was supposed to laugh' (78); and a confronted shoplifter recalls: 'I take it that he's making a deal with me and I don't even think of refusing it.' (42) There is a strong sense, as in Morgan's work, of the violence within nature and society. This is evident in the traps that are laid for rabbits and in the outbreak of war in 'Billy Mason from Gloucester'. In *Outside Paradise* as a whole, violence in the outer world extends to home life which ideally is supposed to provide sanctuary, in the stepfather's behaviour in 'Not Singing Exactly' described above and in the abuse which the narrator in 'A House of One's Own' suffered as a child.

The violence in the farming community, war and the home, generally associated with men, raises questions about the nature of masculinity itself and how it is culturally configured. But this text also suggests the empowerment of women. Partly this lies in comeuppance as when the shoplifter is able to raise the stakes in the deal by taking what she had tried to steal as well as securing freedom from prosecution. More significantly it lies in the voice that women have acquired. Abuse, violence and oppression are now articulated and women are acquiring the means to assert themselves in terms of language and behaviour. Donoghue's *The Woman Who Gave Birth to Rabbits*, discussed in Chapter 2, can be seen as exploring how women, especially working-class women, across the last 300 years or so, have lacked but have begun to obtain the language to speak for themselves against their oppression, social, cultural and economic, and to articulate their desires. James's *Outside Paradise* is an example of a twenty-first-century text interested in exploring not only the connection between gender, desire and power but also the assertive voice of largely Welsh working-class women in this respect.

Given the attention in women's literature to what was previously marginalized, it is not surprising that ways of seeing are important motifs in such writing. In many texts, the emphasis is on what is in the corner of the eye or at the margin of consciousness. This is the subject of the next chapter.

Notes

1   Siân James, *Outside Paradise* (Cardiff: Parthian Books, 2001).
2   Lynda Johnston and Gill Valentine, 'Wherever I Lay My Girlfriend, That's My Home', in David Bell and Gill Valentine (eds), *Mapping Desire* (London and New York: Routledge, 1995), p. 100.
3   Ibid.
4   Julia Kristeva, 'A New Type of Intellectual: The Dissident', cited and trans. in Anna Smith, *Julia Kristeva: Readings in Exile and Estrangement* (Basingstoke: Macmillan, 1996), pp. 28–9.
5   Smith, *Julia Kristeva*, p. 35.

6 Fields of Vision

Referring to literary awards won in Wales by a historical novel with a lesbian protagonist, Jane Aaron and Wynn Thomas suggest that in twenty-first-century Wales there is 'a current desire to see differences in sexual as well as ethnic orientation more openly acknowledged in a more heterogeneous Welsh culture'.[1] They are referring here to the emergence of a more inclusive society which writers, such as those discussed in Chapter 3, have no doubt played some part in creating, even though there may still be a long way to go.

Emma Donoghue, Stevie Davies and Sarah Waters, through their acclaimed fiction, have made important contributions to pushing back the boundaries of what is acceptable, acknowledged and explored in terms of sexuality, especially same-sex relationships. However, as we have seen from some of the fiction discussed in the previous chapters, writers who push at the boundaries of desire are often concerned to expose not so much 'unspoken' as 'unspeakable' desires. In contemporary Welsh and Irish fiction written by women this is a recurring theme not least because women have often been the principal victims of violence and abuse and of what is still hidden in many families and communities. In the recent fiction examined in the previous chapters, this would include the suffering of children at the hands of bullying parents or stepparents, such as Jack in Davies's *Kith and Kin* (2004) or Dave in James's short story 'Not Singing Exactly'. What happens in these homes raises questions about the role of the mother; whether she is complicit as in Davies's novel or bullied and scared herself as in James's story. But both these texts hint that what the children suffer is not simply violence but a sexually tinged violence. In James's short story 'A Home of One's Own', the female protagonist explicitly experiences sexual abuse. In countries such as Wales and, especially, Ireland where the home is part of the rhetoric of the nation, this kind of thing has existed in what has virtually been a 'blind spot' or has been partially observed by what we may call a 'lazy eye', not concerned enough to take action. The vicar's response to what his new parishioner tells him about her father would suggest that in his priesthood in a small Welsh village this is not something that he has encountered or thought much about.

In previous chapters, I have argued that the tropes of gender, desire and power embrace other themes such as family, community and nationhood because of the ways in which gender, sexuality and desire are implicated in the wider social discourses and power structures. But they also pose questions about the field of vision itself. As far as women's writing is concerned, the concept of a 'blind side' is a recurring literary trope, because many women, such as Julia and Helen in Sarah Waters's wartime novel, *The Night Watch*, are only able to pursue their sexuality behind the backs of others. Thus, Julia and Helen exist as a couple literally and metaphorically in their landlord's blind spot. The discussion of the book in Chapter 3 stressed the night watch as a metaphor, among other things, for surveillance and intrusion into the private. But it is also worth reiterating here that the night watch is significant for what it does not notice as much as for what it sees. For women writers exploring women's sexuality in a historical context, what is out of sight is particularly important because the history is a long process of the private and marginalized becoming centred in the public consciousness. Indeed, as Waters's narrative of Kay, Julia and Helen makes clear, what is now socially acceptable was, only half a century ago, clandestine, risky and dangerous and it took, as in Kay's case, a considerable amount of courage to be in public what one really wanted to be.

A further reason why the field of vision is a recurring motif in women's writing and writing about gender, desire and sexuality generally is that the participant, whether observed or as a participant narrator, does not always have her own sexuality fully in view. This is the case in the relationship between Mara and Frankie in *Kith and Kin*. In remembering the friendship between them, Mara also reconstructs it, realizing that so much at the time had been at the margins of her consciousness. In Donoghue's *Stir-fry* Maria's 'coming out' in mid-twentieth-century Dublin is as much a discovery for her of what she is coming out into. When she finds herself by chance spying on her flatmates making love, she is witnessing what has always been out of sight.

In other texts, what characters bring forward from the margins of their psyche is much more unpalatable than in Mara's case. An obvious example, discussed in the previous chapter, is Mr Bristow in Siân James's 'Losing'. Here James is interested not simply in describing the violence but in the way in which Mr Bristow seems to be able to push the violence to the back of his mind and behave with his young visitor as if nothing had happened. She is also interested in how such households as the Bristows are able to survive.

The expression of desires that are at best only partially understood is a feature not only of individual but also communal psyches. This is true, of course, even of the audiences in the Welsh valleys who turn out in Leonora Brito's 'Dat's Love', discussed in Chapter 2, to see the young, ethnic and mixed race women performing African-American routines, in Sarah's case mockingly. It is even truer of the Dublin engineering students in *Stir-fry*, mentioned in Chapter 3, who follow a tradition of throwing women students into the University pond. Here, Donoghue is interested not only in those who are actively involved but also those who watch, the 'lazy eyes' who see what is going on and allow themselves to be complicit in it. The way in which the community behaves toward Hetty for befriending a deserter in James's story, 'Billy Mason from Gloucester', discussed in the previous chapter, and the way in which a Belfast community behaves in punishing Marta in Linda Anderson's *To Stay Alive*, discussed in Chapter 4, is only possible because they, too, must be blind to what they are doing. Indeed, juxtaposing the Dublin students with these other more violent and aggressive communities suggests how the individuals involved might in time 'progress' from one level of bullying to another. One of the most disturbing features of Anderson's account of the Belfast public punishment is the complicity of the women and another is the way in which the men do not appear to recognize their own sadism and cruelty. Of course, in order to engage in war as a combatant or a supporter, one has to be able to push so much out of view and think of people in terms of negative categories such as 'deserter' and 'whore'. This is one of the explanations why the soldiers in *To Stay Alive* are able to abuse Rosaleen as they do. But the soldier's language, as discussed in Chapter 4, is based on his distorted and short-sighted view of women.

The 'blind spot' is an effective literary trope in many of the texts we have discussed because it literally allows the authors to extend their field of vision, but also because of the way in which it raises issues about 'complicity', 'guilt' and 'innocence'. This chapter is concerned with two writers, Catherine Merriman and Mary Morrissy, who employ the motifs of near-sightedness and the 'lazy eye' quite extensively in their short fiction. Indeed, some of the texts imply that there can be no such thing as 'innocence' per se, equating it with a 'lazy eye'. That is to say, an eye that by circumstances or refusal or cowardice is not as fully engaged as it should be.

The 'blind spot' as a concept

Writing in English from Wales embraces not only authors who have been born and raised in Wales but also writers who have moved to the country and made it their home. Catherine Merriman was born and raised in London and educated at the University of Kent. However, her career as a writer is inseparable from Wales where she has lived since 1973. *Getting a Life* (2001),[2] her third collection of short stories, marks the maturity which her own short fiction as well as that of women's writing generally in Wales had reached by the turn of the century. A recurring trope in this collection of previously published or broadcast work is the 'blind spot'. Like the 'blind side' in a driving mirror, it is a space of danger outside of what is normally in our field of vision. This danger ranges from actual violence in 'Delivery', where a young boy is struck by an axe from behind, to potential violence in 'One Step Away from Trouble', where Doggy, who accuses the narrator of having sex with his wife who has recently left him, sidles up to the narrator in a bar literally from his 'blind side', to the perceived possibility of rape and murder in 'Eating Sugar'.

One of the most entertaining and original short stories from Wales around the subject of partial sightedness is Sarah A. Todd's 'Last Night's Dinner'.[3] It features a young woman, living in her own apartment, who begins imagining animals there. Her misery begins with a cow in her wardrobe but soon she finds a pig and a chicken. Eventually, it is revealed that the animals are connected to what she has recently eaten or is currently eating. The story may be read as an argument for vegetarianism but it is about more than that. Abby frequently eats meat and chicken without really thinking about where it comes from. In this, she is assisted by the food industry, restaurants and society as a whole which package food and meals in a way that distances them from their flesh-and-blood origins. It takes Abby and her friend a while to make the connection because they use the deliberately alienated language of the food industry themselves, thinking and talking about a 'BLT', a 'Quarter Pounder' and a 'Chicken McNugget'. The reality of raising animals for food, keeping them in factory conditions and the 'reality' of slaughter and food preparation are outside Abby's field of vision.

A much more disturbing short story on the theme of what lies outside of consciousness is Janet Holcroft's 'The Sugar Pig' published in the same collection of short fiction as the previous story.[4] It concerns the regular visits that a young girl, Carrie, makes, with her parents' consent, to her aunt and uncle, a couple who had lived next door to her grandmother. Aunt Lenka is a Hungarian refugee who married a man she met during the Second World War in a London underground station. At their home, Carrie enjoys exotic foods that are new to her and receives presents. However, on one evening shortly before Christmas everything changes because the girl sees, without fully understanding, what she has not previously noticed. Entering her uncle's sitting room she finds pornographic magazines under his chair's cushion and lewd calendars on display. On that occasion, when she sits on his lap she becomes, without fully understanding why, uncomfortable about his proximity to her and the way in which he is holding her. When her father comes to collect her she is ready to leave and no longer willing to return. Along with her parents, she has failed to see her uncle's true face, as indeed has her aunt, who has pushed his unsavoury interests to the back of the house and of her own mind.

In order to understand the significance of the 'blind spot' for a writer, or indeed any artist, we have to turn to Michel Foucault's 'The Order of Things' (1970) where the analysis of knowledge opens with Foucault's discussion of Diego Velázquez's painting *Las Meninas*. This painting interests Foucault because there are three gazes in it – that of the artist, that of the model and that of the spectators – and the painter is caught between standing back from his canvas, allowing us to see him, or moving forward and becoming invisible. Between all these observers there is what Foucault calls 'an uncertain point'.[5] Moreover, there is a mirror in the picture which allows us to see what is outside the reach of these gazes but which comes into visibility when the picture is viewed as a whole.

Even so, the mirror in the painting is duplicitous, seemingly offering straightforward representation but actually causing us to ask what it is that is not reflected in this mirror. Throughout *Getting A Life*, Merriman appears to be interested in what is in the equivalent of Velázquez's mirror. The stories appear to offer us straightforward representation but they also give us one or more 'uncertain points'.

At the borders of vision

In 'Eating Sugar', as in the best of the stories in *Getting A Life*, there are numerous 'uncertain points' or 'blind spots'. Alex and his wife Eileen, visiting their daughter who is resident in Thailand, find their role as their daughter's guardians overturned as she, more familiar with the language and the country than they are, finds herself looking after her parents. The gist of the tale is that the three of them visit a waterfall in rural Thailand and return from the climb to discover that the market from which they had set out has packed up and gone. Alex and Eileen's anxieties are heightened when they are joined by four Thai men who have come down from the waterfall behind them. It is significant that the strangers make their presence known to the family as 'male voices behind them' (19). This immediately associates them with the flies that attack the backs of Alex's legs. Although they show the Welsh family kindness, Alex and Eileen are troubled by them. Throughout, Alex spends his time looking at them in a 'rear view mirror', as it were, suspecting that they mean to rob them or even worse. The story intersperses the long wait for a vehicle, which the men tell them is coming, with the escalating tension felt by Alex and Eileen. The exotic picture that tourists usually have of the country is transformed: 'The Land of Smiles; but also of pirates, and bandits. A poor country where palaces were roofed in gold.' (22) Alex becomes increasingly worried about what is happening outside his view and, of course, since the men do not speak good English and Alex speaks no Thai, his field of vision is always partial:

> This place was dangerous. Danger on all sides. The heat. The dark. The men. The forest. The voracious tumultuous forest. You were so aware, here, of civilisation as ephemera. How, if you just turned your back, all would revert to wilderness. (25)

His fear is not only of what could happen when their backs are turned but of what is happening within his own mind. Whilst even Eileen is keeping one eye in the 'rear view mirror', he has entered that space almost entirely. The men offer them beer and fruit which in his state of mind he interprets as a manoeuvre to distract him – 'Trying to take my mind off what is happening' (27) – so that they can sneak up on him from behind.

The role reversal in this story turns on the fact that parents are like drivers, constantly looking behind but having to avoid thinking too much about what is at the margins of their vision. Alex, feeling that he is obliged to look out for his wife and child, despite the fact that they are both adults, becomes 'an overwrought child' himself (26):

> It was the helplessness children must feel. There had been a role reversal here. Suzanne, their brave twenty-one-year old daughter transformed this side of the world to a competent, patient, encouraging parent. He and Eileen her anxious, fractious, dependent charges. (19)

Suzanne is a better parent because she does not allow herself to be overwhelmed by fears of what might happen. Ironically, Suzanne and the Thai men inadvertently treat Alex like a child at its mother's breast, offering him oral distractions to quieten him, in this case beer and fruit.

In many of the stories in *Getting A Life*, the space outside the usual field of vision is also a place of insight and revelation, turning what has been perceived as 'normality' upside down. In 'One Day', William's mother, who owns the hotel he manages, is losing her sight so that her son, to whom for both their sakes she must now transfer the hotel, is literally on the sidelines of her vision. His own 'blind spot' is what the hotel is doing to him. Working all hours of the day, he has no leisure, no real friendships and no love life, as he confesses to a young female guest, Fiona, who is interested in a career in hotel management herself. But his short-sightedness is evident also in his affairs with guests, about which his mother knows nothing. Moreover, many of the guests choose the hotel because it occupies a space that is in some ways 'out of sight':

> Holidaying women off the leash, off the beaten track, determined to enjoy themselves. Usually women in their late twenties, thirties – the

sisters were both well into their thirties – past the age of shyness, or romantic notions. (75)

William's attentiveness is driven by sexual desire. At the beginning of the story, our attention is drawn to how the 'thick lenses of his mother's spectacles made them look opaque' (73). In fact, William ignores how opaque his own lenses are. His mother is unable to distinguish between the different breakfast juices but William is unable to distinguish between women, seeing them all in terms of their sexual availability and their physicality. He notices Fiona in her 'shorts and skimpy halterneck top' (76); Katherine's legs he observes 'were crossed at the ankle, her painted toenails almost touching his chair cushion' (81); and Geraldine makes an impression on him because she is 'lying on her front, wearing shorts and a loose, sleeveless top' (81). Fiona, however, comes to him almost from his 'blind side'. When she does so, she takes him into a place of uncertainty because she is so different from the others: 'She was genuinely interested. She was not flirting. He was not flirting.' (77) Whereas she talks fully to him, the others speak to him 'from the side', as it were. Geraldine is hardly ever as straightforward as Fiona. Her language is duplicitous and she enjoys sexual innuendo. When she comments that the hotel has 'beautiful views' she is referring obliquely to herself. At one point, 'fixing William with her dark glasses and lifting her front on to her elbows' she deliberately reveals ' a hanging pair of small white breasts' (82). Here references to vision are very significant. Geraldine's dark glasses mean that she can watch William looking at her breasts without making eye contact with him whilst offering him something mysterious and unknown. She encourages him to look into his own unknown depths. Katherine, obliquely commenting upon his lack of overt response, mischievously remarks how short-sighted his mother is. Their patronizing comments as he passes through the terrace are delivered from the side, literally and figuratively from his 'blind spot': 'Still busy. Poor boy'; 'A manager's job is never done'; 'Legalised slavery I'd call it' (84). The point from which they are speaking is not only his 'blind spot' but an 'uncertain' space where there is a tension between his dignity as a professional and his interest in the attractive guests for casual affairs.

Geraldine is able to dominate him because she deliberately positions herself at this 'uncertain point'. She always seems to be in the corner of his eye or to approach him from the margins of his vision. At dinner, he allocates the side of the restaurant where she is sitting to a waitress instead of looking after the guests there himself, pushing her out of his sight. But, later, at the bar, she appears suddenly at his side again, tapping him on the shoulder. Even when she arranges to sleep with him, it is done through innuendo – she asks him for 'room service' – and shortly afterwards he sees her laughing behind her hand. But when he follows her to her room, the affair breaks down at the moment he sees what he had failed to notice all the time she was standing in front of him. It is a pair of binoculars which has been missing in the hotel for days and upon which an elderly, regular guest is dependent. He realizes that Geraldine has stolen the binoculars and has used them to spy on him in the morning when his habit has been to walk shirtless along the beach. But what he now sees in addition to the binoculars are the regular affairs which have been a substitute for a fulfilling relationship. He realizes the dangerous nature of what he has been doing. The sudden return of his moral consciousness, resulting in him ordering Geraldine and her sister pompously from the hotel, leaves Geraldine half-naked, humiliated and scorned. Her revenge the following morning is to empty the contents of the vacuum cleaner into the breakfast buffet dishes before leaving. This is deliciously appropriate for she is returning to him in a highly public manner what he has managed successfully over the years to brush under the carpet.

Secret desires

In 'Aberrance in the Emotional Spectrum', the 'blind spot' is both literal and metaphorical. The story is based around what is called a Canine Olfactory Spectrometer, capable of displaying human emotions as colours. The narrator realizes at one point that the colours emitted by an individual when in a state of sexual arousal may be particularly forceful and would enable them to refine the nature of the Spectrometer. He and his colleague Felicity, whom the reader suspects he may be interested in himself, persuade the technician to have sexual intercourse with her in front of the Spectrometer. The narrator finds himself cast in the role of voyeur watching the two have sex. But in the course of this, he realizes that Felicity emits a blue colour, signifying 'a relaxed unemotional calmness' (62). This seems 'particularly strong when her body – and so possibly her gaze

– turns to the one way glass', which he admits he finds 'vaguely disconcerting' (69). As he watches, the screen goes blank leaving what is going on between the two literally out of sight. But this 'blind spot' is not simply in the Spectrometer; it is also demonstrates the narrator's psychic short-sightedness. He realizes that Felicity has coolly and calculatingly set him up to view a situation which she knew would make him jealous: 'My eyes are now truly open. The woman is a menace to her colleagues. What a tramp.' (71) The language here suggests, of course, that his eyes are not 'truly open'. It is not simply Felicity that got him into this situation.

A complex story that is literally structured around what people fail to see is 'The Pursuit of Beauty'. It is set in the National Portrait Gallery and based around a young boy's frequent visits there to follow a girl whom he would like to get to know. Mark is in the corner of her eye, secretly following her and building up courage to speak to her. Patsy is aware of him but mostly he remains just out of sight. Meanwhile a security guard, whom Mark becomes aware is watching him, is always in the corner of his eye. Whilst Mark is building up a positive fantasy of Patsy, all the time he is fearful that she will reject him. Thus, constantly looking over his shoulder at Patsy or the guard, and worrying about whether she will like him, he appears nervous and risks being seen by others, such as the security guard, as a stalker, literally someone who starts out at the margins of another's consciousness.

Mark agrees to accompany the guard who finally approaches him because he believes that he has appeared to be acting suspiciously. But he also does so because there is another guard always at the edge of his consciousness – the one who arrested him for shoplifting when he was younger. The climax of the story, literally and metaphorically, is the masturbation session that takes place between them in the security office. Throughout the episode – in which Mark is taken into his 'uncertain point' – the guard reassures him that he knows Mark better than he knows himself. The narrative shifts from a focus upon what has been at the margins of Mark's field of vision, partly accounting for his behaviour, to a sexuality that has previously been even further out of view. This is highlighted in the way in which the guard now stands before him whilst throughout the story he has been mainly in Mark's side vision and by Patsy dropping out of sight:

The man's nearness was overpowering. The uniform, the knowing, smiling face. His bulk filled the world. Mark couldn't think. Patsy was a tiny dot somewhere at the edge of the universe. A tiny, receding, vanishing dot. (156)

The violence in 'Delivery' and 'Getting A Life' is more vivid than in the works we have discussed so far. In 'Delivery', an elderly man, Harry, living alone, attacks his nephew's son with an axe, forcing him to dress up in his deceased wife's dress, and in 'Getting A Life', a petty criminal protects a female police officer from an assailant and incurs serious injuries himself. In both stories, the violence erupts from the depths of the chaos into which the protagonists are plunged. Their disordered minds are reflected in the physical environments in which they live and in each case they have to confront what they have pushed to the margins of their consciousnesses. In Harry's case, it is the fact that he could have saved his wife's life. Crucial to confronting what they have suppressed is the act of returning to the location in which the past is trapped. Harry returns to the bedroom:

> . . . where the double bedstead, unslept in for thirty years, still stood in the middle of the room. The bare mattress was velvety with dust. He opened the wardrobe and touched her dresses. Silly styles. He had loved the full, fussy, petticoated frocks the girls wore in his own youth . . . (110)

In 'Getting A Life', Stephen returns to the flat in which he lived before he found himself labelled a hero:

> It took him an hour and a half to walk back to his old block of flats. Jeez, they looked depressing. Even in the dark. Especially in the dark. There were small mountains of cardboard rubbish either side of the block entrance. Broken glass crunched underfoot. What a dump this place was. Literally. He hated it. He certainly had no regrets. He was glad he'd moved. (200)

The emphasis upon the 'blackness' underscores the fact that he has not only returned to the flat but also to what has been out of sight. It is a place where he has 'dumped' a lot of what he should have confronted so that the flat is figuratively as well as literally a dump. It is also a place where he confronts uncertainty – hence the broken glass crunching under his feet – and comes to the realization that he is right to have moved on.

Again, it is what is beyond the protagonists' field of vision that is important to the narrative. Harry believes that his family are plotting behind his back, which makes him feel depressed and alone. Intriguingly, it is his nephew's son who causes him to look into the 'rear view mirror' where, as in Velázquez's painting, not everything is reflected. There are hints that what is not reflected is disturbing indeed. At first, it is only hinted at:

> He was a boy. As tall as his father, but slim as a whip. Blonde hair tucked behind his ears. Something glinted on an earlobe. An earring? Jewellery? But he was, undoubtedly, a boy. (104)

The language here, too, like the mirror, does not reflect everything. As is the case with some of the guests in 'One Day', meaning seems to come in from the side, as it were. The image of the blonde hair behind the ears suggests something that is hidden and the reference to 'something glinted' causes us to wonder what it is that glints in Harry's eyes for a moment. The repetition of the fact that he was a boy underscores his feminization in Harry's view, whilst the simile comparing the boy to a whip introduces a sadomasochistic note that is taken up later. The boy does not appear to speak straightforwardly to Harry, for whom what is said draws attention to something at the edge of his psyche: '"Hello, Mr Daniels". The boy's eyelashes batted like a girl's. "It'll be a pleasure."' (104) The homoerotic element that is half articulated here is more overt later in the story when Harry confronts the guilt and uncertainties that have haunted him since his wife's death:

> So fresh and pure, standing there in his grey sweatshirt with a hood at the back, his blue jeans. And his face: the beauty of his profile, the sweep of his silky hair, the glint of gold at his ear. The boy's eyes had reached the window and halted, resting on the hanging dress. His lips parted, but he said nothing. (112)

Whilst the boy's eyes reach the window – implying clarity of vision – in fact he and the reader, through Harry's focalization, are still looking into a 'rear view mirror' where everything is fragmented and magnified at the same time. The different elements, emerging from the depths of Harry's consciousness where so much has been buried, are not a coherent whole.

In 'Getting A Life', Sarah's involvement in arresting Steven begins with an aside, a sexual innuendo that gets her posted to his stake out. Throughout her dealings with Steven, she only glances at what is in her 'rear view mirror' – that she finds him physically attractive. Whilst she tries to act on this knowledge, he is unwilling to become involved with her partly because he cannot remember what happened in the room when he was supposed to have saved her life and partly because he has his own problems to confront. Indeed, his attempted suicide is a watershed in his life and in the story. It fails because he takes so many aspirin on an empty stomach that he vomits, figuratively expelling the past, which he has to do before he can move on in his life. Nevertheless, despite the fact that Sarah is unable to enter a lasting relationship with Steven, she remains an important catalyst in his recovery.

Although 'Delivery' and 'Getting A Life' are violent stories, they are positive in so far as the protagonists are able to find some kind of salvation and redemption when they reach rock bottom. At one level, this is a theme that recurs in the work of many Catholic writers. Merriman's collection of stories is comparable to writings by Catholic women in that she seems interested in the role of a mediator in bringing an individual out of anxiety and despair. Several of the stories in *Getting A Life* push back the boundaries of what we might think of as a mediator in this respect: in 'Delivery', most disturbingly of all, it is Harry's nephew's son forced to wear his deceased wife's dress; in 'Getting A Life', it is a woman police officer who persuades Steven to use the compensation and reward awarded him by the court to find the father he has never known in Italy; and in 'Eating Sugar', it is a couple's daughter. In other stories, not concerned with suffering as such, for example, 'One Day', revelation comes about because of a mediator, in this case a young student with ambitions of entering hotel management.

The religious connotations are quite pronounced in 'Getting A Life', in which Steven saves the life of a person who has him in shackles. The allusion to the crucifixion is taken up at the end of the story when Sarah learns that Steven has entered a new life, literally returning to his father. In the meantime, when she visits his flat, she finds, like Mary looking for Christ in the tomb, that he has gone. The photograph that she eventually receives from Steven provides her with an image where the emphasis, as in the resurrection narrative, is upon 'transformation' and 'transcendence'.

Limit and transgression

The principal themes in 'Getting A Life' are important also to the Irish writer Mary Morrissy in whose collection of short stories, *A Lazy Eye* (1993),[6] the field of vision is an important motif. Morrissy, born in Dublin in 1957, won the Hennessey Award in 1984 for her short stories. Although *A Lazy Eye* develops a number of specifically Irish themes, it shares many of the preoccupations of the Welsh women writers discussed previously, including the way in which our sense of self changes over time and with changes in our own bodies; the differences between generations in the way in which desire is viewed; same-sex relationships and friendships; the concept of being in a state of limbo; and an interest in partial sightedness. But the collection's principal preoccupation is with places where an individual is brought up against physical and imaginative and/or cultural limits. In 'A Lazy Eye' it is a sleeper compartment and a cramped house; in 'A Moment of Downfall' it is a classroom and a convent; and in 'A Curse' it is a house in which a young girl is brought into close proximity with her employer. Although there are allusions to Catholicism throughout the stories, they are 'post-Catholic' in so far as they move beyond the Catholic centricity of revolutionary Ireland and the De Valera Republic.

In order to understand the importance of limit and transgression to Morrissy, it is useful at this point to turn briefly to what the French cultural historian Foucault has said about them. Foucault suggested that the twentieth century would discover 'the related categories of exhaustion, excess, the limit and transgression' and that in the absence of God, the perceived presence which Foucault believed had invested life with a totality of meaning, '"modern society" would become preoccupied with the limit of thought, and indeed we might add vision'.[7]

'A Curse' is based around a young girl's growing infatuation with the man by whom she is employed as a babysitter. Partial sightedness is important to this story in so far as Mr Skerrit does not see the extent of her feelings for him or the consequences of indulging her. Meanwhile, she frequently looks in her 'rear view mirror' where she sees the reality of the situation she is in: 'It was only when she came across evidence of his shared life with Joy that she felt twinges of envy . . . And she knew sooner or later Joy would come home.' (222) Here the 'rear view mirror', as in Merriman's work, reveals a space of potential danger but also of revelation.

Like many of the characters in Clare Morgan's *An Affair of the Heart*, she too is in a state of limbo, no longer fully fitting into her parents' home and not quite a member of the Skerrit household. She imagines 'the expelled air of her father's lungs still trapped in the house' (208) and sees the Skerrit house as signifying 'newness and modernity' (209). But her father's home is also losing its relevance for her and is becoming 'just things to sit on and use' (209). In this respect, Clara signifies the Ireland at the end of the twentieth century in limbo between the valued past associated with the fathers of Ireland, the founders of the Irish Republic, and the young, modern Ireland ushered in with the Lemass economic reforms of the 1960s, referred to earlier in Chapters 1 and 3, and Ireland's eventual membership of the European Union. The relationship between Clara and the Skerrit family always exists at the boundary between their modernity and her parents' past. Offering Clara apparent freedom, it is also a place where she is trapped. She crosses the boundary when she hears them talking about her behind her back at Rose's christening. It is at this point that, like many of Merriman's characters, she stares into her 'rear view mirror'. But what happens here is that she is plunged into an even more dangerous limbo, having stabbed the baby in her hip with a nappy pin.

As suggested earlier, De Valera's Ireland was a place of entrapment rather than liberation as far as women were concerned because of the way in which they were associated with the home in the 1937 Constitution. But post-1970s Ireland brought disappointment as well as promise. Clara's father's voice provides a telling commentary from the past upon the new 'shoddy workmanship' as he calls it (210). Whilst Mr Skerrit comes to be seen by Clara as the kind of man she hopes to marry, she notices him 'rolling his shoulders as if something in his back was being crushed' (210). In many respects, the Skerrits epitomize the brash, modern, consumerism of metropolitan Ireland: 'Mrs Skerrit would walk in on a wave of heavy perfume. She wore extravagant spangly dresses, off-the-shoulder styles which showed up the fragile bones around her neck.' (210) The fragility of her bones suggests the precarious nature of the way she and her husband live in the spontaneity of the present – she is appropriately named 'Joy' – where money has eclipsed rootedness in a meaningful past. This rubs off on Clara so that she comes to see the Skerrits 'as her private property . . . a world apart' (213). Clara's mother makes clear how the Skerrits enjoy a lifestyle which pushes the past out of sight. They live almost entirely in the present and the future.

Clara's present and future is to a considerable extent created by the mass media. When she settles into the Skerrit home on evenings when they are out, she finds that it is easier 'to imagine herself as an extension of the television world she watched so avidly' (211). Television, as mentioned in Chapter 1, played a significant role in liberating the people of Ireland from the monological authority of the Catholic Church – television brought priests and politicians into the home where they might be judged by the people themselves – and the mass media was crucial to ushering in the new postmodernity. But whilst it enabled the Irish, especially the young, to reach out, literally and metaphorically, beyond traditional boundaries and limits, it also offered the young a virtual reality. Clara desiring the glamour of the Skerrits's life is inseparable from the influence of the mass media upon the young.

Yet, paradoxically, Clara is part of the mass media world of twentieth-century Ireland and yet not part of it, just as she is part of, but always outside, the Skerrit household. Their house is as different from her own as is that of the teenage protagonist from that of the sisters whom she visits in 'Hester and Louise' in Siân James's *Outside Paradise* discussed in Chapter 5. The difference between the home which the young women visit and their own home in both stories is a matter of luxury. In 'Hester and Louise' it lies in the way they treat her – brushing her hair with an ivory-backed brush and moisturizing her face, neck and shoulders – as well as the luxurious nature of the house itself, with thick carpets everywhere. It is indicative of what the narrator, like Clara in 'A Curse', aspires to and values at this point in her life. The Skerritts's bathroom 'had pink carpet which lapped up the side of the bath and made the room seem like a tilted ship' and Clara notices that it 'did not smell of antiseptic and spearmint toothpaste, as the bathroom at home did, where everything was locked away in a cabinet over the basin' (212).

Absent pasts

The way in which our sense of self changes with time and circumstance, an important motif in Clare Morgan's *An Affair of the*

Heart, is central to 'The Playhouse'. Like Morgan's 'A Day in the Life of Princess Crystal', it is concerned with the changing relationship between two female friends. In Morgan's story, they are very different, partly because of their different national backgrounds: Jennifer is Irish and Marielle is Anglo-German. The story traces their relationship from the time when they took a home together to what happens to that relationship when Marielle marries and has a child. In Morrissy's text, the third-person narrative explores the relationship between the two female friends largely from the perspective of one of them, Helen. Helen once knew everything about Sue. But the drowning of her second child, an event that occurred literally in her 'blind spot', becomes a private grief that puts Sue beyond Helen.

Sue's house casts ominous shadows into the garden, signifying the traumas that have shaped her life differently from Helen's and now puts a barrier between them. However, it is not simply the loss of her child. Married to Frank, who also casts a shadow between his wife and Helen when he enters, Sue is now a different woman from the one Helen remembers. The abandoned toys in the garden signify the abandoning of Helen. When Sue's daughter shows her the playhouse where she takes her friends, Helen asks if she is one of her friends but gets no reply, highlighting her estrangement from the family. Indeed, visiting Sue for Helen is like visiting the playhouse. Whilst she thinks about how their relationship has changed, Sue does not. Helen is now only in the corner of Sue's vision.

In Chapter 1, I referred to all women's writing bearing the trace of the history of confrontation and struggle and of empowerment and disempowerment from which it has emerged. The way in which the De Valera Republic defined women's role in terms of the family and the domestic introduces a different, specific perspective on the way in which women's literature is inevitably born out of a history of struggle and confrontation. Throughout women's writing, the home, as discussed in Chapter 5 in relation to Siân James's *Outside Paradise*, is often a place of oppression. As we saw then, this is not necessarily overt oppression and violence. For many young women in Ireland, the home was a place where there was no privacy. In 'A Lazy Eye', Bella remembers 'the ramshackle house on Vandeleur Green, the crowded bedrooms, the lack of privacy and space, the pans of white bread and the cheap cuts of meat.' (55) The cramped house reflects the cramped nature of the family; the physical confinement signifies the psychological entrapment.

'A Lazy Eye' is about the way in which a young woman comes up against limits that would dictate her servility. When Bella is put out of her sleeping compartment and off her train because she has menstruated over the sheets, she behaves with a dignity that is not shown toward her. Defined by others as an act of transgression, her menstruation becomes an occasion upon which she is able not only to make a stand but also to push against limit. As the train pulls away, 'She stared defiantly after it; she was determined to be dignified. She had after all been waiting for this moment all her life.' (54) Apart from the cramped house, the single most important thing in Bella's life that seems to have oppressed her is not her father as such but her father's acceptance of less than she thinks he could have been as a person. At one level, in her mind, his so-called 'lazy eye' signifies a mental laziness so that she has an image of him which she finds humiliating for him and for herself: 'He worked as a bank porter, standing to attention in a marbled lobby, his gold buttons gleaming, holding the door for customers.' (44) The 'lazy eye' becomes a symbol for his lack of moral courage. Imagining that as a doorman the only way he would meet 'a violent, public death was at the hands of men in balaclavas and sawn-off shotguns', she concludes that 'he was too comical and biddable a man to be killed thus' (44). However, as a child, she thought of the lazy eye as 'the evil eye, all-seeing, masterful' (44). She remembers that her father's gaze 'veered shiftily to the right as if something very lewd was going on behind people's backs' (44). In other words, she thought of someone with a 'lazy eye' as being able to see what others cannot.

The inheritance of her father's condition singles Bella out at home and in the school, though not as dramatically as she would have liked. At home, her spectacles are frequently the subject of everyone's attention and care is always taken to ensure that they are not accidentally broken by someone. In other words, the family protects her vision which is different from anyone else's. At school, she puts up with nicknames like 'specky two-eyes' (45) because they give her a kind of status. The story itself demonstrates the 'all seeing' that Bella associated with the lazy eye as a child. For it makes a connection between Bella's stigmatization as a young girl and her menstruation as a young adult. The 'folklore' that develops around Bella's eye when she is forced to wear a patch to correct the eye – 'Some were convinced that Bella did not have a second eye; others that she had been badly scarred and it was too unsightly to expose' (45) – is analogous to the way in which the train attendant associates her menstruation with 'animals', 'perversions' and evil-doing' (52–3). It leaves her with the kind of incredulity she experienced in the playground stories about her eye: 'Don't they know that women bleed?' (54)

What is also highlighted in this story is the way in which this kind of oppression is not fully appreciated by many women. The complicity of the other girls in defining Bella by her lazy eye is analogous to her fellow traveller Irma's lack of support for her on the train and her dutiful, unsympathetic translation of the attendant's abuse. In this respect, the definition of what constitutes a 'lazy eye' changes in the course of the story. Whilst it can signify an eye that sees what others do not, it also suggests, by literal translation, an eye that is too lazy to see. Who, the story seems to ask, really has a lazy eye, Bella or the attendant and Irma? Moreover, the location of the train, somewhere in Germany, gives this definition of a lazy eye a darker, much more serious political connotation. In highlighting Irma's cooperation with Bella being put off the train – 'She helped Bella pack with the same glassy indifference with which she translated the attendant's French' (54) – the story alludes to the extent to which the holocaust in those countries was only possible with the complicity of 'respectable' Germans and fellow Jews. At the end of the story, Bella remembers how she felt when the patch was first taken off her spectacles: 'her vision unobscured, her lazy eye finally cured' (54). Clarity of vision brings a realization of the seemingly unending daily struggle against humiliation and others' lazy eyes.

Divided attentions

The story 'Divided Attention' is a combination of memory and remembered imagination. It, too, is concerned with blind spots but develops them into what are parallel universes in which people live. In the story, the female narrator, who has been having an affair with a married man, recalls receiving phone calls from a 'heavy breather'. As he repeatedly phones back, she uses the silent listener as she might a priest in the confessional. Indeed, she imagines him in a telephone box which is the size and shape of a confessional box. During her phone calls, she admits her relationship with a married man but also to phoning his wife and himself anonymously, vicariously participating in the family life which he has been reluctant to talk about with her and which she has blocked off during the affair.

In other words, like the heavy breather who rings her, she also becomes a stalker.

The obscene caller occupies a 'blind spot' as indeed did she when she visited her lover's home, standing behind trees, out of sight from the doors and windows. But there is much else that is out of sight or partially seen, too, including Larry's wife, since he was conducting the affair in secret, and the affair itself because neither of them fully sees what they are doing to themselves and others. Moreover, he does know that his lover is secretly stalking him. Only partially seen by the Catholic Church and wider society, too, are the married people having secret affairs.

The narrator has to battle against her caller's heavy breathing and groaning as she 'confesses' to him. This parallels to some extent how she has to fight against guilty thoughts about her lover's wife and children. It seems that it was easier for both of them when they pushed thoughts of his family out of consciousness; she only learns the names of his children when she phones his wife. Once she learns their names, the affair becomes more difficult for her. In other words, the heavy breather-cum-confessor encourages her, like the priest in the confessional, to look honestly at what she is doing. The story also disturbingly equates the caller, the Catholic priest and the reader in a kind of voyeuristic activity whilst exploiting the voyeurism in order to link art and confession. The caller becomes a kind of mediator who is able to help the narrator to get closer to the morality that she is transgressing because he is himself a sexual sinner.

If 'Divided Attention' conflates the voyeur, the confessor and the priest, 'Two China Dogs' connects the disparate worlds of religion and the fairground. It is a narrative of a boy with a birthmark, known colloquially as a 'port wine stain', on his face. He is born to a woman made pregnant by a fairground man who gives up the fair to become her husband and to earn his living as a handyman. On his father's death, his aunt, Madge, takes him to the fair community which rekindles the tradition of the fairground 'freaks' that his father told him about. The conflation of Catholicism and the fairground is encapsulated in the objects on the mantelpiece in his parents' parlour. They include the two china dogs which his mother had won at the fair on the night of his conception and a statue of the Virgin Mary. Indeed, somewhat like the 'heavy breather' in Divided Attention', he assumes the role of the Virgin Mary as mediatrix: women come to him because of his birth mark as they visit statues of the Virgin Mary and other relics associated with her. This is a concept to which we will return in the next chapter in a discussion of Morrissy's novel, *Mother of Pearl* (1996), which relies heavily upon Catholic concepts, many of which it criticizes. The notion of the Virgin Mary as a mediatrix is based upon the belief that she can intercede with Christ on the part of sinners, securing them redemption. Moreover, there are a number of biblical allusions associated with the boy: the birthmark is reminiscent of the mark of Cain and at one point he is associated with the betrayed Christ. Primarily, he stands between the 'perfect' and the 'imperfect' as if his imperfection enables others to reach the 'other' world more easily. He confesses at one point that 'I have learned the power of imperfection' (159).

But in this story, the 'power of imperfection' is double edged for his face is also a 'dark booth'. In this respect, he challenges the traditional concept of the Virgin Mary as a mediatrix. A key line in the story is his reflection: 'When I go back there to see my mother I walk into a mirror that has reversed.' (159) Whilst this refers primarily to his 'real' mother, within Catholicism it invokes simultaneously the Virgin Mother. Thus, the Virgin Mary not only points penitents toward Christ but encourages them to look into their 'rear view mirror' which offers insight into what is dangerous. Indeed, he is located between the normal and the 'monstrous' of his father's day – the midget, the leopard man and the Siamese twins – as well as between the divine in the human and the monstrous that seems to challenge the notion of the divine in the human plan. He serves to remind us that the blurred boundary between the human and the non-human embraces the incarnation of the monstrous as well as the divine.

A godless universe

In 'Rosa', Morrissy develops a motif that is important to both 'Two China Dogs' and 'Divided Attention' – the extent to which we are a subject in our own lives and an object in another's. This story concerns two sisters, one of whom, Rosa, becomes pregnant by a man who abandons her to have the baby alone. Over the Christmas period, she and her sister eventually leave the baby in a yuletide crib to starve to death, crying alone, in a department store where the sister works.

The notion of one being an object in someone else's life is encapsulated in the story's religious theme. It begins with the Pope's declaration of a Holy Year from Rome which has an impact upon lives in a small town as far away as rural Ireland. Even the department store's decision to have a crib rather than the usual Father Christmas is a result of its participation in a narrative emanating from elsewhere. Indeed, if we return to the Bible, it is possible to see the baby Jesus as not a subject in his own life but a player in a divine destiny that was predetermined, as Rosa's baby is an object in her mother's life rather than a subject in her own.

There is an uneasy tension throughout the story between Rosa's assumption of control over her own destiny – initially changing her name from Rosie to Rosa and finally deciding to free herself of her unwanted child – and the way in which her sister believes that she is increasingly a subject in Rosa's life more so than in her own. She confesses to the reader: 'I live on the edges of her dark, livid world until it seems that without her I would barely exist . . .' (27) This realization becomes disturbing when she comes to understand the nature of this world in which she is increasingly a player. Even when she feels that she has 'passed over into Rosa's world' she believes that there 'were corners of it into which she retreated that I could only guess at' (31). The phrase 'passed over' invokes the juxtaposition of the material and the spiritual worlds. In a sense, Catholicism is poised on the cusp of these two worlds in which the individual is always surrounded by icons, themselves a conflation of the material and the spiritual, that point in the direction of what cannot be understood. This is encapsulated in the image of Rosa at the crib containing a doll of the baby Jesus, whose sense of mystery is enhanced by the fact that it is black: 'She made quite a pious picture, a heavily pregnant girl kneeling before the crib, tinselled angels hanging above her.' (28) The phrase 'pious picture' stresses that this is more image than reality but also raises questions about the boundary between 'image' and 'reality', as does the replacement of the doll with Rosa's own child and Rosa's comparison of herself with a shop window mannequin: 'As we went home, Rosa glanced at her newly confirmed shape in shop windows. Serpentine mannequins, their fingers arched mockingly like Balinese dancers, their heads tilted quizzically, smiled back at her.' (30) The tinsel anticipates a postmodernity in which images have become increasingly removed from any transcendental meaning and have become signs that carry no significance beyond themselves or their relationship with other signs. In that postmodernity, the flesh and blood child and the plastic doll are interchangeable. The tinsel points not to any religious, spiritual or communal meanings but to a consumer-oriented world that is fundamentally no more than an economic system. Where in that world, in which the human and non-human are interchangeable, the story asks at this point, are spirituality and morality located?

At one level, the 'pious picture' is a piece of religious iconography formed of a flesh and blood person. The image of Rosa kneeling is embedded in her own life; it is an act in which she feels she is the participant. But it is also an image of the penitent sinner which Catholicism repeats over and over again, so that Rosa is also the object in a larger narrative of serial images. Whilst her own name 'Rosa' retains the trace of her birth name, it essentially positions her within the Mariolatry of Catholicism. At another level, the pious picture is rooted in Rosa's own unfathomable psychology: 'She would come back to our rooms barefoot, soaked through, her hair wringing, her sodden shoes in her hand, their dye leaving faint red patches in the hollows beneath her ankle bones.' (28) The emphasis upon her naked feet highlights the self-inflicted suffering of the penitent inspired by the Passion of Christ. The dye filling the hollows of her ankles invokes the bloodied feet of the crucified Christ. Taken together, her bare feet, her soaked body and the allusions to the crucifixion suggest a 'theatre of pain' which connects her own mental torment with the Catholic iconography of suffering. The story 'Divided Attention', discussed above, is a post-Catholic text in that the implicit conflation of a 'heavy breather' and a Catholic priest challenges the ostensible spiritual purity of the Catholic Church. This story is post-Catholic in the way in which Rosa subverts the Catholic ideal of the dutiful daughter who aspires to be a perfect mother; her name, of course, suggests the Virgin Mary. The image of the child in the crib, screaming endlessly into a void, is a spectacularly darker version of stories of unwanted babies being drowned by their mothers in twentieth-century Catholic Ireland where contraception and abortion were illegal. Rosa and her sister are undeterred by the lingering, cruel nature of the baby's death, whilst the child's unanswered screams invoke a compassionless, Godless universe.

Although Morrissy's work is critical of Catholicism, it explores the wider spiritual implications of its images and symbols. Indeed, both Morrissy and Merriman pursue what might be called the 'spiritual' dimension of people's lives, if we think of spirituality as embracing the 'non-material'. 'Eating Sugar' concerns the tourist's understanding of other cultures; 'One Day' and 'Delivery' explores moral consciousness; 'Aberrance in the Emotional Spectrum' examines sexual jealousy; 'The Pursuit of Beauty' involves the relationship between one's sexuality and identity; 'Divided Attention' explores the morality of sexual behaviour; and 'A Curse' involves the conflict between non-material and material aspirations. Some key works that highlight this wider conception of 'spirituality' are the subject of the next chapter.

Notes

1   Jane Aaron and M. Wynn Thomas, ' "Pulling You through Changes": Welsh Writing in English Before, Between and After Two Referenda', in Wynn Thomas, *Welsh Writing in English*, p. 305.
2   Catherine Merriman, *Getting A Life* (Dinas Powys: Honno, 2001).
3   In Patricia Dunker and Janet Thomas (eds), *The Woman Who Loved Cucumbers* (Dinas Powys: Honno, 2002), pp. 23–8.
4   Ibid., pp. 49–56.
5   Michel Foucault, *The Order of Things: An Archaeology of the Human Sciences* (1966; rpt London: Tavistock, 1970), p. 13.
6   Mary Morrissy, *A Lazy Eye* (1993; rpt London: Vintage, 1996).
7   Michel Foucault, 'Preface to Transgression', in Michel Foucault, *Language, Counter-memory, Practice: Selected Essays and Interviews*, ed. D. F. Bouchard, trans. Bouchard and S. Simon (Ithaca, New York: Columbia University Press, 1977), p. 49.

7 Religion, Spirituality and Identity

Although it has become commonplace to talk of two languages in Wales and Ireland, the cultural situation in each of these countries is much more complex than this. Over the last fifty years, Ireland and Wales have become increasingly diverse in their linguistic composition and more recognition is being given to the many different community languages, especially in the towns and cities of south Wales. Of course, south Wales has always been linguistically diverse, and the same is true of the religious composition of its population.

This book began by discussing how concepts such as 'race', 'history', 'desire' and the 'self' changed in the previous century so as no longer to have fixed and singular meanings. At one level, it may be acknowledged, as is evident in the texts examined, that they have always been fluid, changing over time. But, at another level, they have latterly become more inclusive. Thus, it is possible to talk of post-'History' where we conceive of 'History' itself as the product of particular discourses and recognize that it would be more meaningful to think rather in terms of particular 'histories'. The same is true of the concept of religion, so that now it seems possible to talk of post-'Religion' and even, as one of the novels discussed in this chapter illustrates, post-Catholic where the approach to both recognize 'religion' and different versions of Catholicism, which has itself changed over time, without privileging one perspective as the Religion or, even, the Catholicism. Although Irish writers are approaching the Irish Catholic past in ways that are more critical and inclusive than previously, and even reading the Bible in different and exciting ways, 'religion' and 'spirituality' have been separated since the late twentieth century. What constitutes 'spirituality' for many people includes what we might think of as 'religion' but also many other aspects of our lives, including family and community, in which religion has always been implicated. This does not mean, though, that religious concepts and thought have no relevance to late twentieth- and twenty-first-century writing. The fiction that in Wales and Ireland push back the boundaries of desire, gender and power often embrace ideas about religion and spirituality just as in previous chapters we noted how they explore concepts of family, community and nation. In the case of Wales and Ireland, this is not surprising as religion has evidently shaped the nature of Ireland and, in a different way, has also historically influenced Welsh communities and sensibilities.

Many of the contemporary texts from Wales and Ireland that explore the eclectic nature of postmodern spirituality are written by authors who themselves grew up in families where religious and spiritual boundaries were more clearly, if sometimes oppressively, drawn. But this does not mean that religious communities were not complicated and contradictory. The complexity of the Jewish community, which has had a strong presence in parts of Wales, and the modern Jewish family are highlighted in the Cardiff-born writer Bernice Rubens's groundbreaking novel, *The Elected Member* (1969).[1] In her 'memoir', *When I Grow Up*,[2] Rubens provides an insight into how a Jewish Welsh family behaved and thought very differently from their Protestant or Nonconformist Welsh neighbours in response to the prospect of war and what was happening in Germany. They also received very different sorts of information about events in Europe:

> It was a Friday, a day on which practising Protestants collected their *Church Times*, the Catholics their *Tablet*, and the Jews their *Jewish Chronicle*. The Friday fix for all ... And of course there was the general news. Most of it relating to Jewish topics and all of it dire. Dire warnings of a possible second world war, fearful rumours of the fate of German Jews. In those winter days of 1938, long before the displacement of thousands of nationals all over the world, the word 'refugee' was synonymous with Jew. It needed no attribute, and in the Jewish community of Cardiff it was a buzz-word that hummed in every conversation. (35)

The language here reveals a great deal. Protestants, Catholics and Jews are referred to as if they occupy separate boxes. Each is supported by its own discourse. In the case of the Jewish community, the links are with other Jewish communities more so than to other Cardiff communities or even to Cardiff itself. Noticeably,

Rubens speaks of 'the Jewish community of Cardiff' which privileges religious affiliation over the community's geocultural location. It is a community that is bound together by a particular level of intimacy: 'a buzz-word that hummed in every conversation'. It thinks in international rather than local or even national terms. The Jewish community stands apart from the other Welsh communities: 'Few of the Welsh or English believed the terrible stories of their plight, and wondered what all the fuss was about. But Jews believed it, because many of them had been there before.' (34)

At one level, *The Elected Member* is about a middle-class, dysfunctional Jewish family in which the celebrated son becomes an object of shame and a signifier of the destruction of the family's ideals and aspirations. A brilliant forty-one-year-old barrister, he suffers a series of mental breakdowns, exacerbated by taking drugs. The novel opens with him waking in his parents' bed which has 'his' side and an 'inherited' side upon which there are 'nightmares' and 'terrible wakenings' (7). The bed signifies the division in his own psyche between his postmodern self and the traditional Jewish culture in which he has been brought up and in which he is intended to participate.

It is also a novel that explores mental illness as a cultural and social signifier. As in Rubens's well-known novel about illness, *Milwaukee* (2001),[3] to which I will return later, there is a detective element to this text: here Norman's father, Rabbi Zweck, embarks for a while upon a search for his son's supplier of drugs and this leads him unwittingly to a prostitute whom Norman used. It is also a psychoanalytic novel in which meaning is located as much in the spaces between words as in the words themselves. The Rabbi's dream of his son in the hospital, clutching a wastepaper basket that is too heavy for him to lift, is particularly important to this aspect of the book. Here the novel anticipates *Milwaukee* in the way in which it contrasts an inner mental struggle which can only be understood by the person embroiled in it with the way in which that person is observed by those on the outside. The medical language, such as the term 'hallucinations', used to describe Norman's condition does not do justice to the intensity of his suffering. Moreover, the novel stresses how even some of the doctors dealing with the mentally ill believe that their condition is somehow a product of sin brought upon the sick by themselves. The discussion of hallucination in this novel is interspersed with theological questions; one of the nurses points out to Rabbi Zweck that he might have thought differently about Norman's hallucinations if instead of silverfish he had seen a burning bush.

Sin, guilt and redemption

Norman's hallucinations revolve around the appearance of 'silverfish' but also he is clearly obsessive about his own ageing body and has visions of his dead mother. During his mental breakdowns, he speaks crudely, almost as if he is speaking in 'tongues'. This seems to give expression to an alternate identity that is at odds with his usual image as a respectable lawyer from a relatively well-off, middle-class Jewish family. According to Jewish thought, redemption begins when one has reached rock bottom. The descent into lust and depravity is evident not only in Norman's language but in his having sex with his sister and his visits to a seedy brothel. In keeping with the tenets of Jewish theology, these experiences mark the beginnings of redemption. At the end, faced with his father's heart attack, the truth about his part in the suicide of the man he secretly loved and his role in his sister's misery, Norman feels his Jewish faith awakened within him.

Like the majority of Irish novels concerned with Catholicism, *The Elected Member* is anchored in family relationships caught up in religious conflict, sin, guilt and the search for redemption. In such texts, these relationships are usually characterized by estrangement from the family as a whole, from others and even from one's self:

> That's what it was like, lying there, an opting out, a withdrawal from all his doubts, a retreat from his own and others' suspicions, a gentle turning away from all uncertainty. He closed his eyes and gave himself up wholly to the peace and joy that invaded him. His father looked at his face, and watched the slow spreading of his son's smile. (37)

Referring to 'peace' and 'joy', the language here has religious connotations, but Norman's experience is not religious in the conventional sense. His father, at one point, despite everything that he has said, is in danger of believing that his son can actually see hordes of silverfish. His sister is also a cause for concern, still wearing a schoolgirl's white ankle socks at forty and having nothing in common with her brother other than that they share 'the same parents, the same miserable childhood, and the same mutual embar-rassment'. (22) She is resentful of Norman for his effects on his father, of her father for the love she feels duty-bound to owe him and of her sister Esther for marrying and opting out of the family.

Characters in this novel are never fully themselves because of the guilt or hatred they carry around with them. In some respects they carry another life in theirs: Norman, responsible for dictating the letter that was sent to the man with whom he was secretly in love and that led to the man's suicide, takes drugs in order to 'kill' the David within him; Esther is riddled with hatred of Norman for the part he played in ruining her life when he encouraged her to reject David in favour of someone else; and Rabbi Zweck carries hate for his daughter Esther upon whose elopement he blames his wife's death.

Guilt and complicity are themes which inform a great deal of Jewish writing. In this novel, it surfaces not only in the individual cases mentioned above but also in the incarceration of Norman. In doing so, and typically of Welsh and especially Irish writing about religion, the themes of guilt, complicity and redemption are broad-ened to include more than only the family and individual trauma. Norman is taken into a psychiatric hospital, helped by his father and sister. Here the text raises the issue of their complicity in his confinement.

The concern with complicity such as this in Jewish writing is a veiled way of returning to a central issue in twentieth-century Jewish history which would have been particularly important to Jewish authors writing within three decades of the Holocaust; that is to what extent were some of the Jewish people themselves complicit in their own extermination? What happens to Norman can be compared to the incident in Mary Morrissy's short story, 'A Lazy Eye', discussed in the previous chapter, in which Bella is put off the train, significantly somewhere in Germany, because of the complicity of her fellow female traveller. This episode, too, as noted in Chapter 6, seems to imply that the persecution of the Jews in Nazi Germany was made possible partly through the prejudice of Germans holding official positions and partly though the complic-ity of fellow Jews. In Rubens's novel, Norman's sister, coinciden-tally named Bella, too, refuses to lift the shop counter to let the doctors take her brother through the shop. Waiting for a customer to do so, she thinks she has resisted becoming involved in her brother's fate. But, of course, she is as implicated by remaining inactive as those who remained silent when Jews in Nazi Germany and Europe were rounded up and taken to camps. The doctors who take Norman in their car admit that they have to misrepresent the hospital to patients, and relatives, in order to facilitate their cooperation, a strategy reminiscent of the misrepresentation of the camps during the war. When Bella phones the hospital to discover how Norman is, both she and her father are willing to believe the lie. Similarly, later, when Norman phones her and says he wants money for toiletries and chocolate, she only temporarily pretends to believe him. She knows that he wants money to buy drugs and becomes his accomplice, as she has been in the past by turning a blind eye to his stealing the shop's takings. When Norman's father discovers the brothel that his son has been visiting and is excited by the prostitute he finds there, he denies what is patently obvious to the reader. When he touches her breast he tells himself that it is to cover it with her dressing gown. But one of the most serious acts of denial in the novel is Norman's refusal to admit that he is in love with his friend David and his responsibility, as suggested above, for the letter which Esther sends to David that results in his suicide.

Norman's final case, as a lawyer, in the middle of which he breaks down, is one involving another family – the Steinbergs. The Steinbergs accuse Mrs Cass's son, whom they know to be an unemployed thief, of taking her ring from her corpse. Bertie denies seeing the ring and Norman turns the table on his own clients by arguing that only they who saw the ring could have stolen it. The theme of refusing to see runs throughout the text – all but Norman deny the existence of the silverfish – and in the Steinberg case Norman argues ironically that Bertie should be sent to an asylum because he refuses to see. Guilt is determined not by what people do but by what they choose not to see, echoing the guilt of those who saw what was happening in Germany in the 1930s and 1940s but chose not to do so. The madness of the family and of the hospital mirrors the madness of the persecution of the Jews in Germany and the Holocaust: 'madness became acceptable if it were mad enough, and if it went on for long enough.' (157)

Family lies

Thus, an important theme in this novel is the necessity of facing the truth. It focuses upon the need for Norman's father and for his sisters to do so. One of the key lies told in the book is Norman's mother's falsifying of her son's age in order to make his knowledge of languages seem all the more impressive. The result is that he celebrates his barmitzvah when he is sixteen years old. The need to face the truth is also interwoven with the need for forgiveness. Bella's sister who secretly married a non-Jew hopes that her father will not die before he has forgiven her. Confronted at his death by an unmarried daughter and a mentally broken son, Rabbi Zweck eventually finds himself seeking redemption.

The text alludes to Jewish history through the choice of language, words such as 'chosen' and 'event' recur. There is a suggestion that the Holocaust may have been inevitable given the construction of the Jewish people as 'chosen'. Alone, Bella wonders whether the family was responsible for Norman's illness. A significant image is the way the sleeves of Norman's suits – themselves the symbol of the successful lawyer celebrated by the family – are intertwined with those of his mother's clothes in the wardrobe. Norman himself feels that he has been 'chosen' by the family as a scapegoat, which he deeply resents. In fact, his father 'chooses' him because of his success. The fact that Norman is a successful barrister is important to his father. Bella, on the other hand, needs Norman to be a failure in order to cope with her own sense of failure. She also needs to be able to treat him as a child, evident when she visits him in hospital, because it makes it easier for her to deny that she and her brother once had sex. The difficulties for the family of determining when Norman's illness started parallels the difficulties for historians of determining when the Holocaust began. Norman also believes that he has been 'elected' to witness the suicides in similar circumstances of two people, David and the so-called 'Minister' in the mental hospital. He believes he has been burdened by 'God's neuroses' and that he has been asked to carry his parents, sisters and others.

On his return from the hospital, Norman's father goes to his son's bedroom in order to search for information about what has happened to him and about the drugs he has been taking, hoping to find Norman's source. The chaotic papers he begins to search through, arranged non-chronologically, stand in contradistinction to the order which his family has presented to the outside world. They signify the personal and familial chaos behind the respectable barrister. It is at this moment that Rabbi Zweck begins to recall his own life story, thinking back to when he first came to England as a Lithuanian Jew, to settle in a Jewish community in London. His experience is typical of that of the Galut Jew. In exile, his Jewish identity is compromised despite the fact that he becomes a Rabbi. In his early years as an immigrant, he speaks Yiddish using English words for new technology and cultural forms for which there is no Yiddish term. Eventually, he becomes an English speaker whose language is punctuated with Yiddish. Stimulated by his son's mental illness to rethink the chronology of his own life – his arrival in a new country, marriage, children and wife's death – he journeys into the past to rediscover and reclaim Abraham Zweck who became consumed by the persona of Rabbi Zweck and has survived in his own life like the Yiddish phrases that interrupt his English. Whilst searching Norman's room he discovers his 'naturalization' papers. The word 'naturalization' is double edged, suggesting the official process by which he became a British citizen but also the way in which he has become absorbed into what was once a foreign culture to him. This is paralleled by the way in which the patients are absorbed into the mental hospital and are 'naturalized' as members of that institution. Although the 'naturalized' shuffling figures in pyjamas and slippers are seen positively by the hospital, there is a deep-rooted sense of loss about them and they are described as 'sad metronomes' (167). Norman's pink pills 'naturalize' him, in more senses than one.

Rabbi Zweck, remembering the Jewish shopkeeper who persuaded him to think about going into business when he first arrived in Britain, begins to contemplate our capacity to be absorbed into cultures and narratives which are 'other' to us. Recalling how he married that shopkeeper's daughter and in inheriting her father's business made a home in one of the first places he discovered in England, Abraham realizes that he has not actually moved very far.

Mother of forgiveness

Mother of Pearl (1996), Mary Morrissy's first novel, is a very different work from Bernice Rubens's *The Elected Member*. Divided into four parts, it concerns the stealing of a newborn child. The 'criminal' is a woman made childless by an operation to cure tuberculosis, but the crime is one which in turn violates the sacredness in which mothering and motherhood are held in Catholicism in Ireland and Northern Ireland. The first part of *Mother of Pearl* focuses on Irene, the woman who steals the child; the second part on Rita Spain née Golden, the child's real mother; and the third part on the return of the child (now named Mary) to her lawful family. The fourth part once again focuses on Irene and the novel returns briefly to the place where it all started.

In many ways, *Mother of Pearl* is structurally a more difficult work than Rubens's novel. However, as in *The Elected Member*, its principal character is estranged from her parent. In this case, it is a daughter who is incarcerated by her family in an institution, but this time it is a sanatorium because she has tuberculosis. Whilst Rubens's novel is concerned with prejudices around mental illness, Morrissy exposes the myths and fears surrounding tuberculosis. In deconstructing the way in which the disease was viewed and treated in the middle of the twentieth century, Morrissy's focus is very similar to that of Susan Sontag.[4] Tuberculosis is associated with moral and spiritual failings in the individual, seen as physically represented in the physical wasting and exhaustion that it causes. Furthermore, it is linked to physical dirt and a lack of cleanliness, perceived as analogies of moral impurity: 'She had, by her illness, disgraced the household, her mother believed. It spoke of poverty, a lack of hygiene.' (4) Sontag, discussing the way in which tuberculosis, cancer and Aids have been rendered in figurative language, argues fiercely for an approach to illness that takes it out of the metaphorical language in which it is usually couched. In many respects, this is very similar to the project which Morrissy undertakes in *Mother of Pearl*. But instead of being concerned to strip illness and disease of the metaphorical language in which they are (mis)represented, she is concerned with divorcing women, mothering and motherhood from the figurative language through which they have traditionally been represented in Irish Catholicism.

The Elected Member, as suggested above, reflects Jewish theology in the way in which it takes Norman, his family and the reader down to spiritual depths where, according to Jewish theology, redemption begins. *Mother of Pearl*, too, is structured around an important dimension of the particular religious context in which it has its origins and it, too, concerns redemption. In this case, the novel turns on the role of the Virgin Mary as a mediatrix in helping to bring sinners to Christ, a role referred to in the previous chapter. In doing so, it reconfigures various perspectives on the Virgin Mary as a mediatrix and, most particularly, as Mater Dolorosa, a subject already considered in the discussion of Stevie Davies's *Kith and Kin* in Chapter 3. As numerous scholars have pointed out, the Virgin

Mary is not the fixed referent she is sometimes taken to be. The origins of her various roles, such as Mater Dolorosa and Mater Gloriosa, are historically specific.[5] But what makes the figure of the Mater Dolorosa particularly relevant to Morrissy's novel is that it stresses her participation in humankind's pain and suffering. Morrissy goes further than the Christian tradition associated with 'Our Lady of Sorrows' and identifies the suffering of women, specifically, with her. Mary's role as 'Mother of Sorrows' is linked to her capacity to intercede with her son on behalf of suffering humanity. The title of the novel may be descriptive, referring to the mothers of the child named Pearl. But as a litany in the text makes clear, 'Mother of Pearl' is one of the names of the Virgin Mary to whom the novel may be addressed: '*Mirror of Justice, Seat of Wisdom, Mystical Rose, Morning Star, Tower of Ivory, Mother of Christ, Mother of Divine Grace, Mother Most Pure, Mother of Pearl . . .*' (139) Thus, the novel might be read as addressed to the Virgin Mary herself, on behalf of women, alluding to her part in the salvation of humankind through her role as a compassionate mediator between Christ and humanity.

However, as I have pointed out in an earlier study of this novel,[6] if the title of the book is intended to suggest that it is a plea to the Virgin Mary, the novel is complicated by the ambivalence toward Catholicism and toward Mary which it displays. This function of bringing relief to the condemned is parodied in the sanatorium in the different kind of 'relief' that Irene brings to men condemned by tuberculosis:

> She had her rules. She would never let them penetrate her. If they wanted gratification they must do it themselves. She could touch them, but they must never lay a finger on her. Irene would remain a virgin; she was saving herself. *This* was her calling, she believed, her life's work. (23–4)

At one level, Irene humiliates herself by becoming a male masturbation object. But she retains a female power invested in her through women's association with the Virgin Mary.

The motif of Mary as intercessor runs throughout the novel. Rita Spain, the stolen child's real mother, who does not actually want her, finds that the incense and the litany in Church makes her feel 'blessed and released'. Her name, an anagram for 'Rita's pain', stresses her association with suffering women, of which there are many in the Bible as Morrissy's novel reminds us. At one point in the book, Rita's daughter compares her biological mother in her imagination to 'Elizabeth, mother of John the Baptist, grown hopeless with the passing years, for whom a child would be a miraculous favour granted by the message of an angel' (186). This association is ironic, given Irene's role as a kind of mediatrix in the hospital and the fact that she is unable to have children, because from the middle ages to the present day women who have had difficulty in conceiving have sought help from Mary. This is in itself ironic because women find themselves praying for help to a woman who supposedly gave birth as a virgin and without pain.

In my previous study of this novel, I argued that *Mother of Pearl* alerts us to a feminist reading of the Bible.[7] This point is pertinent to the present study also but for different reasons. A feminist reading of the Bible highlights how its women are, like Irene, rarely ever the subjects of their own narratives. The list of women in the Bible who have difficulty having children includes many who are important not for themselves but because they are a part of a significant man's life story. Thus, Rachel is mentioned not for herself but because she is the wife of Jacob, and Hannah because she is the mother of Samuel. What ought to make Hannah significant but is frequently overlooked is that she apparently endured even more suffering than most women, described in the Bible as a 'bitterness of soul' (1 Samuel 1:10), so that she 'wept, and did not eat' (1 Samuel 1:7). Not only are such women, like Morrissy's Irene, shamed because they are unable to bear children but they are further humiliated by having to procure fertile women for their husbands: Sarah gives Abraham her Egyptian maid Hagar while Rachel gives Jacob her maid Bilhah and has to observe Jacob having children by her sister Leah and by Leah's maid Zilpah.

In invoking these women, and the 'heroic' spaces that they occupy, through the allusion to Elizabeth's infertility, the novel challenges the pressure which the Church and the Bible generally places on childless women. In fact, the Catholic Church teaches that children are a blessing from God, who 'settles the barren woman in her home as a happy mother of children' (Psalm 113:9). Only when Rita and her husband move to Mecklenburgh with their second child, Stella, does she feel they are 'a proper family' (148). This reinforces how the pressure placed on ordinary women by the Catholic Church, as argued in Chapter 4, requires a kind of 'heroism' from women who would seek to resist it.

Irene's situation is made doubly ironic because the Catholic Church professes to recognize that 'sterility neither prohibits nor invalidates marriage'.[8] In fact, the holiness that accrued to the Virgin Mary because she gave birth to the Son of God, and the way the Catholic Church consequently encourages women to become brides of Christ, is cryptically parodied in Irene's marriage to 'God' in the name of her husband 'Godwin'. Moreover, his story is itself parodic of aspects of Jesus's upbringing, shifting the emphasis from Mary as the vessel of God to Mary as a more independent being:

> A father was never mentioned and Stanley grew up barely believing in him. His mother had seemed to him large and mysterious enough, like a capricious cathedral, to have produced him on her own. He never felt a void in the household, nor was she curious about a man who had never become flesh, who existed only because Stanley knew he must have. (28)

A further parallel between Rubens's and Morrissy's novels is that in each a central protagonist suffers because of pressure which is put on them, and which in turn is related to the religious community in which they find themselves. Thus, Norman is pressured to become what his Jewish parents, craving success and respectability, want him to become. Irene is coerced into stealing a child by the pressure that the community places upon her. Indeed, in the wider context of Morrissy's novel, it is ironic that her being sent away to the sanatorium is explained to the community by implying that it is because she is pregnant. The pressure applied to Irene in the first part of the book is such that like Norman she is more an object in other people's narratives than a subject in her own.

Forgiving memories

Bernice Rubens's *Milwaukee* is a combination of genres. A novel of family memory which journeys into the past, it is also a psychoanalytic text about the return of what is repressed, a mystery novel in which a private detective is employed to discover the truth about a GI from the past, and a novel about the theology of forgiveness which in its final pages brings together three generations of forgiving. But it is also a revenge text in which a mother takes revenge on her daughter for supposedly bringing about her father's death through the shame of becoming pregnant by a GI in the war; in which a daughter takes revenge on her mother for having lied to her about her father; and a mother takes revenge in turn on her daughter for having, partly at her grandmother's instigation and partly on a whim of mean mindedness, hatched a plot that breaks up her mother's marriage. It is also a book about the psychology of dying.

Like *The Elected Member*, *Milwaukee* is a novel of boundaries where border territories and limbo states are important. It concerns the last weeks in the life of Annie, a woman who has entered a hospice which, as she herself observes, is somewhere between a hotel and a hospital. Although told in the third person, the story is effectively narrated from a state between the present and the past and between life and death. As in Davies's *Kith and Kin*, it unfolds through recollections of the past in instalments. These recollected incidents include Annie's pregnancy arising from fleeting moments of sex with a GI during the war; her father's funeral; her daughter's search for her biological father; the break-up of her best friend's relationship; her daughter's accusation that she has been raped by her stepfather; the discovery that her daughter's supposed biological father is a bigamist; the discovery that her daughter has married her supposed biological father; and the revelation of the true facts about her daughter's pregnancy.

The pieces of the novel fit together to solve a puzzle buried in the past, a process signified by Annie's jigsaw. She hopes that she will have enough time to solve the puzzle slowly and as painlessly as possible. But her desire to solve the puzzle is linked to a deeper, religious need to be connected not only to her family but, as in *The Elected Member*, with redemption. She hopes to have sufficient time to recall everything, to be able to forgive those involved and, most important of all, to receive forgiveness herself. Although, like *The Elected Member*, this is a novel rooted in the Jewish concepts of atonement and forgiveness, there are allusions to the Virgin Mary which cross over into Catholic religious doctrine.

The narrative is much more schematic than in *Kith and Kin* and might be said to drift in and out of memory, mirroring the way a dying patient drifts in and out of consciousness. In the first part of the novel, Annie seems to be in control of her memory but as she comes nearer death the memories seem to control her. The loneliness of her private engagement with memory stands in contrast to the intimacy between her and her best friend, Clemmie, who seems almost like a spiritual guide to Annie on her journey. At times memory and the present appear to merge as the narrative turns from one time frame to another, sometimes in a single sentence that might refer to either. At one point, for example, Annie excuses herself from a conversation in the hospice because she has to attend, in her memory, her father's funeral.

The use of instalments in *Milwaukee*, however, is not simply a modernist narrative technique that highlights the complex, non-linear relationship between past and present. It is underpinned by genuine insight into the minds of those who suffer a lingering death. Annie has 'packed not for dying but for remembrance, for retro-spection, and even for nostalgia' (6). For Annie, as for one of her initial best friends in the hospice, remembering past pains and joys slowly and in instalments is a survival technique. The most difficult memories are the hardest to open, like the letter from Freddie asking for a divorce. She reads that letter in the way she remembers it – in instalments. She also drinks while reading it, hoping that the alcohol will induce a coma. Not only does this anticipate the coma into which she will eventually fall in the hospice, it mirrors the way in which she will there run from memories. Eventually, the contrast between the physically inert body and the intense activity of her mind becomes heightened. Nowhere is this more evident than in the way in which her body tenses and her jaws become locked as she relives one of the most painful memories – her daughter's accusation that Freddie has raped her, that resulted in Annie's subsequent loss of trust in her husband.

This is a novel dominated by the absent present – Mary's unknown father, a dilemma repeated in her own daughter's case – and also by the repressed. The return of the repressed haunts the narrative as it does Annie herself. At one point, she remembers suddenly meeting in a supermarket one of the other two friends who got into the back of the army truck with the GIs with whom they had sex. Whilst Annie has repressed many of the facts, Molly, who has been unable to have a relationship with a man since, remembers every detail of that fateful night. However, after having met with Annie again, she embarks upon a series of relationships with younger, and increasingly younger, men. Molly is a risk both to Annie's state of mind and to the promise of salvation for her. But she provides Annie with a piece of evidence that proves, at least to her, that the man whom Mary claims is her GI father is not. Molly remembers that he had a tattoo of a bird on his wrist. We might think of the bird as possibly the American Eagle, but, given the GIs' conquest of the girls, it was more than likely a bird of prey.

Like *The Elected Member*, the novel seems to follow the Jewish concept that redemption becomes possible when one reaches the depths of despair and sin. What Molly tells Annie about Ruth is a particularly alarming instance of the return of the repressed for, following losing her virginity to a GI, she has married a man on whom she appears to have wreaked revenge, indulged in regular one-night stands and taken to drink. She has died relatively young, ostensibly of a heart attack but more likely by committing suicide. The official cause of death reminds us of the death by heart attack of Annie's best friend Clemmie's partner, after his lover Richard left him for a younger man. Clemmie's view is that he had died of a broken heart, which is in a sense divine justice for the hurt his leaving had inflicted on her.

Rejection, especially of a sibling by her parent or vice versa, is a recurring motif in Rubens's work. In *Milwaukee*, Annie's rejection by her father is paralleled in an inverted way by her daughter's rejection of her stepfather when she discovers her, supposedly, biological father. In calling him 'Dad', and pointedly displacing Freddie, Mary brings to Annie's mind a further detail she had repressed. In a letter which Mary had written to her grandmother, Annie had seen herself referred to as 'her mother' rather than the warmer and familiar 'Mum'.

Here, as in other texts by Rubens, the rejected sibling is a figure which the author uses to explore where misery, or in this case 'outrage', comes from. Mary's sudden rages and bitterness might be accounted for as a genetic inheritance from her father or it may be the result of believing, possibly instinctively at first, that she has been lied to by her family. Mary's sneering attitude toward her mother and the way she continually taunts her when she brings home the man she says is her father is the physical manifestation of what has haunted her for years – a few moments of sex with an unknown GI in the back of a dirty army truck. Mary, obtaining a place at Oxford University, reminds Annie of what she lost through becoming pregnant with Mary when she was her age. At one point, Annie takes a journey on the London Circle Line, riding round and around, in an attempt to escape the tension at home after Freddie has temporarily left her. The image of the circle seems to signify Annie's life. Mary is not only a reminder of what she has lost. Her anger toward her mother is a reminder to Annie of her own anger toward her mother for not standing up for her against her father. The lives of mother and daughter turn out to parallel each other. They seem cursed by the grandmother's proverbial saying that the apple never falls far from the tree. The Edenic allusion here is appropriate because just as Annie is made pregnant by an unknown soldier, her daughter is made pregnant by an unnamed man whilst a student at Oxford University. When it turns out that Mary was pregnant and that she hatched the plot against her mother because it 'was worth a try' (188) she seems, in her mother's eyes, to have inherited also her mother's meanness.

As is the case with Mary Morrissy's *Mother of Pearl*, women's outrage, as well as loss, is at the centre of *Milwaukee*. But the character who most signifies this, Mary, is also central in other ways, too. At key moments of her life, Annie is waiting for Mary: for her birth (which takes her away from school as well as her parents because she is sent to her aunt and uncle's); for her return home with her biological father; and for her to visit her in the hospice. Although not as developed as in *Mother of Pearl*, religious allusions are important to this text also. The choice of Mary's name encourages us to compare her mother's experiences as a virgin in a dirty truck with the birth of Christ to a virgin in a stable. Annie's endless waiting for her invokes the Catholic trope of waiting for the return of the Virgin Mother. Mary actually marries a man whose brother is called Joseph, and her husband describes himself as a carpenter on their wedding certificate. If Rubens's Mary is the negative image of the Virgin Mary, Annie and Mary's relationship is the obverse of the ideal mother-child relationship signified by the Virgin Mary and child. When Mary returns with her biological father, Annie wants and is glad to be rid of her. Later in the novel, there is a significant allusion to the Bible when Annie recalls the occasion when she is accused by her daughter of being behind her husband's arrest for bigamy. In the hospice, she recalls this as the time when Mary 'denied' her (188), the language invoking Christ's denial by Peter. Mary's child, like that of the Madonna, has no father; in marrying her child's supposed father she echoes, in an inverted way, the Madonna as bride of the Father.

Masquerade, based around desire, betrayal and deceit, is at the centre of this novel as it is in many of Rubens's works. When Annie's daughter discovers that Freddie is her stepfather, and that she was born out of wedlock in the war to an ordinary GI and not a war hero, her entire family life is exposed as a masquerade. In one of Annie's key memories, in which her daughter brings home the GI she alleges is her biological father, masquerade is heaped on masquerade. Mary's grandmother behaves like a 'producer' or 'showman', orchestrating the whole affair and resuming the earlier identity she had as a wife. Her supposed father is involved in a masquerade which causes Annie to indulge in a masquerade, too, feigning a poor memory in order to expose him. Mary herself, of course, knows only too well that the man is not her father and that she was made pregnant not by him or her stepfather but by a stranger whose name she does not know. Her alleged father, Jimmy, is himself a man of many parts, which vary from violent husband with three children, to a GI who is intent on reclaiming his past, to a confidence trickster and eventually to an employee in a fast food restaurant taking the name of 'Harry'. Annie's best friend Clemmie's partner, too, has indulged in a performance around desire, guilt and betrayal. Having masqueraded as a conventional, heterosexual husband, he reveals that he is homosexual and leaves her for a younger man. In keeping with one of the principal motifs of Judaic theology, the text holds on to the possibility that in the descent into lust and betrayal it is possible to find redemption. Indeed, in both Jewish theology and in the text, the former is a prerequisite of the latter.

One of the novel's key masquerades is different from the ones which have already been described. At the centre of the novel and important to Annie's survival in the hospice is the character of Mrs Withers, 'high on death and its paraphernalia', whose entire persona is a masquerade. In her case, though, the performance is a strategy to cope with the prospect of death and the way her life has been haunted by mortality. Despite Annie's initial hostility toward her, she becomes a crucial presence for Annie as she fights off death in order to have enough time to achieve the forgiveness she craves. In the last pages of the text they die within hours of each other.

Whilst *Milwaukee* contains traces of the religious contexts from which it emerges, it engages with a concept of spirituality that embraces more than faith and hope in the conventional religious sense. The spiritual enters the lives of most of the principal characters. Annie is looking for 'forgiveness' and 'redemption'. But what she is hoping for is not to be forgiven by God. She wishes to achieve a redemption that comes from making sense in her own mind of what has happened and by being forgiven by those involved. Thus, family is an important part of what she thinks of as the spiritual, as is rationalizing those areas of her life about which she feels guilty. Her daughter's spiritual life is constructed around the need to know her father and her true lineage. In summary, the novel explores the boundaries between spirituality and the importance of settling one's relationship(s) to the wider human community. What is especially important is how one thinks of oneself and how one is configured by others.

Re-linking

Turning to one of the key novels written by a Welsh woman in the last few decades, Siân James's *Storm at Arberth*[9] seems as different from Morrissy's *Mother of Pearl* as the latter is from *The Elected Member*. However, it shares with Morrissy's novel a focus on the suffering of women. The word 'miserable' is again one that recurs in *Storm at Arberth* (1994), but not with the same degree of regularity as in *A Small Country*, noted in Chapter 4. Misery in this text is located in the mismatch between aspiration and the messy complexity of real lives, especially for women. This is exemplified in some of the minor stories that punctuate the narrative, such as the woman Marian meets on her return from having had sex with her husband's friend, Alex, and in the story of Gwenda Rees who commits suicide in the war after she is made pregnant by an American soldier. The mystery around her death – why she travelled to Bournemouth and may have wished her body would not be found – suggests the pressures on her. Marian summarizes the chaotic condition of the lives of the women in this novel when, after one night of sex with her friend's husband, she wants to cry out: 'I'm in the same boat . . . We all are. Sally and I and even pretty Hannah. Why do we have such beautiful dreams, such ridiculous dreams? Where do they come from? Life is never easy, never what we want it to be.' (134)

However, the novel is not simply concerned with the mismatch between 'dream' and 'reality' and the complexity of lived experience even though these are salient motifs. It explores a theme that Marian identifies: 'There's something very unstable about people.' (144) For James, this instability opens the mind onto areas that are beyond conventional ways of thinking. Sometimes this can prove dangerous, as in Norman's case in Rubens's novel. But it can bring fresh insights and the kind of creativity which Johnston in novels such as *The Railway Station Man*, discussed in Chapter 4, suggests is important for women in wresting control of their language and thinking from dominant, male-centred discourses. In *The Elected Member* and *Mother of Pearl*, the instability in Norman and Irene, respectively, is brought about by the pressure of external circumstances. But their instability also disrupts life for many around them, such as Norman's immediate family and the family he represents in his infamous last case, and in *Mother of Pearl* a family totally removed from Irene whose baby she steals. Beneath the surface of what happens in these texts is a general sense of the instability within life generally over time. In *Storm at Arberth*, the changes that come about in life through illness, age and external circumstances are reflected in the highly changeable weather, evident in the episode in which Sally escapes to Foel Graig. Indeed, the principal events throughout the novel are accompanied by storms and severe weather.

The word 'religion' at one level derives its meaning from a word originally suggesting 're-linking' and this is one of the key motifs of the novel. 'Re-linking' is an important dimension also in *The Elected Member* and *Mother of Pearl*. The former leads to a point where father, son and the family are brought together, as well as where the Judaic notion of redemption is rediscovered. Morrissy's novel reconnects the reader with a feminist Bible but also with the concept of the Virgin Mary as a mediatrix which in turn is a plea for intervention in the sufferings of humanity. *Storm at Arberth* re-links the reader to alternatives to conventional theological wisdom and to an older pre-Christianity spirituality through Foel Graig, which is a pre-Christian site.

Foel Graig anchors, as it were, the book's interest in an older way of looking at the world which can be invigorating, as Marian finds when she goes there with Gerald after her friend Sally has disappeared:

> Marian got out of the car, and to her surprise, felt immediately invigorated. The mountains were beautiful, wild and ancient and free. Drifts of heather, mauve and pink, on the dark grey shale, long blue shadows, blue distances. A huge sky, flocked with pearly clouds. A whipping wind. Everything fresh and new-rinsed. (148)

The language here moves, as in the description of key events in Jennifer Johnston's *A Railway Station Man* and Stevie Davies's *Kith and Kin*, to colour and movement. As in Johnston's novel, James is interested in freeing the mind of its usual referents. This involves the return to something that is 'ancient' and 'wild', as if it is only possible, as in Helen's skinny dipping, to find intellectual and bodily freedom in contact with the uncontained elements. As in Mara's account of lying with her friend Frankie, the language dovetails into the colour 'blue'. Here the colour seems to have been chosen for its association with 'boundarylessness', as the phrase 'blue distances' implies. But what is invigorating can also be threatening. The sensation of seeing 'everything fresh and new-rinsed' is balanced against a 'whipping wind'. Both are, in their different ways, thrilling as Sally observes when she sees a storm coming:

> 'The weather's breaking', she said, 'Look at the clouds rushing at the mountains. And now, look how angry they are. There'll be thunder and lightning any moment now.' (65)

The language in this passage, in contradistinction to the description of Foel Graig, is overtly anthropomorphic. It is as if the 'thrill' of the storm pushes back the boundaries of what it means to be human, angry and 'breaking'. Here Sally occupies a space between the present calm and the storm that is about to happen. Indeed, this seems to be the basis for the way in which the pre-Christian is conceptualized in the novel.

Pre-Christian spirituality enters the novel in two principal ways. First, as Sally Rushton says: 'Paganism makes more sense of the world.' (61) What this actually means is spelt out by her elderly acquaintance Gerald: 'At least paganism contains joy as well as sorrow and cruelty.' (61) This perspective on paganism is used by James as a prism through which to view different relationships and personal/familial narratives in a small town in Pembrokeshire. What the pagan perspective highlights is the way in which desire, as in so many of the texts discussed in this book, embraces, like many Celtic stories, passion, betrayal and guilt. At one point, James invokes the pre-Christian, Celtic narrative of Lleu and his wife. Lleu's wife, made from flowers by Gwydion the Magician, falls in love with huntsman Gronow Pebyr and plots against her husband's life.

Many of the contemporary narratives interwoven in the novel are also of love and betrayal. The central story is that surrounding the relationship between two female friends, Sally Rushton and Marian. Sally comes to stay with Marian in her Welsh cottage after Marian's husband has left her. But eventually Marian discovers what she had always suspected but refused to admit: that Sally and her husband, now deceased, had had an affair and that she had been made pregnant by him. She is revealed as someone who had numerous affairs and even made a pass at her own daughter's lover. Mrs Dainton observes of Sally: 'She seems to smell of love and intrigue.' (62) The juxtaposition of love and intrigue echoes the concern with a risky, dangerous kind of love in Stevie Davies's *Kith and Kin* and Leonora Brito's 'Dat's Love'. This central narrative is supported by subplots which are equally risky in the kind of love with which they are concerned, including a homosexual relationship between Marian's employer, Paul, and a younger man who is married and has children. Once again, it is clear how desire pushes at the boundaries not only of sexuality but of family and community. The theme of desire, passion and betrayal raises its head also in the case of Marian herself. She has sex with Alan, who is in a relationship with a woman called Hannah. On leaving his house, she sees the other, younger woman's photograph. Immediately, it is as if she has appeared from Marian's 'blind spot'. As in a car's rear view mirror, there is an immediate clash between the future into which Marian has been looking and what has been behind her. Acknowledging what she has done, Marian appeals to the photograph: 'If ever you hear about me, please believe that I came here quite innocently and left broken-hearted.' (128) Thus, paganism, in its acceptance of a range of emotions, seems to encapsulate the complexities and contradictions of human hearts and communities better than Christianity, which in its singular, moral vision is always inevitability at odds with the messy 'reality' of most people's lives.

There are times in the novel, though, when it is not clear how the trope of the volatile weather should be read. On occasions, it accompanies moments of moral dilemma or immoral behaviour. When Alan tells Marian about Sally, the weather seems to respond appropriately: 'The storm broke over them with ferocious suddenness, the rain drenching them before they'd managed to make the ten or twelve yards to the house.' (86) A storm occurs when Gareth confides in Sally and makes Gerald Maitland remember the truth about his marriage: how he lied to and cheated on his wife while professing to love her. It is a truth which makes a mockery of the inscription on her gravestone, 'beloved wife of Gerald Maitland' (123). There are different ways of reading these juxtapositions. The storm that breaks when Marian learns about Sally might signify that something so long denied and held in abeyance is finally out in the open. The image of the breaking waters has a female connotation that is not inappropriate to the story here. Alternatively, the thunder and lightening may be a signifier of some kind of moral judgement, as they are difficult to free of their Old Testament-cum-Gothic associations with judgement and retribution. Or, the storm may be an image of the kind of 'reality' that desire is, which only paganism is able to encapsulate.

The epitaph on Gerald's wife's gravestone reads, 'Blessed are the pure in heart' (123). Taken from Christian religion, it seems meaningless when set against the 'real' world of passion and betrayal which is depicted in this novel. Indeed, it reminds us of Maeve Binchey's Star Sullivan, discussed in Chapter 4, whose insistence upon being pure in heart isolated her and prevented her engagement with those around her, even her friends. Very few if any characters in *Storm at Arberth* might be described as 'pure in heart'. Many, at different times in their lives, have been racked by desire, betrayal and guilt: Gerald, Gareth, Sally and eventually Marian.

As in a number of the novels and short stories discussed in this book, passion and betrayal are often interwoven with a sense of almost overwhelming loss. This is also encapsulated in the Lleu story in which his wife is punished by being turned into an owl, crying 'Gronw, Gronw, for their lost love' (76). Unlike the cry of the gulls in Bernice Rubens's *I Sent A Letter to my Love* (1975) which appears to mock humankind, the owl's screech is a haunting manifestation of the loss which characters such as Miss Morris, remembering her lover killed in Burma fifty years before (76), and Alice Dainton, remembering her grandfather who died aged forty after a life of mainly work (71), both have to bear.

The second way in which the pre-Christian is incorporated in the novel is through the way in which it suggests that the Celtic sensibility was repressed by a Christian ontology. The primary focus, though, is upon the way in which 'female'- or, more specifically, 'mother'- oriented myths have been repressed. Thus, attention is drawn to how Rhiannon is reduced to being a King's consort (60) and, in an oblique reference also to the repression of Mariolatry, to the occlusion of Rhea, the Virgin Mother of Zeus, in Greek culture. It is a point of view that is articulated primarily through the figure of Sally, who also tells Alice Dainton that she dislikes reductive words like 'Goddess' and 'Priestess' (63). But it is also expressed in the way in which castle and town stand in contradistinction to each other. The castle is associated with oppression whilst the town is associated with pre-Christian Celtic culture.

As suggested above, the novel itself does not readily champion the pre-Christian over the Christian or the past over the modern. But there is a concern, as in Davies's *Kith and Kin*, with the way in which rural Wales, especially in the post-hippy era, has been associated with alternatives to conventional religion and seen as providing opportunities to re-link with older forms of spirituality. Sally, a drama teacher, is open to a broader range of physical perceptions than Marian, who is much more pragmatic and cerebral. With Gerald she is barefoot and enjoys, like Zack in *Kith and Kin*, feeling the grass through her feet, as if she were reconnected with the earth.

In *Storm at Arberth*, the alternative spirituality which some of the characters find in Wales is contextualized with Wales as 'other', a perspective that can be traced back through the nineteenth century all the way to Shakespeare and beyond. The linguistic 'otherness' of Wales is signified by the signposts which offer English monoglot speakers from outside Wales only a jumble of letters that they find impossible to pronounce. But the novel is primarily interested in the sense of being in a 'foreign country', of having entered the 'other', in ontological rather than purely linguistic terms, not that the two can be satisfactorily separated. At the heart of this is a sensibility which cannot be divorced from the landscape which takes on an 'air of mystery' and what seems to be the 'strange light' that falls 'on the small stunted trees and the gorse bushes and the melancholy hills' (97). However, the novel is not simply making a case that the Welsh landscape is 'melancholy' and 'other' which has been made many times before in many genres. It engages with a sensibility whose perceived 'otherness' can only be articulated with reference to the non-verbal – to physical space, colour and movement.

Entering a foreign country is a metaphor that functions at many different levels in the novel. Of these, the most important is the different territories which characters like Marian and Gareth enter sexually. The confusion English speakers encounter on seeing a Welsh language road sign is a metaphor for the disorientation that most of the characters, crossing over into new spaces in their private lives, experience. After having sex with Alan, Marian feels that 'For two hours she'd been someone else, someone she'd never come across before, and wouldn't have approved of if she had.' (106)

When she expresses a momentary wish to stay with him, 'It seemed like someone else talking' (108). Not surprisingly, this motif of disorientation is in turn linked with images of spatial confusion – in Alice's room, Sally has to walk 'through the maze of furniture' to reach the window (62) – and poor light. Marian has to see through all the half light and shadows that have surrounded Sally to discover the truth about her.

Even from these few novels, albeit explicitly concerned with religion and spirituality, a number of trends emerge. Sexuality, desire and spirituality are implicated in the lives of nearly all of the principal characters. Their lives are usually complex and messy: from Norman's relationship with his sister, his interest in another man and his father's arousal by a prostitute; to Irene's services to other tuberculosis patients and her theft of another woman's baby; to Annie and her daughter's one-night stands with men they do not even know the names of; to Marian's relationship with her deceased husband's friend and her married employer's gay relationship. Each of the texts exposes the difficulties of placing the complicated lives of ordinary people into a religious or spiritual framework that can make sense of them.

Storm at Arberth suggests that life is so complex and contradictory that pre-Christian spirituality is better placed to make sense of it than Christianity. Even the texts that emanate from more conventional religious backgrounds push at the boundaries of theological concepts. Rubens adapts concepts from Judaic theological thought, particularly ideas around forgiveness and redemption, but these concepts are developed through a more inclusive understanding of them. Thus, redemption is seen as possibly being achieved through understanding one's own life. This is especially the case where the individual life has been shaped by what might be seen as transgressive desires. However, in Rubens's texts being able to forgive others is an important concept. For Mary Morrissy, a woman's spiritual life should be rooted in a feminist understanding of religious principles. *Mother of Pearl* is an especially important Irish contribution to a discussion of late twentieth-century spirituality because of the way in which it draws attention to the notion of a 'feminist' Bible which recognizes the many women, and their sufferings, that are configured in the Old and New Testaments. At one level, the reader, like Sally, can find in these novels alternatives to conventional religion. But they offer, more profoundly, a postmodern spirituality. There are numerous, different ideas, concepts and practices in these books that cannot readily be brought together in a singular, fixed religious concept.

Each of the texts discussed in this chapter has a context – Jewish Theology, Irish Catholic or pre-Christian – in which they are best read. However, these contexts are composed of discourses which in their own way each text reconfigures. Thus, at the heart of all these novels there is a space in which their corresponding but also competing discourses meet or collide. Here, there is a postmodern spirituality prepared to recognize the eclectic nature of what in the twenty-first century might be thought of as embracing the spiritual life. It includes many of the subjects that have been raised in previous chapters, such as the importance of recognizing previously silenced or marginalized voices and histories; the significance of desire and of understanding how our lives are implicated in wider social discourse and power structures; recognizing the 'heroic' spaces that many women occupy even in their ordinary lives; how our consciousnesses are dependent upon a blind spot into which we look too rarely; and how our spiritual needs and concerns are fluid, changing like our sense of our selves, over time.

Notes

1   Bernice Rubens, *The Elected Member* (1969; rpt Abacus, 2003).
2   Bernice Rubens, *When I Grow Up* (London: Little Brown, 2005).
3   Bernice Rubens, *Milwaukee* (2001; rpt London: Abacus, 2002).
4   Susan Sontag, *Illness as Metaphor* (1978; revd New York: Picador, 2001).
5   See, for example, Jaroslav Pelikan, *Mary Through the Centuries* (New Haven: Yale University Press, 1996); and Marina Warner, *Alone of All her Sex: The Myth and Cult of the Virgin Mary* (1976; rpt London: Picador: 1990).
6   Peach, *The Contemporary Irish Novel*, p. 163.
7   Ibid., pp. 162–3.
8   Sean Finnegan, *The Essential Catholic Handbook: A Summary of Beliefs, Practices, and Prayers* (Norwich: Canterbury Press, 1997), p. 247.
9   Siân James, *Storm at Arberth* (Bridgend: Seren, 1994).

Select Bibliography

Aaron, Jane, *et al.* (eds), *Our Sisters' Land: The Changing Identity of Women in Wales* (Cardiff: University of Wales Press, 1994).

Baudrillard, Jean, *Symbolic Exchange and Death*, ed. M. Gane, trans. Iain Hamilton Grant (1976; rpt London: Sage, 1993).

Bell, David, and Valentine, Gill, *Mapping Desire* (London and New York: Routledge, 1995).

Bhabha, Homi K. (ed.), *Nation and Narration* (London and New York: Routledge, 1990).

Bohata, Kirsti, *Postcolonialism Revisited* (Cardiff: University of Wales Press, 2004).

Butler, Judith, *Bodies that Matter: On the Discursive Limits of Sex* (London and New York: Routledge, 1990).

Butler, Judith, *Gender Trouble: Feminism and the Subversion of Identity* (London and New York: Routledge, 1990).

Connolly, Claire (ed.), *Theorizing Ireland* (Basingstoke: Palgrave Macmillan, 2003).

Coward, Rosalind, *Female Desire: Women's Sexuality Today* (London: Paladin, 1984).

Finnegan, Sean, *The Essential Catholic Handbook: A Summary of Beliefs, Practices, and Prayers* (Norwich: Canterbury Press, 1997).

Foucault, Michel, *The Order of Things: An Archaeology of the Human Sciences* (1966; rpt London: Tavistock, 1970).

Foucault, Michel, 'Preface to Transgression', in Michel Foucault, *Language, Counter-memory, Practice: Selected Essays and Interviews*, ed. D. F. Bouchard, trans. Bouchard and Sherry Simon (Ithaca, New York: Columbia University Press, 1977).

Freud, Sigmund, *An Outline of Psychoanalysis*, ed. J. Stratchey (1949; rpt London: Hogarth Press, 1969).

Gates, Henry Louis, Jr (ed.), *Black Literature and Literary Theory* (1984; rpt London and New York: Routledge, 1990).

Gibbons, Luke, *Transformations in Irish Culture* (Cork: Cork University Press, 1996).

Harasym, Sara (ed.), *Gayatri Chakravorty Spivak: The Post-colonial Critic. Interviews, Strategies, Dialogues* (London and New York: Routledge: 1990).

Harte, Liam and Parker, Michael (eds), *Contemporary Irish Fiction: Themes, Tropes, Theories* (Basingstoke: Macmillan, 2000).

Hebdige, Dick, 'Subjects in Space', *New Formations*, 11 (1990) vi–vii.

hooks, bell, *Yearnings: Race, Gender and Cultural Politics* (Boston: South End Press, 1990).

Joannou, Maroula, *Contemporary Women's Writing: From The Golden Notebook to The Colour Purple* (Manchester: Manchester University Press, 2000).

Keith, Michael, and Pile, Steve (eds), *Place and the Politics of Identity* (London and New York: Routledge, 1993).

Kiberd, Declan, *Inventing Ireland: The Literature of the Modern Nation* (1995; rpt London: Vintage, 1996).

Klein, Melanie, *The Selected Writings of Melanie Klein*, ed. J. Mitchell (Harmondsworth: Penguin, 1991).

Kosofsky Sedgwick, Eve, *Tendencies* (London and New York: Routledge, 1994).

Lloyd, David, *Anomalous States: Irish Wriitng and the Post-colonial Moment* (Dublin: Lilliput, 1993).

Llwyd, Alan, *Cymru Ddu: Hanes Pobl Dduon Cymru* (Black Wales: A History of Black Welsh People) (Wrexham: Hughes & Son (Publishers) Ltd, 2005).

McCarthy, Conor, *Modernisation, Crisis and Culture in Ireland 1969– 1992* (Dublin: Four Courts Press, 2000).

Peach, Linden, *The Contemporary Irish Novel* (Basingstoke: Palgrave Macmillan, 2003).

Pelikan, Jaroslav, *Mary Through the Centuries* (New Haven: Yale University Press, 1996).

Rose, Gillian, *Feminism and Geography: The Limits of Geographical Knowledge* (Cambridge: Polity Press, 1993).

Rose, Jacqueline, *Why War? – Psychoanalysis, Politics and the Return of Melanie Klein* (Oxford: Blackwell, 1993).

St Peter, Christine, *Changing Ireland: Strategies in Contemporary Women's Fiction* (Basingstoke: Macmillan, 2000).

Smith, Anna, *Julia Kristeva: Readings in Exile and Estrangement* (Basingstoke: Macmillan, 1996).

Smyth, Gerry, *The Novel and the Nation: Studies in the New Irish Fiction* (London: Pluto Press, 1997).

Sontag, Susan, *Illness as Metaphor* (1978; revd New York: Picador, 2001).

Thomas, M. Wynn, *Internal Difference: Twentieth-century Writing in Wales* (Cardiff: University of Wales Press, 1992).

Thomas, M. Wynn, *Corresponding Cultures: The Two Literatures of Wales* (Cardiff: University of Wales Press, 1999).

Thomas, M. Wynn, (ed.), *Welsh Writing in English* (Cardiff: University of Wales Press, 2003).

Warner, Marina, *Alone of All Her Sex: The Myth and Cult of the Virgin Mary* (1976; rpt London: Picador: 1990).

Index